Access 2000
For Windows®

FOR
DUMMIES®

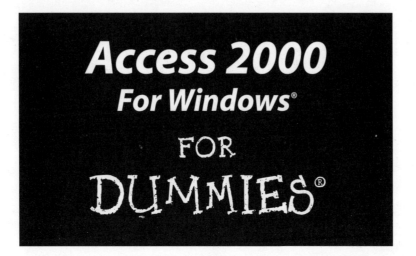

Access 2000
For Windows®
FOR
DUMMIES®

by John Kaufeld

Hungry Minds™

HUNGRY MINDS, INC.

New York, NY ◆ Cleveland, OH ◆ Indianapolis, IN

Access 2000 For Windows® For Dummies®

Published by
Hungry Minds, Inc.
909 Third Avenue
New York, NY 10022
www.hungryminds.com
www.dummies.com (Dummies Press Web site)

Library of Congress Control Number: 99-61116

ISBN: 0-7645-0444-4

Printed in the United States of America

10 9

1O/SQ/QS/QR/IN

Distributed in the United States by Hungry Minds, Inc.

Distributed by CDG Books Canada Inc. for Canada; by Transworld Publishers Limited in the United Kingdom; by IDG Norge Books for Norway; by IDG Sweden Books for Sweden; by IDG Books Australia Publishing Corporation Pty. Ltd. for Australia and New Zealand; by TransQuest Publishers Pte Ltd. for Singapore, Malaysia, Thailand, Indonesia, and Hong Kong; by Gotop Information Inc. for Taiwan; by ICG Muse, Inc. for Japan; by Intersoft for South Africa; by Eyrolles for France; by International Thomson Publishing for Germany, Austria and Switzerland; by Distribuidora Cuspide for Argentina; by LR International for Brazil; by Galileo Libros for Chile; by Ediciones ZETA S.C.R. Ltda. for Peru; by WS Computer Publishing Corporation, Inc., for the Philippines; by Contemporanea de Ediciones for Venezuela; by Express Computer Distributors for the Caribbean and West Indies; by Micronesia Media Distributor, Inc. for Micronesia; by Chips Computadoras S.A. de C.V. for Mexico; by Editorial Norma de Panama S.A. for Panama; by American Bookshops for Finland.

For general information on Hungry Minds' products and services please contact our Customer Care Department within the U.S. at 800-762-2974, outside the U.S. at 317-572-3993 or fax 317-572-4002.

For sales inquiries and reseller information, including discounts, premium and bulk quantity sales, and foreign-language translations, please contact our Customer Care Department at 800-434-3422, fax 317-572-4002, or write to Hungry Minds, Inc., Attn: Customer Care Department, 10475 Crosspoint Boulevard, Indianapolis, IN 46256.

For information on licensing foreign or domestic rights, please contact our Sub-Rights Customer Care Department at 650-653-7098.

For authorization to photocopy items for corporate, personal, or educational use, please contact Copyright Clearance Center, 222 Rosewood Drive, Danvers, MA 01923, or fax 978-750-4470.

For information on using Hungry Minds' products and services in the classroom or for ordering examination copies, please contact our Educational Sales Department at 800-434-2086 or fax 317-572-4005.

Please contact our Public Relations Department at 212-884-5163 for press review copies or 212-884-5000 for author interviews and other publicity information or fax 212-884-5400.

About the Author

John Kaufeld got hooked on computers a long time ago. Somewhere along the way, he discovered that he really enjoyed helping people resolve computer problems (a trait that his Computer Science pals generally considered a character flaw, but that everyone else seemed to appreciate). John finally achieved his B.S. degree in Management Information Systems from Ball State University, and he became the first PC Support Technician for what was then Westinghouse outside Cincinnati, Ohio.

Since that time, he's logged nearly a decade of experience working with normal people who, for one reason or another, were stuck with a "friendly" personal computer that turned on them. He's also trained more than 1,000 people in many different PC and Macintosh applications. The vast majority of them not only survived the experience, but thrived on it. Today, John is president of Access Systems, a computer consulting firm. He still does troubleshooting, conducts technical and interpersonal skills seminars for up-and-coming computer gurus, and writes in his free moments.

John's other IDG titles include *FoxPro 2.6 For Windows For Dummies, Paradox 5 For Windows For Dummies, Games Online For Dummies,* and the best-selling *America Online For Dummies,* 5th Edition. John lives with his wife, two children, and a tolerable American Eskimo dog in Indianapolis, Indiana.

Dedication

To Jenny, because without you I'd be completely nuts.

To J.B. and the Pooz, for reminding Daddy to smile when all he could do was write.

To IDG Books, for the opportunity of a lifetime.

My sincere thanks to you, one and all.

Author's Acknowledgments

Another one's out the door. . . .

As with any good magic trick, there's more to putting out a book than meets the eye. Kudos and candy (lots of chocolate!) to my Project Editor, Pat O'Brien, and Copy Editor, Jerelind Charles, for their diligent efforts in making my ramblings follow commonly accepted semantic guidelines. An equally significant quantity of thanks (and chocolate) are thrown in the direction of my Technical Editor, Scott Hofmann, MCSD (saaaa-LUTE!), for making sure that I'm not making this stuff up.

As always, my sincere thanks go to Diane Steele, the Executive in Charge of a Bewildering Array of Problems, for her support and encouragement, and for the opportunity of a lifetime. Finally, thanks to Tom Lehrer, whose musical comedy kept my brain from (ack!) becoming serious as I finished the book.

Publisher's Acknowledgments

We're proud of this book; please send us your comments through our Online Registration Form located at www.dummies.com.

Some of the people who helped bring this book to market include the following:

Acquisitions, Editorial, and Media Development

Project Editor: Pat O'Brien

Acquisitions Editor: Joyce Pepple

Copy Editor: Jerelind Charles

Technical Editor: Scott Hofmann, MCSD

Editorial Manager: Mary C. Corder

Media Development Manager: Heather Heath Dismore

Editorial Assistant: Paul E. Kuzmic

Production

Project Coordinator: E. Shawn Aylsworth

Layout and Graphics: Angela F. Hunckler, Brent Savage, Jacque Schneider, Janet Seib, Rashell Smith, Michael A. Sullivan, Brian Torwelle

Proofreaders: Christine Berman, Jennifer Mahern, Brian Massey, Nancy Price, Rebecca Senninger, Ethel M. Winslow, Janet M. Withers

Indexer: Anne Leach

Special Help

Billie A. Williams, Donna Love, Suzanne Thomas, Paula Lowell

General and Administrative

Hungry Minds, Inc.: John Kilcullen, CEO; Bill Barry, President and COO; John Ball, Executive VP, Operations & Administration; John Harris, CFO

Hungry Minds Technology Publishing Group: Richard Swadley, Senior Vice President and Publisher; Mary Bednarek, Vice President and Publisher, Networking and Certification; Walter R. Bruce III, Vice President and Publisher, General User and Design Professional; Joseph Wikert, Vice President and Publisher, Programming; Mary C. Corder, Editorial Director, Branded Technology Editorial; Andy Cummings, Publishing Director, General User and Design Professional; Barry Pruett, Publishing Director, Visual

Hungry Minds Manufacturing: Ivor Parker, Vice President, Manufacturing

Hungry Minds Marketing: John Helmus, Assistant Vice President, Director of Marketing

Hungry Minds Online Management: Brenda McLaughlin, Executive Vice President, Chief Internet Officer

Hungry Minds Production for Branded Press: Debbie Stailey, Production Director

Hungry Minds Sales: Roland Elgey, Senior Vice President, Sales and Marketing; Michael Violano, Vice President, International Sales and Sub Rights

◆

The publisher would like to give special thanks to Patrick J. McGovern, without whom this book would not have been possible.

◆

Contents at a Glance

Introduction 1

Part I: Which Came First: The Data or the Base? 7

Chapter 1: The 37-Minute Overview 9
Chapter 2: Finding Your Way Around like a Native 25
Chapter 3: Calling the Online St. Bernard and Other Forms of Help 37

Part II: Truly Tempting Tables 49

Chapter 4: Designing and Building a Home for Your Data 51
Chapter 5: Relationships, Keys, and Indexes (And Why You Really Do Care) 77
Chapter 6: New Data, Old Data, and Data in Need of Repair 89
Chapter 7: Making Your Table Think with Formats, Masks, and Validations 99
Chapter 8: Making Your Datasheets Dance 115
Chapter 9: Table Remodeling Tips for the Do-It-Yourselfer 129

Part III: Finding the Ultimate Answer to Everything (Well, Not Everything) 139

Chapter 10: Quick Searches: Find, Filter, and Sort 141
Chapter 11: Pose a Simple Query, Get 10,000 Answers 153
Chapter 12: Searching a Slew of Tables 167
Chapter 13: Lions AND Bears OR Tigers? Oh, My! 177
Chapter 14: Teaching Queries to Think and Count 185
Chapter 15: Calculating Your Way to Fame and Fortune 195
Chapter 16: Automated Editing for Big Changes 209

Part IV: Turning Your Table into a Book 219

Chapter 17: AutoReport: Like the Model-T, It's Clunky but It Runs 221
Chapter 18: Wizardly Help with Labels, Charts, and Multilevel Reports 233
Chapter 19: It's Amazing What a Little Formatting Can Do 251
Chapter 20: Headers and Footers for Groups, Pages, and Even (Egad) Whole Reports 273

Part V: Wizards, Forms, and Other Mystical Stuff 293

Chapter 21: Spinning Your Data into (And onto) the Web 295

Chapter 22: Making Forms That Look Cool and Work Great 309

Chapter 23: If Love Is Universal, Why Can't I Export to It? 323

Chapter 24: The Analyzer: Your Data's Dr. Freud, Dr. Watson, and Dr. Jekyll 331

Part VI: The Part of Tens 339

Chapter 25: Ten Timesaving Keyboard Shortcuts 341

Chapter 26: Ten Common Crises and How to Survive Them 345

Chapter 27: Ten Tips from the Database Nerds 351

Index 357

Book Registration Information ....Back of Book

Cartoons at a Glance

By Rich Tennant

"Your database is beyond repair, but before I tell you our backup recommendation, let me ask you a question. How many index cards do you think will fit on the walls of your computer room?"

page 49

"OH YEAH, AND TRY NOT TO ENTER THE WRONG PASSWORD."

page 7

"MY GIRLFRIEND RAN A SPREADSHEET OF MY LIFE, AND GENERATED THIS CHART. MY BEST HOPE IS THAT SHE'LL CHANGE HER MAJOR FROM 'COMPUTER SCIENCES' TO 'REHABILITATIVE SERVICES.'"

page 293

"WELL, SHOOT! THIS EGGPLANT CHART IS JUST AS CONFUSING AS THE BUTTERNUT SQUASH CHART AND THE GOURD CHART. CAN'T YOU JUST MAKE A PIE CHART LIKE EVERYONE ELSE?"

page 219

page 139

page 339

Fax: 978-546-7747
E-mail: richtennant@the5thwave.com
World Wide Web: www.the5thwave.com

Table of Contents

· ·

Introduction 1

You Don't Need to Be a Nerd to Use This Book 1
Sneaking a Peek at What's to Come 2
    Part I: Which Came First: The Data or the Base? 2
    Part II: Truly Tempting Tables .2
    Part III: Finding the Ultimate Answer to Everything
      (Well, Not Everything) 3
    Part IV: Turning Your Table into a Book 3
    Part V: Wizards, Forms, and Other Mystical Stuff 3
    Part VI: The Part of Tens 3
What the Funny Text Means 3
Finding Points of Interest 4
Setting Sail on the Voyage 5

Part I: Which Came First: The Data or the Base? 7

Chapter 1: The 37-Minute Overview 9

In the Beginning, There Was Access 2000
    (But It Wasn't Running Yet) 10
Opening an Existing Database 12
Touring the Database Window 14
Finding Candy amongst the Grass Clippings 15
Making a Few Changes 18
Reporting the Results 19
Saving Your Hard Work 21
The Great Backup Lecture 22
Making a Graceful Exit 23

Chapter 2: Finding Your Way Around like a Native 25

Making Sense of the Sights 26
Windows Shopping for Fun and Understanding 28
    The database window 28
    The datasheet window 29
    The form window 31
    The query window 32
Belly Up to the Toolbar, Folks! 32
Menus, Menus Everywhere (And Keystrokes That Work as Well) 34
Playing with the Other Mouse Button 34

Chapter 3: Calling the Online St. Bernard and Other Forms of Help **37**

When in Doubt, Press F1 38
  Combing the Contents 41
  Asking the Answer Wizard 42
  Inspecting the Index 42
The Whatzis Menu Option 44
Your Modem Knows More Than You May Think 45
It's on the Tip of My Fax 45
Talking to a Human 47

Part II : Truly Tempting Tables *49*

Chapter 4: Designing and Building a Home for Your Data **51**

Database Terms to Know and Tolerate 52
  Data (your stuff) 52
  Fields (the homes for your stuff) 53
  Records (the homes on one block) 53
  Table (the blocks in a neighborhood) 54
  Database (a community of neighborhoods) 54
Frolicking through the Fields .55
A Smattering of Fields to Get You Started 57
Flat Files versus Relational Databases: Let the Contest Begin! 58
  Flat files: Simple answers for simple needs 59
  Relational databases: Complex solutions to bigger problems 59
  So, what does all of this mean to you? 60
Great Tables Start with Great Designs 61
It's Finally Time to Build the Database 63
Creating Tables at the Wave of a Wand 68
Building Tables by Hand, Just as in the Old Days 73

Chapter 5: Relationships, Keys, and Indexes (And Why You Really Do Care) **77**

The Joy (And Necessity) of a Primary Key 78
Divulging the Secrets of a Good Relationship 80
Linking Your Tables with the Relationship Builder Thingie 82
Indexing Your Way to Fame, Fortune, and Significantly
  Faster Queries 86

Chapter 6: New Data, Old Data, and Data in Need of Repair **89**

Dragging Your Table into the Digital Workshop 89
Adding a Little Something to the Mix 92
Changing What's Already There 95
Kicking Out Unwanted Records 96
Recovering from a Baaaad Edit 97

Chapter 7: Making Your Table Think with Formats, Masks, and Validations **99**

Finding the Place to Make a Change 100
To Format, Perchance to Better See 101
Text and memo fields 102
Number and currency fields 103
Date/time fields 104
Yes/No fields 105
What Is That Masked Data? 106
Using the Input Mask Wizard 106
Making a mask by hand 108
Validations: The Digital Breathalyzer Test 112

Chapter 8: Making Your Datasheets Dance **115**

Wandering Here, There, and Everywhere 115
Seeing More (Or Less) of Your Data 117
Changing the column width 118
Changing the row height 119
Reorganizing the columns 120
Hiding a column 122
Freezing a column 124
Fonting Around with Your Table 125
Giving Your Data the 3-D Look 127

Chapter 9: Table Remodeling Tips for the Do-It-Yourselfer **129**

This Chapter Can Be Hazardous to Your Table's Design 130
Putting a New Field Next to the Piano 130
Saying Good-bye to a Field (And All Its Data) 133
A Field by Any Other Name Still Holds the Same Stuff 134
Changing a field name in Design view 135
Changing a field name in Datasheet view 136

Part III: Finding the Ultimate Answer to Everything (Well, Not Everything) *139*

Chapter 10: Quick Searches: Find, Filter, and Sort **141**

Finding Stuff in Your Tables 142
Finding first things first (and next things after that) 142
Tuning a search for speed and accuracy 143
Sorting Out Life on the Planet 145
Filtering Records with Something in Common 147
Filter by Selection 147
Filter by Form 148
Removing your mistakes (or when good criteria go bad) 151

Chapter 11: Pose a Simple Query, Get 10,000 Answers **153**

Database Interrogation for Fun and Profit 154
On Your Way with a Simple Query — Advanced Filter/Sort 155
   Peering into the filter window 156
   Building a simple query — er, filter 157
Plagued by Tough Questions? Try an Industrial-Strength Query! 160
Build a Better Query and the Answers Beat a Path
   to Your Monitor 160
Toto, Can the Wizard Help? 164

Chapter 12: Searching a Slew of Tables **167**

Some General Thoughts about Multiple-Table Queries 167
Calling on the Query Wizard 169
Rolling Up Your Sleeves and Building the Query by Hand 172

Chapter 13: Lions AND Bears OR Tigers? Oh, My! **177**

Comparing AND to OR 178
Finding Things between Kansas AND Oz 178
Multiple ANDs: AND Then What Happened? 179
Are You a Good Witch OR a Bad Witch? 180
AND and OR? AND or OR? 182

Chapter 14: Teaching Queries to Think and Count **185**

Totaling Everything in Sight 186
Counting the Good Count 188
Counting with Crosstab 189
Does It All Add Up? 190
There's More to Life Than Sum and Count 193

Chapter 15: Calculating Your Way to Fame and Fortune **195**

A Simple Calculation 196
Bigger, Better (And More Complicated) Calculations 200
   Add another calculation — go ahead, add two! 200
   Using one expression to solve a different question 201
   Making Access 2000 ask 202
   Working with words 203
Expression Builder to the Rescue 204

Chapter 16: Automated Editing for Big Changes **209**

First, This Word from Our Paranoid Sponsor 209
Quick and Easy Fixes: Replacing Your Mistakes 210
Different Queries for Different Jobs 211
You're Outta Here: The Delete Query 212
Making Big Changes 214

Part IV: Turning Your Table into a Book *219*

Chapter 17: AutoReport: Like the Model-T, It's Clunky but It Runs *221*

AutoReport Basics for High-Speed Information 222
Putting the Wheels of Informational Progress into Motion 222
Previewing Your Informational Masterpiece 225
    Zooming around your report 226
    Calling on the pop-up menu 228
Truth Is Beauty, So Make Your Reports Look Great 228
    The Margins tab 229
    The Page tab 230
    The Columns tab 231

Chapter 18: Wizardly Help with Labels, Charts, and Multilevel Reports *233*

Creating Labels 233
Using the Chart Wizard in Your Report 239
Creating More Advanced Reports 242
    The first step: Starting the wizard and picking some fields 243
    More groups! More groups! 245
    Sorting out the details 247
    The home stretch 249

Chapter 19: It's Amazing What a Little Formatting Can Do *251*

Taking Your Report to the Design View Tune-Up Shop 252
Striking Up the Bands (And the Markers, Too) 253
Formatting This, That, These, and Those 255
    Colorizing your report 257
    Moving things around 258
    Bordering on beautiful 260
        Coloring your lines and borders 260
        Widening your lines and borders 261
        Adding special effects to your lines and borders 261
    Tweaking your text 263
Taking a Peek 264
AutoFormatting Your Way to a Beautiful Report 266
Lining Everything Up 267
Drawing Your Own Lines 269
Inserting Page Breaks 270
Sprucing Up the Place with a Few Pictures .271
Passing Your Reports around the (Microsoft) Office 272
    From Access to Word 272
    From Access to Excel 272
    From Access to Mail Merge 272

Chapter 20: Headers and Footers for Groups, Pages, and Even (Egad) Whole Reports 273

  Everything in Its Place 274
    Grouping your records 277
    Changing a section's size 281
  Fine-Tuning the Layout 282
    Dressing up your report as a whole 282
      Playing with page headings 282
      Keeping the right stuff together 284
    Formatting individual sections of your report 284
    Taking it one item at a time .285
  Filling in Those Sections 285
    At the head of the class 285
    Expressing yourself in footers 287
    These feet were made for summing 289
    Page numbers and dates 291
      Hey, what page is this? .291
      When did you print this report, anyway? 292

Part V: Wizards, Forms, and Other Mystical Stuff . . .293

Chapter 21: Spinning Your Data into (And onto) the Web 295

  Access 2000 and the Internet: A Match Made in Redmond 296
  Can't Hyperlinks Take Something to Calm Down? 297
    Adding a hyperlink field to your table 298
    Typing hyperlinks (and using them, too) 300
  Pushing Your Data onto the Web 302
  Advanced Topics for Your Copious Nerd Time 307

Chapter 22: Making Forms That Look Cool and Work Great 309

  Tax Forms and Data Forms Are Very Different Animals 309
  Creating a Form at the Wave of a Wand 311
  Mass Production at Its Best: Forms from the Auto Factory 314
  Ultimate Beauty through Cosmetic Surgery 316
    Taking a form into Design view 318
    Moving fields 318
    Adding lines and boxes 319
    Changing the field tab order 320

Chapter 23: If Love Is Universal, Why Can't I Export to It? 323

  Importing Only the Best Information for Your Databases 324
    Translating file formats 324
    Importing or linking your files 326
  Sending Your Data on a Long, One-Way Trip 327

Chapter 24: The Analyzer: Your Data's Dr. Freud, Dr. Watson, and Dr. Jekyll 331

It Slices, It Dices, It Builds Relational Databases! 331
Documentation: What to Give the Nerd in Your Life 336
Let the Performance Analyzer Work on Someone Else's Tables 338

Part VI: The Part of Tens *339*

Chapter 25: Ten Timesaving Keyboard Shortcuts 341

Select an Entire Field — F2 341
Insert the Current Date — Ctrl+; (Semicolon) 341
Insert the Current Time — Ctrl+: (Colon) 342
Insert the Same Field Value as the Last Record
    Ctrl+' (Apostrophe) 342
Insert a Line Break — Ctrl+Enter 342
Add a New Record — Ctrl++ (Plus Sign) 343
Delete the Current Record — Ctrl+− (Minus Sign) 343
Save the Record — Shift+Enter 343
Undo Your Last Changes — Ctrl+Z 343
Open the Selected Object in Design View — Ctrl+Enter 344

Chapter 26: Ten Common Crises and How to Survive Them 345

You Built Several Tables, but Put Them in Different Databases 345
You Type 73.725, but It Changes to 74 by Itself 346
You're Almost Completely Sure That's Not the Question
    You Asked 346
And When You Looked Again, the Record Was Gone 347
The Validation That Never Was 348
The Sometimes-There, Sometimes-Gone Menus 348
You Can't Link to a FoxPro or dBASE Table 349
You Get a Key Violation While Importing a Table 349
Try as You Might, the Program Won't Start 349
The Wizard Won't Come Out of His Castle 350

Chapter 27: Ten Tips from the Database Nerds 351

Document As If Your Life Depends on It 351
Don't Make Your Fields Way Too Big 352
Real Numbers Use Number Fields 353
Better Validations Make Better Data 353
Use Understandable Names 353
Take Great Care When Deleting 353
Keep Backups 354
Think First and Then Think Again 354
Get Organized and Keep It Simple 354
Know When to Ask for Help 355

Index *357*

Book Registration Information . . . .*Back of Book*

Introduction

● ●

*B*eing a normal human being, you probably have work to do. In fact, you may have *lots* of work piled precariously around your office or even stretching onto the Internet. Someone, possibly your boss (or, if you work at home, your Significant Other), suggested that Access 2000 may help you get more done in less time, eliminate the piles, and generally make the safety inspector happy.

So you picked up Access 2000, and here you are. Whee!

If you're confused instead of organized, befuddled instead of productive, or just completely lost on the whole database thing, *Access 2000 For Windows For Dummies* is the book for you.

This is a book with a purpose: to explain Access 2000 without turning you into a world-class nerd in the process. What more could you want? (Well, you *could* want a chocolate malt, but Marketing said that I couldn't package ice cream beverages with this book.)

You Don't Need to Be a Nerd to Use This Book

Becoming a nerd is totally out of the question. In fact, you need to know only a few things about your computer and Windows to get the most out of *Access 2000 For Windows For Dummies*. In the following pages, I presume that you

✔ Have Microsoft Windows 98, 95, or NT 4, and Access 2000 for Windows on your computer (if you have the whole Office 2000 suite, that's fine, too)

To install Office 2000 on a Windows NT system, the NT system must have Service Pack 3 or 4 installed. If Access 2000 already runs on your system, don't worry about the Service Pack; you're good to go. If Office 2000 says you need an NT Service Pack, try downloading the Service Pack from `http://support.microsoft.com/support/ntserver/Content/ServicePacks/`

✔ Know the basics of Windows 95, 98, or NT (whichever one you use)

> ✔ Want to work with databases that other people have created
>
> ✔ Want to use and create queries, reports, and an occasional form
>
> ✔ Want to make your own databases from scratch every now and then
>
> ✔ Have perhaps used other versions of Access (although this is certainly not a requirement)

The good news is that you don't have to know (or even care) about table design, field types, relational databases, or any of that other database stuff to make Access 2000 work for you. Everything you need to know is right here, just waiting for you to read it.

Sneaking a Peek at What's to Come

To give you an idea of what's ahead, here's a breakdown of the six parts in this book. Each part covers a general topic of Access 2000. The part's individual chapters dig into the details.

Part I: Which Came First: The Data or the Base?

Right off the bat, this book answers the lyrical question "It's a data-*what?*" By starting with an overview of both database concepts in general and Access 2000 in particular, this book provides the information you need to make sense of the whole database concept. This part also contains suggestions about solving problems with (or even *without*) Access 2000. If you're about to design a new Access database to fix some pesky problem, read this section first — it may change your mind.

Part II: Truly Tempting Tables

Arguably, tables (where the data lives) are at the center of this whole database hubbub. After all, without tables, you wouldn't have any data to bully around. This part gives you the information you need to know about designing, building, using, changing, and generally coexisting in the same room with Access 2000 tables.

Part III: Finding the Ultimate Answer to Everything (Well, Not Everything)

If tables are at the center of the Access universe, then queries are the first ring of planets. In Access, queries ask the power questions; they unearth the answers you *know* are hiding somewhere in your data. In addition to covering queries, this part also explains how to answer smaller questions using Find, Filter, and Sort — Query's little siblings.

Part IV: Turning Your Table into a Book

Seeing your data on-screen just isn't enough, sometimes. To make your work *really* shine, you have to commit it to paper. Part IV covers the Access report system, a portion of the software entirely dedicated both to getting your information onto the printed page and to driving you nuts in the process.

Part V: Wizards, Forms, and Other Mystical Stuff

At some point, technology approaches magic (one look at the control panel for a modern microwave oven is proof of that). This part explores some of the mystical areas in Access, helping you do stuff faster, seek assistance from the wizards, and even venture into a bit of programming. If the Internet's limitless possibilities pique your online fancy, look in this part for info about the new Web connectivity features in Access 2000. They're really amazing!

Part VI: The Part of Tens

The words "...*For Dummies* book" immediately bring to mind the snappy, irreverent Part of Tens. This section dumps a load of tips and cool ideas onto, and hopefully *into,* your head. You can find a little bit of everything here, including timesaving tips and the solutions to the most common problems awaiting you in Access 2000.

What the Funny Text Means

Every now and then, you need to tell Access to do something or other. Likewise, there are moments when the program wants to toss its own comments and messages back to you (so be nice — communication is a two-way street). To easily show the difference between a human-to-computer message and vice-versa, I format the commands differently.

Here are examples of both kinds of message as they appear in the book.

This is something you type into the computer.

This is how the computer responds to your command.

Because this *is* a Windows program, you don't just type all day — you also mouse around quite a bit. Although I don't use a cool font for mouse actions, I *do* assume that you already know the basics. Here are the mouse movements necessary to make Access 2000 (and any other Windows program) work:

- ✔ **Click:** Position the tip of the mouse pointer (the end of the arrow) on the menu item, button, check box, or whatever else you happen to be aiming at, and then quickly press and release the left mouse button.

- ✔ **Double-click:** Position the mouse pointer as though you're going to click, but fool it at the last minute by clicking twice in rapid succession.

- ✔ **Click and drag** *(highlight)***:** Put the tip of the mouse pointer at the place you want to start highlighting and then press and hold the left mouse button. While holding the mouse button down, drag the pointer across whatever you want to highlight. When you reach the end of what you're highlighting, release the mouse button.

- ✔ **Right-click:** Right-clicking works just like clicking, except that you're exercising the right mouse button instead of the left mouse button.

Of course, the Access 2000 menu comes in handy, too. When I want you to pick something from the main menu bar, the instruction looks like this:

Choose File⇨Open Database.

If you think that mice belong in holes, you can use the underlined letters as shortcut keys to control Access 2000 from the keyboard. To use the keyboard shortcut, hold down the Alt key and press the underlined letters. In the example above, the keyboard shortcut is Alt+F, O. Don't type the comma — it's just trying to make the command easier to read.

If you aren't familiar with all these rodent gymnastics, or if you want to learn more about Windows in general, pick up a copy of one the many *Windows For Dummies* titles by IDG Books Worldwide. Every version of Windows has one!

Finding Points of Interest

When something in this book is particularly valuable, I go out of my way to make sure that it stands out. I use these cool icons to mark text that (for one reason or another) *really* needs your attention. Here's a quick preview of the ones waiting for you in this book and what they mean:

Tips are *really* helpful words of wisdom that promise to save you time, energy, and perhaps some hair. Whenever you see a tip, take a second to check it out.

Some things are too important to forget, so the Remember icon points them out. These items are critical steps in a process — points that you don't want to miss.

Sometimes, I give in to my dark, nerdy side and slip some technical twaddle into the book. The Technical Stuff icon protects you from obscure details by making them easy to avoid. If you're in an adventuresome mood, check out the technical stuff, anyway. You may find it interesting.

The Warning icon says it all: *Skipping this information may be hazardous to your data's health.* Pay attention to these icons and follow their instructions to keep your databases happy and intact.

The wheel on the new Microsoft IntelliMouse adds some interesting innovations to Access 2000. This icon marks timesaving tips featuring the newest addition to the bag of mousy tricks.

Setting Sail on the Voyage

Now nothing's left to hold you back from the wonders of Access 2000. Cleave tightly to *Access 2000 For Windows For Dummies,* consign the Microsoft manuals to a suitable dark hole, and dive into Access 2000.

- ✔ If you're brand-new to the program and don't know which way to turn, start with the general overview in Chapter 1.

- ✔ If you're about to design a database, I salute you — and recommend flipping through Chapter 4 for some helpful design and development tips.

- ✔ Looking for something specific? Try the Table of Contents or the Index, or just flip through the book until you find something interesting.

Bon Voyage!

Part I
Which Came First: The Data or the Base?

The 5th Wave   By Rich Tennant

"OH YEAH, AND TRY NOT TO ENTER THE WRONG PASSWORD."

In this part . . .

Everything starts somewhere. It's that way with nature, with science, and with meatballs that roll down your tie. So what more fitting way to begin this book than with a look at where databases start — as a glimmer in someone's mind.

This part opens with a heretical look at problem solving, and then moves along to cover the new Access 2000 program itself. A little later in the part, you discover the secrets of good data organization and where to find help when the world of Access 2000 has you down.

All in all, this part is a pretty good place to start — whether you're new to the whole database concept, or just to Access 2000. Either way, welcome aboard!

Chapter 1

The 37-Minute Overview

In This Chapter

▶ Starting the program

▶ Opening a database that's already there

▶ A good database is more than tables

▶ Finding a record

▶ Changing a record

▶ Printing a report

▶ Asking for help

▶ Saving your changes

▶ Getting out when you're done

*I*t's confession time. This chapter probably takes longer than 37 minutes to finish, if you read the whole thing. Then again, you may spend *less* time than that if you're already somewhat familiar with the program, or if you're a speed-reader. Either way, the chapter *does* give you a good overview of Access 2000 from start to finish (and I mean that literally).

Because the best way to get into Access 2000 is to literally *get into* it, this chapter leads you on a wild, galloping tour of the software, covering the highlights of things you and Access 2000 probably do together on a daily basis. This chapter is something of a "Day in the Life" story, designed to show you the important stuff while pointing you to other areas of the book for more information.

If you're new to Access 2000, this chapter is a good place to start. If you're already familiar with the older versions of Access, I recommend that you skim through this chapter anyway to see how things have changed. Enjoy the trip!

In the Beginning, There Was Access 2000 (But It Wasn't Running Yet)

The machine is quiet, the screen sits dark and devoid of image, and you aren't getting much work done. Nice as it is, the situation can't go on forever — the time has come to start Access 2000.

Unlike in the old days (way back in the 1980s), when waking up your computer and running a database program could be terribly complicated, starting Access 2000 is simple. Here are the steps:

1. **Mentally prepare yourself for the task at hand.**

   If it's before lunch, have a cup of coffee. After lunch, try chocolate.

2. **Click on the Start button and then click on Programs on the pop-up menu.**

   So far, so good. But now comes the tricky part: finding Access 2000 itself.

3. **If the Programs menu has an entry for Access 2000 (see Figure 1-1), click on that entry to start the program.**

   When you start the program, the Microsoft advertisement — er, logo — screen appears, followed shortly by the friendly dialog box in Figure 1-2. If you see this dialog box on-screen, Access is successfully running, so go on to the next section.

   If you can't find the Access 2000 icon in the Programs menu, then your company's computer people apparently hid the icon somewhere else on the menu. Look for a special menu under the Start menu named something like Applications or Microsoft Office (as in Figure 1-3). If you *still* can't find Access 2000, or if the program won't start, invest in a box of brownies and then bribe your favorite computer guru for help.

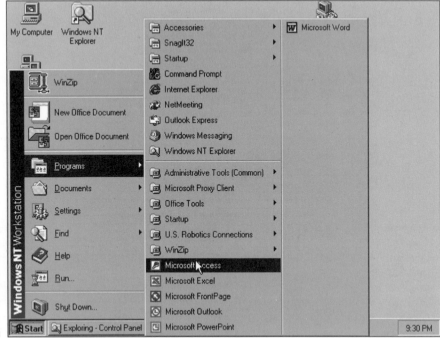

Figure 1-1:
For a smart
program,
Access 2000
doesn't hide
very well.

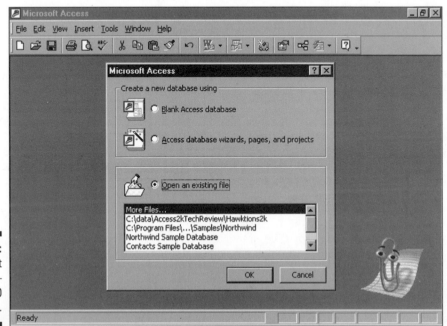

Figure 1-2:
Success at
last —
Access 2000
is running.

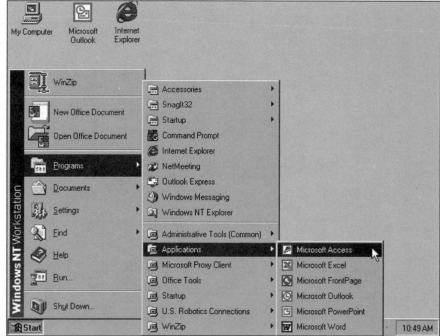

Figure 1-3:
Sometimes
Access 2000
makes you
look a little
harder.

Opening an Existing Database

Bringing the program to life is a good start, but that isn't the ultimate goal. After all, Access 2000 without a database file is like a CD player without a CD: Nice to look at, but you can't dance to it. Loading your database is next on the hit list.

Database files fall in two distinct categories: those that already exist and those that don't. The odds are good that you're working with a database that already exists (after all, you only build a database once, but use it forever). If so, then read on — this section is for you. If you're having a once-in-a-turquoise-lunar-cycle moment and you want to create a new database, then flip to Chapter 4 for detailed design and creation help.

If you just started Access 2000 and your screen looks like Figure 1-2, opening a database only takes a moment. If the database you want to use is listed at the bottom of the dialog box, just double-click on the database name.

If the database you're looking for isn't in the introductory dialog box, then follow these steps:

1. **Double-click on the More Files option in the introductory dialog box to see a list of the databases in the current directory folder.**

   The Open dialog box appears, looking much like Figure 1-4.

2. **Double-click on the database you're interested in.**

   After a moment, the database loads into Access, and you're ready to work.

If the database you want to use isn't listed in the Open dialog box either, the database is probably in some other directory folder. Skip to Chapter 6 (the sidebar called "Bo Peep needed the Find File option") for help with tracking down the database in your hard disk or network.

If you already worked with Access for a while (printing reports, checking out a form or two, and generally keeping yourself busy), and now you want to open another database, follow these steps:

1. **Choose File➪Open Database or click on the Open Database button on the toolbar.**

   The Open dialog box (still appearing for your viewing pleasure in Figure 1-4) pops onto the screen.

2. **Double-click on the name of the database you want to use.**

   If the database isn't listed, you may need to go on a quick hunt for the little fellow. Skip to Chapter 6 and check out the sidebar called "Bo Peep needed the Find File option" for help with the Open dialog box's database search functions.

Figure 1-4:
The Open dialog box, in all its glory.

Touring the Database Window

When a database opens, it usually appears on-screen looking like Figure 1-5. Click one of the buttons on the left side of the window under the Objects bar to display the various parts (Access 2000 calls them *objects*) of your database: Tables, Queries, Forms, and so on. The rest of the window lists whichever objects you select.

After opening the database, you can fiddle with the parts inside:

* ✔ To open a table, click on the Tables button and then double-click on the table you want to see.

* ✔ To run a report, query, or form, click on the appropriate button and then double-click on the item you want to work with.

* ✔ When you get tired of this database, close it by clicking the Close Window button (the X box in the upper-right corner of the window) or by choosing File⇨Close. If you're a keyboard fan, Ctrl+W does the deed without disturbing the mouse.

* ✔ If you want to know more about working with the cool Access 2000 interface (and all the wonderful ways you can play in it), check out Chapter 2.

If some kind soul invested the time to make your life a little easier, a start-up screen (or *switchboard*) resembling Figure 1-6 appears automatically when you open the database. Don't panic — this is a good thing. The only downside is that your switchboard is probably unique to your company, so I can't tell you anything about the options on it. (Sorry, but my crystal ball broke some time ago.) Find the person responsible for creating or maintaining your Access switchboard and offer to trade some cookies for help.

Figure 1-5:
A normal
database
appears,
looking, um,
normal.

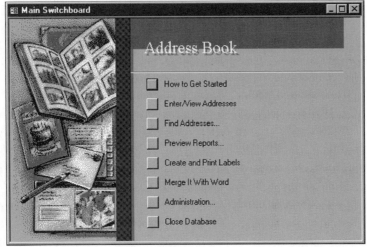

Figure 1-6:
A database
fronted by a
fancy
switchboard
screen.

If your start-up screen does have options like the ones in Figure 1-6, you're in luck. I *can* help you make sense of this start-up screen because it was created using one of the many Database Wizard templates. Check out Chapter 4 for more information about the start-up screen's options and how the whole thing came into being.

Finding Candy amongst the Grass Clippings

I don't understand what the big deal is about getting kids to eat stuff. If you want preschoolers to eat something, just let them take it outside and drop it into the yard first, preferably right after you cut the lawn with a mulching mower. For some inexplicable reason, covering food with freshly cut grass seems to make it all the more appetizing to youngsters.

Finding specific records in your Access table is a little like a toddler's method of whittling through sticky grass in search of candy. Whether you're looking for last names, first names, part numbers, or postal codes, Access 2000 makes finding your target records a whole lot easier — and infinitely less messy.

Here's one way to find records:

1. **Open the table you want to search.**

   If you don't know how to open a table, flip back to the preceding section.

2. **Click in the field you want to search.**

   The blinking toothpick cursor leaps into the field, showing that Access 2000 really heard you (at least *this* time).

3. **Choose Edit⇨Find or click on the Find toolbar button.**

   The Find and Replace dialog box appears (see Figure 1-7).

   Access 2000 displays the name of the current field in the Look In section of the dialog box. To look in a different field, click in the down-arrow next to the field name, and then pick the field from the drop-down list.

4. **Type the text you want to find in the appropriately named Find What text box (see Figure 1-8).**

   Spell carefully, because Access 2000 looks for *exactly* what you type!

5. **Press Enter or click on the Find Next button to start the search.**

   The search begins — and probably ends before you know it. If the program finds a matching record, Access 2000 highlights the data (see Figure 1-9).

   If no record matches your criteria, a big, officious dialog box informs you that Microsoft Access finished searching the records, but found no matches. (If the Office Assistant is on-screen, then instead of getting whacked by the big dialog box, the Assistant quietly tells you about the search results.) If this message appears, click on OK and smile as the dialog box disappears; then double-check what you typed in the Find What text box. You probably just mistyped something. If so, fix it and try the search again.

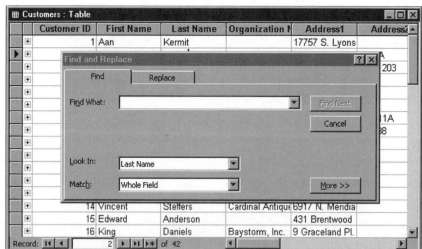

Figure 1-7:
The Find
and Replace
dialog box,
at your
service.

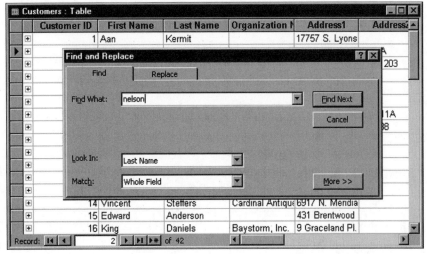

Figure 1-8:
Ready to
seek out a
record.

Access 2000 automatically tries to match a *whole* field in the table with what you typed. So, if you type *Kaufeld* in the Find dialog box, Access 2000 *won't* find a record containing *Kaufeld School of Creative Writing*. Why? Because that entry is not an exact match for *Kaufeld* — it's only a partial match. (Computers are *so* detail-oriented sometimes!) To make Access 2000 accept partial matches as well as full ones, change the Match setting in the Find and Replace dialog box from Whole Field to Any Part of Field.

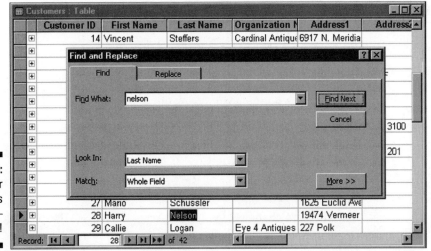

Figure 1-9:
Customer
Nelson is
found —
hooray!

If you *still* can't find the record, either look in Chapter 10 for more details about the Find dialog box or grab a nearby guru and seek personal guidance.

6. Click on Close or press Esc to close the Find dialog box when you're done.

You can do many more tricks with the Find command, so be sure to look in Chapter 10 when you're ready to impress the co-workers.

The right mouse button also provides some tricky ways to find records, but I'm saving those tricks for Chapter 10.

Making a Few Changes

Unfortunately for fruit growers and dairy farmers, life isn't always peaches and cream. Your customers move, the phone company changes an area code, and the digital gremlins mess up your typing skills. Whatever the cause, your job probably includes fixing the various problems in your database. Lucky you.

Changing the stuff in your tables isn't hard. In fact, making changes is almost too easy. I outline the precise steps in the following list. Keep in mind that your changes are *automatically* saved. When you finish working on a record, Access writes the new information to the database *right then.* If you make a mistake, *immediately* press Ctrl+Z to undo your changes — don't put it off until later.

Here's a quick word from the Society of the Perpetually Nervous: Be *very* careful when changing the records in your database. Making changes is easy; recovering from them can be tough. Access 2000 can only help you undo the *last thing you changed.*

When you're ready to change a record, follow these steps:

1. View the table on-screen as a data sheet or in a form.

Either way, your data is hanging out on the monitor and looking cool.

2. Click in the field you want to change.

A flashing toothpick cursor appears in the field, and the mouse pointer changes to an I-beam.

3. Perform whatever repairs the field needs.

All the standard editing keys (Home, End, Backspace, and Delete) work when you're changing an entry in Access 2000. See Chapter 6 for the key-by-key details.

4. **When the field is *just right,* press Return to save the changes.**

   As soon as you press Return, the data is saved — and I do mean *saved.* If you immediately decide that you like the old data better, press Ctrl+Z or choose Edit⇨Undo Typing.

Reporting the Results

Capturing all those wonderful details in your tables is nice, but what's even *nicer* is seeing those records fill a printed page. That's where the Access 2000 report system comes in.

Making your database look wonderful on paper is a cinch with Access 2000. The program has all kinds of report options, plus a reasonably strong Report Wizard to walk you through the hard stuff. Check out Part IV for more about all the really cool report features.

Because printing a report is one of the most common things people do with Access 2000 (who said computers would bring on the paperless office?), the following steps show you how to do it:

1. **If your database display looks like Figure 1-10, click on the Reports button.**

   If you're working with a custom form or a custom-built Access application that's unique to your company, click on the Reports option (or whatever option sounds like that) and follow the system's instructions. Because systems vary so much from company to company, I can't really be more specific. Sorry!

2. **Right-click on the report you want to print.**

   A menu pops up wherever your mouse pointer is.

3. **Choose Print on the pop-up menu (see Figure 1-11).**

   Access 2000 puts a little dialog box in the middle of the screen to tell you how the print job is going. When the print job is complete, the dialog box vanishes without a trace.

   If you change your mind while the report is printing, click Cancel on the so-how's-the-print-job-going? dialog box to stop the process.

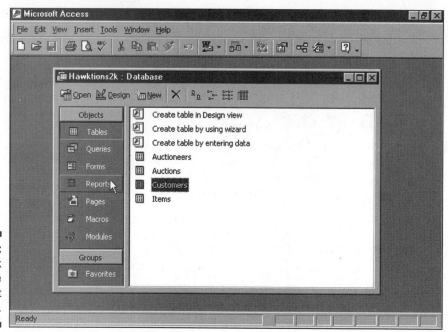

Figure 1-10:
One click
lists all the
current
reports.

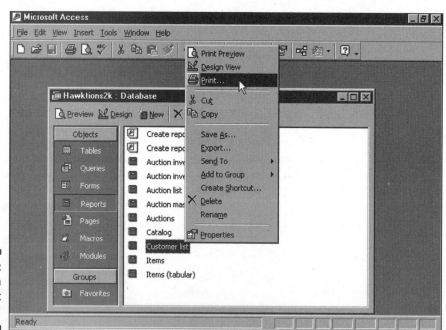

Figure 1-11:
Viola — an
instant Print
menu!

Help is always just a few clicks away

No matter where you are in Access 2000, help is always nearby. Chapter 3 covers all your help options in gory detail, but here's one to get you started.

If you're stumped for what to do next, press the F1 key at the top of your keyboard, which is the Windows universal *help me* key. The F1 key brings up either the ever-helpful Office Assistant or a dialog box that's jam-packed with help topics ranging from an overview of the newest, coolest things about Access 2000 to phenomenally trivial explorations of macros.

Unless you're in the mood to browse, pose your question to the Office Assistant or click the Find tab at the top of the window and search for your topic of interest. Either way, your answer is only a moment away!

Saving Your Hard Work

Actually, I don't have much to say on the topic of saving — Access 2000 saves your work for you. This feature is both good and, well, not so good.

The Access 2000 automatic save feature is good because it's one less detail left lying around to clutter up your life. Whether you entered a bunch of new records or simply fixed a couple that were ever so slightly wrong, your work is automatically safe and sound.

On the other hand, the automatic save feature *isn't* such a good thing because Access 2000 doesn't pay any attention to what it's saving — it just saves everything that's there. If you accidentally wipe out 237 records and then make a couple of errant clicks, you can say *good-bye records, hello backups.*

I said it in a previous section, but it bears repeating: When you're changing the records in your tables, *please* be careful. Messing up a record takes only a second. Don't let this tragedy happen to you. (This has been a public service announcement from your author.)

The Great Backup Lecture

I know you've probably heard this before, but the PC support nerd in me won't let the chapter close without a few words about backing up your databases. Even though I joke about it, doing regular backups is a *vital* part of using Access 2000 (or any program, for that matter).

Why is backing up so important? Take a minute and imagine life without your computer. Don't reminisce about business in the Good Old Days of the 1970s — think about what would happen if you walked in one morning and found *no* computer awaiting your arrival. None. Zippo. The desk is empty — no business letters, no receivables, no customer list, no nothing. Everything was on the computer, but now the computer is history. (It certainly sounds like my definition of a bad day.)

Unless you want to wave goodbye to your business, you need a formal backup plan. Even if it's just you and your computer, write down some notes about how your backup process works. Some specific things to include:

- ✔ **How often is the computer backed up?** A better way to ask this question is "How much data can you afford to lose?" If your information changes daily (like an accounting system, for example), you need to make backups every day or two. If you mainly play adventure games on your machine and use Access 2000 as infrequently as possible, backup every week or two. No universal rule is right for everyone.

- ✔ **Where are the backup disks or tapes stored?** If the backups are stored right next to the computer, they'll be conveniently destroyed along with the computer in the event of a fire. Keep your backups in another building, if possible, or at least in another room.

- ✔ **How do you backup the data?** Write down a step-by-step procedure, along with a method for figuring out what tape or disk set to use in the backup process.

- ✔ **How do you *restore* the data?** Again, create a step-by-step process. Your mind won't be particularly clear if tragedy strikes and you have to restore destroyed data, so make the steps simple and understandable.

After you settle into the backup routine, try restoring your data once to make sure that your system works. You're *much* better off finding this out before the disk dies rather than afterward. Set aside a couple hours to ensure that your efforts will pay off on that fateful day when the disk drive dies. You'll thank me later.

If you're in a corporate environment, it's possible that your local Department of Computer People automatically backs up your data. To find out for sure, give them a call and ask.

Making a Graceful Exit

When it's time to shut down for the day, do so the right way:

1. **If you have a database open, choose File⇨Close or click the Windows 95/98 Close Window button in the upper-right corner of the database window.**

   I'm old-fashioned enough not to trust my program to close everything by itself without screwing something up. Whenever possible, I close my files manually before shutting down the program.

2. **Close Access 2000 by choosing File⇨Exit.**

   Go ahead and shut down Windows 95/98, as well, if you're done for the night. To do so, click on the Start button and then click on Shut Down. When Windows asks whether you're serious about this shut-down thing, click on Yes. After Windows 95/98 gets done doing whatever it is that software does just before bedtime, turn off your computer and make your escape to freedom.

Chapter 2

Finding Your Way Around
like a Native

In This Chapter

▶ What's what with the interface?

▶ Looking at the pretty windows

▶ Checking out the toolbars

▶ Ordering from the menu

▶ Doing tricks with the right mouse button

Cruising around an unfamiliar city is fun, exciting, and frustrating. Seeing the sights, recognizing famous landmarks, and discovering new places to exercise your credit card make it fun. Finding yourself lost deep within a neighborhood that's "in transition" makes it, uh, exciting. Being unable to find your way back in either case makes it frustrating.

If you're comfortable with earlier versions of Access, then driving your mouse through Access 2000 is much like steering your car through your home town — twenty years later. The terrain looks somewhat familiar, but you're in for some surprises — things like "Where'd they move that menu item? It used to be right over, um . . . oh geez, half of the menu is gone — no, wait, it's back. Eeesh . . . I need more coffee."

I know the feeling. Nothing is worse than watching your work pile up while deciphering a new program. This chapter helps you out of that trap by presenting a tour of the sights and sounds of Access 2000. It covers the common things you see and deal with on-screen, from the main window to the toolbar and beyond. Kick back and enjoy the jaunt — it's a great way to get comfortable with Access 2000.

Making Sense of the Sights

Because Access 2000 is, after all, a Windows 95/98 program, the first stop on this merry visual jaunt is the program's main window. Figure 2-1 shows Access 2000 in a common pose, displaying a database window (which I cover later in this chapter).

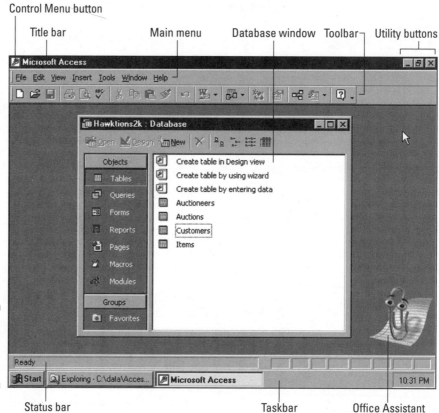

Control Menu button

Title bar   Main menu   Database window   Toolbar   Utility buttons

Figure 2-1:
Access 2000, in all its glory.

Status bar   Taskbar   Office Assistant

To make the most of Access 2000, you need to be familiar with nine parts of the main window. I describe each part briefly in the paragraphs that follow. If you're *really* new to Windows 95/98, consider picking up a copy of *Windows 98 For Dummies* by Andy Rathbone (published by IDG Books Worldwide, Inc.). Having that book will make your life with Windows 95/98 a *lot* easier, I promise.

✔ **Control Menu button:** Click on the Access "key" to open the Control Menu. Frankly, this menu is mostly for doing nerdy stuff. But because you *can* make Access 2000 go away by double-clicking here, I suppose that this button has some redeeming value for the rest of us, despite its nerdy tendencies. In Windows 3.1, the button's picture was a box with a horizontal bar in it. These days, it looks spiffier.

✔ **Title bar:** Every window comes complete with a space along the top for the title. This space has a second purpose, too: It changes color to let you know which program is currently active in Windows.

✔ **Main menu:** Between the title bar and the toolbar sits the Main menu, Keeper of the Digital Peace. Aside from preventing fights between the two bars, this menu is also your main stopping point for Access 2000 commands and functions.

✔ **Toolbar:** Think of the toolbar as an electronic version of Lon Chaney, the Man of a Thousand Faces. Just about every time you do something in Access 2000, this *Bar of a Thousand Buttons* does a quick change to serve up the tools you need. Read more about this slippery character later in this chapter.

✔ **Utility buttons:** These three buttons appear on every window. From left to right, these buttons reduce the current program to a button on the Taskbar, make the current program either fit in a window or take up the whole screen (one button, two tasks — pretty cool, eh?), and close the current window.

✔ **Status bar:** Access 2000 is a talkative system, with words of wisdom to share about every little thing. Whenever Access wants to tell you something, a message appears on the Status bar. On the far right of the Status bar are indicators for keyboard settings such as Caps Lock.

✔ **Database window:** In the midst of this maelstrom sits a serene database window, explained in the next section.

✔ **Taskbar:** Across the bottom of the screen is the Windows 95/98 taskbar, Microsoft's quick-and-easy tool for switching among programs. Each running program has a button on this bar. To use another program, just click on its button.

✔ **Office Assistant:** This helpful fellow shows up in all Office 2000 products, including Access 2000. When you have a question or want some help, give him a click and ask away. (And when you're bored, right-click on it and select Animate for some brief entertainment.)

Windows Shopping for Fun and Understanding

There's more to Access 2000 than the big picture window. The program is chock-full of little windows for every need and occasion. This section looks at four of the most common ones: the database window, datasheet window, form window, and query (you guessed it) window.

For details on how these windows work, what to do with them, and why you should even care, keep trekking through this book. Databases and datasheets appear in Part II, queries star in Part III, and forms have a supporting role in Part V.

The database window

Most of the time when you open a database, it appears in a window like Figure 2-2. This window gives you access to all the cool stuff in your database, provides tools to change things or create new items, and generally helps you manage your database stuff. And it looks cool. Who could ask for more?

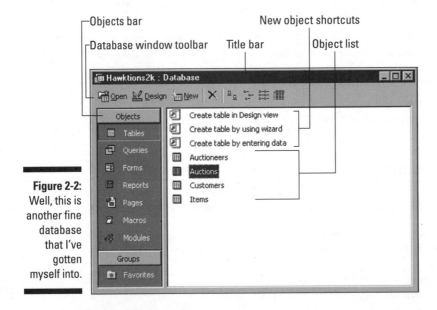

Figure 2-2: Well, this is another fine database that I've gotten myself into.

The *Objects bar buttons* down the left side of the window switch between lists of the *objects* (tables, queries, reports, and so on) that make up the database. Along the upper left side are four database window toolbar *buttons* for working with the database's objects: Open displays the current object, Design lets you change the object, New creates a new object, and the big, bad X deletes the current object (kiss that table good-bye!). The other buttons to the right of the X change how Access 2000 lists the objects that your database contains. Your choices run the gamut from colorful, friendly icons to detailed mini-dossiers. Feel free to try the settings yourself — you can't hurt anything! (Just don't accidentally click the X, okay?)

Your database *may* start up looking like Figure 2-3. Don't let the pretty face fool you, though — this window is just a fancier front hung onto Figure 2-2's database. Seeing something like this window is a clue that you're working with a formal Access 2000 application. The form may be something created with a wizard (like the one in Figure 2-3), or perhaps one of your in-house nerds whipped it up just for you. This special form is called a *switchboard*.

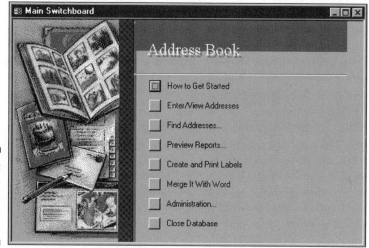

Figure 2-3:
A wizard-created switchboard.

The datasheet window

Is it a table or a spreadsheet? Only its owner knows for sure! Such are the traumas of the modern database. Being mistaken for a spreadsheet, for goodness sake! What's the world coming to?

Looking at Figure 2-4, it's easy to see why people may confuse the two. Yes, that's a *table*. Looks kinda like a spreadsheet, doesn't it? In *datasheet view,* an Access 2000 table appears (and arguably acts) like a simple spreadsheet. The resemblance is only skin-deep, though — this table is really a very different animal.

Table name   Fields

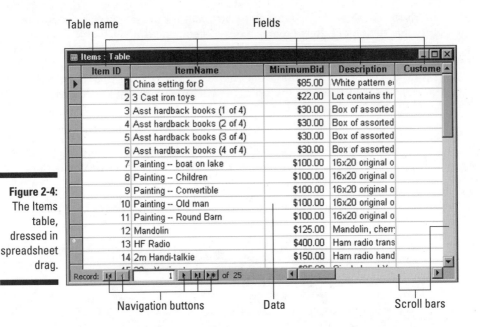

Figure 2-4:
The Items
table,
dressed in
spreadsheet
drag.

Navigation buttons   Data   Scroll bars

The datasheet window shows the *table name* across its top, just as it should. Right under that, the table's *fields* are arrayed across the window. The table's *records* are laid out in rows. Don't worry if you're not exactly sure about the difference between a record and a field. Chapter 4 has all the details about that.

On the right side and lower-right corner are a pair of *scroll bars,* which make moving through the table a real breeze. The *navigation buttons* are hanging out in the window's lower-left side. These buttons are a lot like the controls on a compact disc player or VCR (videocassette recorder). The buttons that have arrows pointing to a bar take you to the first or last record of the table. The arrow-only buttons move you to the next or previous record. Clicking on the arrow and asterisk button adds a new record to the table.

Access 2000 adds a new feature to the database window for all of your related tables (see Chapters 4 and 5 for more about building relationships and quality conversations between tables). When you open a table that's related to others in your database, Access 2000 puts a column of plus signs (+) to the left of the first field in the table. Despite its mundane appearance, this column definitely qualifies for an award like *Way-Cool Technology That's Actually Useful.*

When you click on the plus sign next to a particular record, Access 2000 follows the relationship link to another table in your database and then displays all the data from that other table that goes with the current record in this table. For instance, you may click on the plus sign next to a product in your Catalog table to display all of the current orders for that product. Best of all, the process is automatic — Access handles all of the work for you by itself.

The form window

Form view is the other popular way to look at Access 2000 tables. With forms, the data looks more, well, traditional — none of that sissy spreadsheet-style stuff. A form usually shows the data in a table at the blinding rate of one record per screen, the same way that the nerds of the 1970s worked with their data, using million-dollar computers that had all the intelligence of today's microwave ovens.

Figure 2-5 is a very simple but classic example of an Access 2000 form. Along the top is the ever-anticipated *title bar*. The table's *fields* take up the middle of the form. In the lower-left corner are the same *navigation buttons* you saw and fiddled with in the datasheet window.

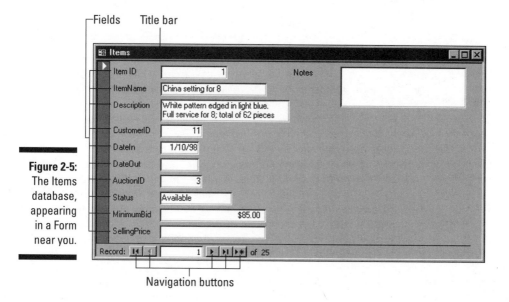

Figure 2-5:
The Items
database,
appearing
in a Form
near you.

If forms really pique your interest, check out Chapter 22 for more information.

The query window

The heart of any database program is its capability to search for information. In particular, the heart of Access 2000 is the query system. And sitting at the heart of the query system is the *query window,* lovingly reproduced in Figure 2-6.

Title bar   Tables

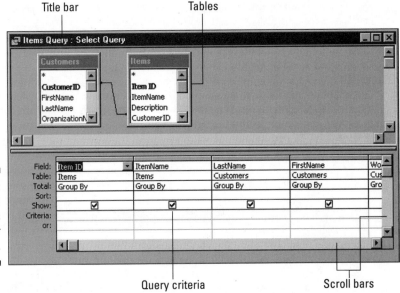

Figure 2-6:
The digital
Holmes
at your
service.

Query criteria   Scroll bars

The top of the window displays the *title bar,* showing the query's given name. The window's top half shows the *tables* involved in the query. If the query uses more than one table, this section also shows how the tables are linked together (or *joined*). The lower half displays the *query criteria* — the instructions that make the query work. Because all this stuff can get large and complicated, the window has several *scroll bars* to help you see everything clearly.

When you run a query, Access 2000 usually displays the results in a datasheet.

Belly Up to the Toolbar, Folks!

Toolbars are the Office 2000 equivalent of sliced bread — they're *that* useful. Access 2000 has a bunch of them, too. You won't ever find yourself without a toolbar around to help.

So what *is* a toolbar? It's that row of cool buttons just below the menu at the top of the screen. Figure 2-7 shows the Database toolbar in action (well, in as much action as any inanimate object ever shows).

Figure 2-7:
The
Database
toolbar, just
sitting there.

The toolbars give you single-click access to the best features of Access 2000. The engineers designed the toolbars to contain the most common functions you need when working with your data. The Datasheet toolbar, for example, includes three buttons that control the Filter tools (tools that help you quickly find things in your database). Instead of working your way through a menu to find these Filter tools, they're out in the open, just a mouse click away.

Because a toolbar exists for literally every occasion, I describe the toolbars throughout the book. Don't worry if you can't remember what all the buttons do — neither can I. If you're button-challenged, too, check out the following sidebar for a useful word about *ScreenTips,* Access 2000's built-in toolbar button-reminder system.

Quick — what does that button do?

Access 2000 has 29 different toolbars. (Okay, it's a nerd statistic, but I'm building up to a point — trust me.) Each toolbar has, um, lots of buttons on it. There's no way that anyone, not even the programmers, can remember what all the buttons do. Besides, who'd want to try?

Unfortunately, toolbars are pretty useless if you don't know what the buttons do. To resolve this problem, Microsoft came up with *ScreenTips* — little pop-up descriptions that appear when you point the mouse at a toolbar button.

To see a button's ScreenTip, just hold the mouse pointer over the button in question. Wait there for a second, and {poof!} the ScreenTip appears. If you position your mouse, wait patiently, and nothing happens, your ScreenTips may be turned off. To turn them on, right-click anywhere on the toolbar and then select Customize from the pop-up menu. When the Customize dialog box appears, click the Options tab. Make sure a check mark appears next to Show ScreenTips on toolbars. Click on Close to make the dialog box vanish.

If you have trouble seeing the little pictures on each button, tell Access 2000 to make them bigger. To do that, right-click on any toolbar and then select Customize from the pop-up menu. When the Customize dialog box appears, click the Options tab. In the lower part of the Options page, click the Large Icons checkbox. Access 2000 immediately makes the icons much bigger — about four times their old size, as a matter of fact. If you decide that big *wasn't* better, just click the checkbox again to turn it off. Click the Close button at the bottom of the window to finish the task.

Menus, Menus Everywhere (And Keystrokes That Work as Well)

Truth be told, there isn't a lot to say about the Access 2000 menus. The main thing that you're sure to notice is that they change every time you do something new. Gone are the days of *one program, one menu*. Now we have *context-sensitive* menus that show different options depending on what you're doing at the moment.

Some things never change, though. Here's a brief rundown of generic menu truisms:

✔ If your mouse dies, you can get to the menu items from the keyboard. Just hold down the Alt key and press the underlined letter of the menu item you want. For instance, press Alt+F to open the File menu.

✔ Some menu items have a specific key assigned to them. The Copy command (Edit⇨Copy on the menu) also works without the menu by pressing Ctrl+C. If an item has a keyboard equivalent, Access lists that key combination right next to the item in the pull-down menu.

Playing with the Other Mouse Button

After surviving years of neglect and general indifference, the right mouse button comes into its own with Windows 95/98. Finally, there's something for it to do. Right mouse buttons of the world, rejoice!

In Access 2000 (just like most applications for Windows 95/98), the right mouse button pops up a list of things you can do with the current on-screen item. In Figure 2-8, I right-click on the Customers table. Access 2000 is right there, offering a list of common things to do with tables. Instead of working through the main menu to copy the current table, for instance, I can right-click and select Copy from the pop-up menu. Talk about a time-saver!

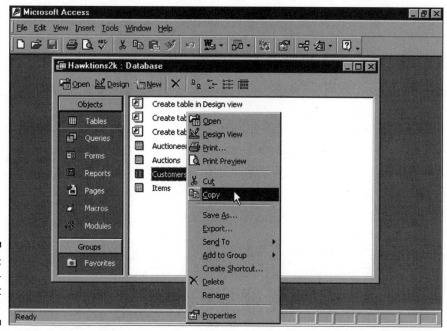

Figure 2-8:
Too cool —
an instant
menu!

Experiment with the right mouse button. Try right-clicking on everything in sight — see what happens. Don't worry about messing up your system because you can't do any lasting harm with the right mouse button. See what you can find!

Chapter 3

Calling the Online St. Bernard and Other Forms of Help

In This Chapter

▶ Introducing the Office Assistant

▶ Checking the Contents, Answer, and Index tabs

▶ Using the Whatzis menu option

▶ Modeming for help

▶ Finding FastTips

▶ Querying humans

*G*etting in over your head is easy, sometimes. For example, mountains are *much* taller after you start climbing than they were when you looked up from the ground. Plus, your equipment *never* seems to fail when you're packing it. Instead, your trusty gear waits until you're in the middle of nowhere, dangling precariously from the crumbling edge of a craggy peak. Then — and only then — does your gear remember its mortal fear of heights and have heart failure.

That's what St. Bernards are for. When you're lost in the alpine wilderness — cold, wet, and alone — it's reassuring to know that a St. Bernard will be along soon. I'm a little unclear about precisely what the dog *does* when it finds you; but at that point, I'd probably settle for the companionship. Access 2000 has its own built-in St. Bernard, although on-screen it looks more like a few dialog boxes than a husky canine. This chapter explores several different ways to find answers to your Access 2000 questions. Knowing where to look for information is as important as knowing the information itself, so browse through this chapter and discover your options.

When in Doubt, Press F1

No matter where you are in Access 2000, help is available at the touch of a key. Just press F1, and the perky Office Assistant leaps into action (Figure 3-1). The Assistant, a new feature of Office 2000, shows up in all the Office 2000 applications. The Assistant replaces the old Answer Wizard and simplifies the help process even more. The Office Assistant even tosses in some entertaining animated moments at no extra charge.

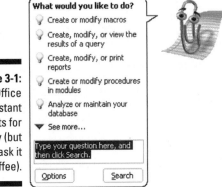

Figure 3-1: The Office Assistant reports for duty (but don't ask it for coffee).

When you call up the Assistant, it tries to figure out what you're trying to accomplish in Access 2000 and suggests 10 Help topics that it thinks are relevant. If one of these topics hits the spot (which, in my experience, happens most of the time), click on the button next to the topic and the Assistant presents the information to you.

The Assistant is a good guesser but doesn't always come up with the right topics. For moments like that, the Assistant includes a do-it-yourself question box along the bottom of the window. Here's a step-by-step layout of how to use this marvel of modern technology to ask the Assistant a detailed question:

1. **Click on the Office Assistant window or press F1.**

   The Assistant's dialog box pops up (looking quite perky, I might add).

2. **In the box at the bottom of the window, type your question in plain language, just as in Figure 3-2.**

   You read it right — in *plain language*. Can you believe it? A program that actually *understands* you. Who knows where this dangerous trend may lead?

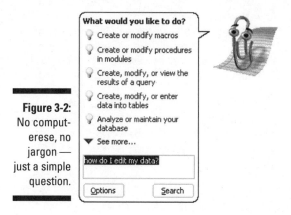

Figure 3-2:
No comput-
erese, no
jargon —
just a simple
question.

3. **Click on Search or press Enter when you finish typing.**

   The Assistant does its thing and displays a list of Help topics that it thinks will answer your question (see Figure 3-3). If none of the topics is quite what you had in mind, rephrase your question and give it another try.

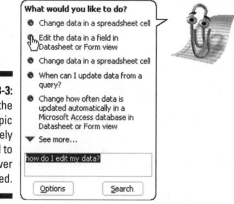

Figure 3-3:
Click the
Help topic
most likely
to lead to
the answer
you need.

4. **Click on the Help topic that sounds like the best match.**

   If, after reading through some Help topics, you still aren't satisfied, close the Help window and then start again with Step 1 to ask the Assistant another question.

The default Assistant is an animated paperclip, named Clippit (no, I'm not making this up — someone actually *named* the cartoon paper clip). Access 2000 ships with several different Office Assistants, so if ol' Clippit doesn't match your working style, feel free to switch. To change the Office Assistant, right-click on the Assistant and then select Choose Assistant from the pop-up menu. Access 2000 presents you with a gallery of options ranging from a mundane Office logo to a nicely rendered cartoon version of Albert Einstein. Click on the Next and Back buttons to cycle through the various Assistants. When you find *precisely* the right one for you, click on OK. You need to have the Office 2000 CD or Access 2000 disk set handy to install the new Assistant.

Sitting behind the Assistant are the Access 2000 traditional Help files. After the Assistant points you to a particular Help topic, the normal Help system takes over. If you're more comfortable with the way Help worked in Access for Windows 95/98, have no fear — the Help system you knew and loved is still available in Access 2000.

To open up the traditional Help system in Access 2000, you must first turn off the Office Assistant. Right-click on the Assistant and then select Options from the pop-up menu. A window with way too many check boxes appears on-screen. You want to uncheck the Use the Office Assistant box by clicking on it. Click on the OK button and you have successfully turned the Office Assistant off until you check the Use the Office Assistant box again.

Now choose Help⇨Microsoft Access Help from the menu bar. The Help window appears, looking much like Figure 3-4. The window splits into two panes, displaying help topics on the left and detailed information on the right. The three tabs across the left side of the window offer different ways to find answers. There's a method here for everyone, regardless of how you like to do research. The following sections explore each of the Help window tabs in order of usefulness: Contents, Answer Wizard, and Index.

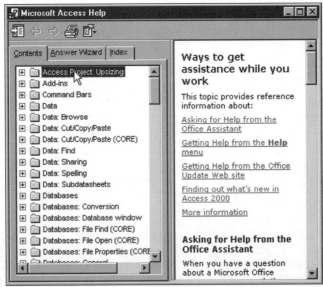

Figure 3-4:
The Help
system is
still ready
to serve.

Combing the Contents

The *Contents tab* is for casual browsers or people who enjoy digging around in a book's Table of Contents in search of something. Here's how to use it:

1. **Click on the Contents tab.**

   The Help window lists the available master Help topics, complete with little manila folder icons next to each one.

   The book icon means that this entry leads to other Help topics or specific Help documents.

2. **Find a Help topic that looks interesting and double-click on it.**

   The system opens the Help topic, changes the closed manila folder icon to an open manila folder (too cute!), and shows you a list of specific Help documents (see Figure 3-5).

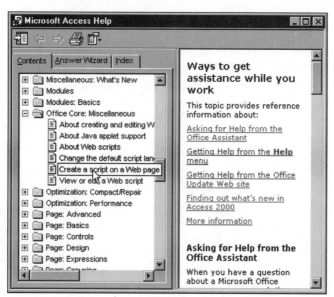

Figure 3-5:
Here's the information I want.

The Help documents are marked with the lines-on-a-page icon (but you probably figured that out on your own).

If you choose the wrong topic, double-click on the topic name again to make it go away.

Also, clicking one time on the plus sign (+) sitting just before the manila folder icon opens or closes the manila folder.

3. **Repeat Step 2 until you find what you're looking for.**

   After you're done reading a Help document, click the Help Topics button to see the Contents page again.

Asking the Answer Wizard

The next Help tab is the *Answer Wizard*. This Help tab is a much-needed update of the old *Find* option, which was absolutely archaic. Thanks to advances in modern technology, the Answer Wizard conjures up the information you need from the keywords you type. Follow these steps to call the Wizard into action:

1. **Click on the <u>A</u>nswer Wizard tab.**

   As you expect, the Answer Wizard page appears on-screen.

   If you're using Help for the first time, the Help system tells you that it has to create a word list before you can do the search. Just patiently follow along with the prompts, and soon you're ready for Step 2.

2. **In the box at the top of the window, type a couple of key words that describe what you're looking for.**

   After you finish typing, hit the Enter key or click Search. The Answer Wizard searches for topics that match your entry and displays a list of possible matches in the big window at the bottom of the screen.

3. **Scroll through the list at the bottom of the window until you find an item that looks like your topic.**

   When (and if) you find a topic of interest (see Figure 3-6), click on the topic to see the Help document.

Inspecting the Index

If you prefer diving into the index rather than rattling through the table of contents, click the *Index tab*. It works just like the index of a book, except that it's automated. Here's how to use it:

1. **Click on the <u>I</u>ndex tab.**

   The screen changes to show the Index page.

2. **Type the term you're looking for in the box at the top of the window.**

   As you type, Access 2000 suggests an alphabetical list of known terms from the existing help topics in a list in the middle of the window. At any point, you may stop typing your phrase, double-click on a keyword in the list, and Access 2000 pops it up into your keyword box.

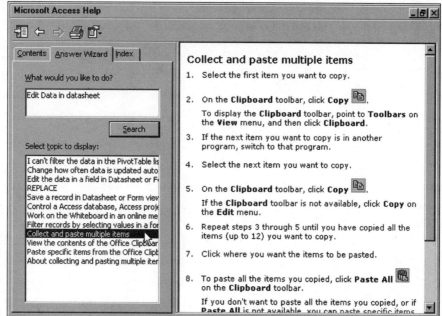

Figure 3-6:
I finally
found my
topic.

Meanwhile, Access 2000, like a savvy politician preparing for a televised debate, is generating a list of responses or help topics near the bottom of the window it thinks will best suit your keyword phrase that you typed in the box at the top of the window. Access 2000 offers a prioritized number of occurrences of your keyword phrase within the help topic (see Figure 3-7 for an example).

3. When you find the topic you're looking for, click to see the Help document.

If a couple of items match your topic, the Help system displays a dialog box like Figure 3-7. If that happens, double-click on your choice to see it.

The Office 2000 Help window works a little like a web browser, mainly because Office 2000 is constructed with parts of a web browser — specifically Microsoft Internet Explorer 5.0. If you have been "surfing" through Access 2000 Help a while and you want to get back to a topic you surfed over a few pages ago, click the left pointing arrow in the help toolbar to return to the previous help topic. The left arrow toolbar button moves you back one help topic at a time. Likewise, you may click the right pointing arrow in the help toolbar to move back to where you were previously.

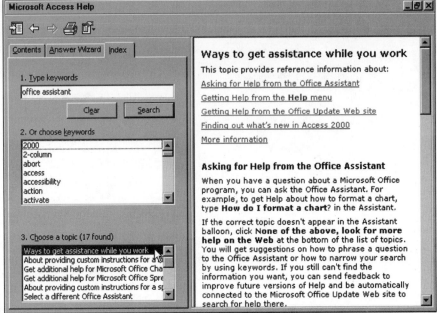

Figure 3-7:
You could
read about
the Office
Assistant
all day.

The Whatzis Menu Option

Whatzis isn't the technical term for this menu entry, but I think it should be (sometimes those programmers need more creativity when naming things). The item in question is the Help⇨What's This menu option — the one with a mouse pointer and question mark on it. I call this the *Whatzis* item — your tool for quickly finding out what any button or menu item in Access 2000 does.

Here's how the little bugger works:

1. Choose Help⇨What's This?

The mouse pointer suddenly grows a large question mark on one side — Access 2000 is telling you that you're now in Whatzis mode.

2. Select the menu item or click on the button you want to know more about.

Access 2000 displays a Help screen with the name of the item and a brief description of what that item does.

3. Click once more to make the helpful little Help screen go away.

Quick and easy answers for those brain-blank moments of life — it just doesn't get any better than this.

Your Modem Knows More Than You May Think

There's gold in them thar online services! If you have access (pardon the pun) to the Internet or an account on America Online, CompuServe, or Prodigy, then a world of answers waits at your modem.

Microsoft maintains official support areas on the major online services, plus a very complete World Wide Web page for the Internet crowd. A host of informal question and answer areas cover Microsoft products as well. Table 3-1 explains how to find the support areas on each system.

Table 3-1	Microsoft Support Areas Available Online	
System	*Access Command*	*Notes*
America Online	keyword PCApplications	Look for *MS Access Q&A* in the message boards under Database Use and Development
CompuServe	go MSACCESS	Devotes whole area to Access; lots of good stuff
Newsgroups	comp.databases.	Requires access to the MS-Access Internet newsgroups
World Wide Web	http://www.microsoft.com/Support/	Requires access to the Web

If you have an Internet e-mail address and enjoy having your mailbox full, you can sign up for the Access mailing list. See the nearby sidebar "Drinking at the never-empty well of a mailing list" for more details.

A slew of *...For Dummies* books are available to help you navigate the online world. Among them are *America Online For Dummies,* 5th Edition (written by yours truly); *CompuServe For Dummies,* 3rd Edition (by Wallace Wang); and *The Internet For Dummies,* 6th Edition (from John Levine, Carol Baroudi, and Margaret Levine Young). Of course, IDG Books Worldwide, Inc., the sponsor of today's program, brings these fine books to you.

It's on the Tip of My Fax

Here's the easiest, most inexpensive way to get information about Access 2000 (or any Microsoft product, for that matter). This way is toll-free, quick, and relatively painless. What is it? (Drum roll please!) It's FastTips, the automated Microsoft information system.

FastTips offers recorded answers to common questions and documents from Microsoft's support library. To use the *answers to common questions* part of the system, you need a touch-tone phone. To receive documents, you also need a fax machine.

The FastTips system is available 24 hours a day, 7 days a week. It even works on weekends and holidays, just as real people like you sometimes do. That's why FastTips is such a great service to know about — it's available at those odd times of the day and night when you have a deadline looming and nowhere to turn for help.

Here's how to reach FastTips:

1. **Get some paper and a pencil and then take a few deep breaths to relax.**

   You're about to tangle with a menu-driven voice response system, so it's important to be in the proper frame of mind for the experience.

   Make sure that you have the fax number handy if you're requesting documents.

2. **Find a touch-tone phone and press 1-800-936-4100.**

   If you're planning to request faxed documents, you *don't* have to call from the fax machine; just know the fax number.

3. **Listen patiently to the first menu and then select the option for Access.**

   As of this writing, Access is option 4 on the main menu, but such things change with time. If they *did* change the menu item, write the new number into this book so that you have it the next time you call.

Drinking at the never-empty well of a mailing list

If your company has Internet e-mail, consider signing up for the Access mailing list to join a never-ending discussion of Access at all levels, from novice to nerd. Aside from filling your mailbox with important-looking messages, the list gives you a way to get answers fast at any time.

To join the mailing list, send a message to LISTSERV@peach.ease.lsoft.com. You can write anything as the subject of your message (the computer on the other end doesn't care). In the body of the message, type SUBSCRIBE ACCESS-L followed by your real name, *not* your e-mail address. The mailing list computer automatically picks up your e-mail address from the message itself.

After you subscribe, your first message explains how the list works, how to send messages to it, and how to get off of the list when you decide you've had enough. Give it a try — mailing lists are great tools!

4. Follow the menu prompts to find the information you want.

The first time you call FastTips, request a map and catalog. The menu has formal options to order these items. Navigating FastTips is just like driving to Cleveland, except without the car. The trip is easier if you know where you're going and what you're looking for. Before trying to do big things with FastTips, get a system map and catalog to review.

If you request a fax, don't worry if the fax doesn't arrive for 10 or 15 minutes. When the system is particularly busy, you may have to wait a little longer. Be patient — use the time for a stretch break.

Talking to a Human

Sometimes, you've had it up to *here* with computers and automation in general. At that point, you just want to talk to a human — any human — who can help solve your problem. Microsoft provides a variety of phone numbers for just such occasions.

On these numbers, you pay for the phone call, but the first two answers are free.

✔ To reach Access 2000 phone support, call 425-635-7050 from the United States. Live human beings are available from 6:00 a.m. to 6:00 p.m. Pacific time, Monday through Friday (except holidays).

In Canada, the free support number is 905-568-2294. The Canadian line is staffed from 8:00 a.m. to 8:00 p.m. Eastern time, Monday through Friday (except holidays).

After two calls, the free ride is over — it's time to get out your credit card and use the *per incident* line.

✔ For fast answers to your Access 2000 problems at any hour of the day or night, call 800-936-5500 from the US or Canada. Unless your company purchased an annual support contract from Microsoft, solutions from this number cost a flat *$55 per incident.* So what's an incident? According to Microsoft, an *incident* is *all the calls related to the same problem* (or something close to that). The bottom line is that if you call several times trying to solve the same problem, you pay for only one call. Of course, the *really* nice thing about paying for support is that these numbers are staffed 24 hours a day. I guess you really *do* get what you pay for.

✔ If you have a light, fluffy question, such as "What's the current version number of Microsoft Access?" (or "What's the weather like in Redmond, Washington?"), call the Microsoft sales department at 800-426-9400. These folks are at the phones, waiting for your call, from 6:30 a.m. to 5:30 p.m. Pacific time, Monday through Friday.

✔ If you are deaf or hearing-impaired and have a TDD or TT modem, call 206-635-4948 between 6:00 a.m. and 6:00 p.m. Pacific time, Monday through Friday.

This number works for all Microsoft products (Word, Excel, PowerPoint, and the others).

Part II
Truly Tempting Tables

The 5th Wave — By Rich Tennant

"Your database is beyond repair, but before I tell you our backup recommendation, let me ask you a question. How many index cards do you think will fit on the walls of your computer room?"

In this part . . .

With Access 2000 well in hand, you begin a life of storing, managing, organizing, and reorganizing data. (By the way, welcome to your new life. I hope you enjoy your stay here.) Because data hangs out in tables, you need to know how to do the whole table thing if you have any hope of making your data do tricks.

This part eases you into the role of Commander of All Tables by covering the basics. You go from creating tables through using tables and on into maintaining and repairing tables. Heck, if you're not careful, you may find yourself attacking the dining room table by the end of Chapter 9.

Chapter 4

Designing and Building a Home for Your Data

. . . .

In This Chapter

▶ Fields, fields everywhere

▶ Sample fields to simplify your day

▶ Flat files and relational databases revealed

▶ Designing your tables

▶ Creating the database

▶ Building a table with the Table Wizard

▶ Assembling a table by hand

. . . .

*T*his may be the single most important chapter in this book. Why? Because really useful databases grow from carefully considered plans. The problem is that nobody ever explains stuff like how to successfully string a bunch of fields together and make a table out of them. For some unknown reason, *they* think you already know how to do it — that it's instinct, like the birds flying south for the winter or my wife finding the best sales in the mall.

If you didn't pop from the womb muttering, "phone numbers and postal codes are treated as text even though they're numbers," (and believe me, I'd worry about you if you did) then this chapter is for you. The following pages divulge the secrets of fields, tables, and databases in Technicolor glory. The chapter covers the database terms you need to know, tips for choosing fields and designing tables, and details on assembling the pieces into great databases.

Although I hate making a big deal out of techie terminology, this time I must. Please, for your own sanity, get a good grip on the information in the first section of this Chapter. The database terms described there appear *everywhere* in Access 2000. Whenever you build a query, design a form, or create a report, the terms stealthily await you, ready to leap out and befuddle the ill-prepared. Steel yourself for their attack by spending time in the terms section, appearing next in this Chapter. (Of course, the *rest* of the chapter is important, too, so feel free to keep reading after mastering the database terms.)

Database Terms to Know and Tolerate

Wait! Don't skip this section just because it's about terminology. I keep the technoweenie content of this book to a minimum, but you simply *must* know a few magic nerd words before your foray into database development.

If you just felt faint because you didn't realize that you are developing a database, just put the book down for a moment, take a few deep breaths, and remember that it's *only* a computer, not something really important like kids, kites, or chocolate mousse.

The few terms you need to know are listed in the following sections. There's a brief explanation of each one, plus a translation guide for people migrating to Access 2000 from other major Windows databases such as dBASE, FoxPro, and Paradox.

The terms are listed in order, starting with the smallest piece of a database and advancing to the largest. It's much like a backwards version of that "flea on the wart on the frog on the bump on the log in the hole in the bottom of the sea" song that my kids sing incessantly some days. The definitions kinda build on each other, so it makes the most sense if you start with *data* and work your way down to *database*.

Data (your stuff)

Data is the stuff that Access stores, shuffles, and stacks for you. Every time you write your name on a form (*last name first,* of course), you're providing data. In a database program's skewed approach to the world, *Your Name* may be stored as one piece of data (your whole name, with or without the middle initial), two pieces (first and last name), or even more pieces (title, first name, middle initial, last name, and suffix). The details depend on how the database designer set up the database's *fields* (that's covered in the next section, so don't worry about it right now).

> ✔ dBASE, FoxPro, Paradox, and almost all other database programs all agree that data should, in fact, be called *data.* Don't expect this degree of cooperation to continue much beyond the term *record,* because that's where it ends.

🖝 Database programs view data differently than you and I do. If you see 16773, you know it's a number — it's an intuitive thing. Access 2000 and the other database programs see 16773 as either a number or a group of characters, depending on what type of *field* it's stored in. There's more about this peculiar behavior in "Frolicking through the Fields" later in the chapter. For the sake of your sanity, please make sure you're comfortable with this little oddity because it can *really* throw you for a loop sometimes.

Fields (the homes for your stuff)

Because nobody wants their data to wander around homeless, the technical wizards created *fields* — places for your data to live. Each field holds one kind of data. For example, to track information about a baseball card collection, your fields may include Manufacturer, Player Name, Position, Year, Team, Condition, and so on. Each of those items is a unique *field* in your database.

🖝 As with the term *data,* dBASE, FoxPro, and Paradox all agree about what a *field* is.

🖝 The programs begin to disagree when you talk about the specific types of fields available. Just because you *always used to do it this way in Paradox* doesn't mean the same method works in Access 2000. For more details, flip ahead to "Frolicking through the Fields," just a couple pages away in this chapter.

Records (the homes on one block)

Having fields is a good start, but if you stopped there, how would you know which last name went with which first name? Something needs to keep those unruly fields in order — something like a *record.* All the fields for one baseball card, one accounting entry, or one of whatever it is you're tracking with Access 2000 are collectively known as a *record.* If you have two baseball cards in your collection, then you have two records in your database, one for each card. (Of course, you *also* have a mighty small card collection, but that goes without saying.)

🖝 In one final burst of similarity, dBASE, FoxPro, and Paradox concur on the term *record* (but the party ends here).

🖝 Each record in a *table* has the exact same fields, but (usually) different data inside those fields. By the way, I slipped *table* into the last sentence because that's the next term you need to know (plus I like the challenge of writing sneaky prose).

Table (the blocks in a neighborhood)

A *table* is a collection of *records* that describe similar data. The key phrase to remember in that last sentence is *similar data.* All the records in a single table contain *fields* of similar data. The information about that baseball card collection might fit into a single table. So would the accounting data. However, a single table would *not* handle both baseball cards *and* accounting entries. Combining the two is a novel concept (and may even make accounting fun), but it's not going to work in Access 2000.

- ✔ Paradox and FoxPro basically agree with Access 2000 about what a table is. (Isn't that nice?)

- ✔ dBASE has its own ideas about this *table* thing. It prefers the term *database file.*

- ✔ Did you notice that I said the baseball card collection *might* fit in one table? I'm not hedging my bet because I think that the table can't physically hold entries about all your cards. Instead, you may use a few *related* tables to hold the data. That's all you need to know for now, but this is an important topic to understand. Be sure to peek at "Flat Files versus Relational Databases: Let the Contest Begin!" later in this chapter for the whole scoop.

Database (a community of neighborhoods)

An Access 2000 *database* (or *database file* — the terms are interchangeable) is a collection of everything relating to a particular set of information. The database contains all the tables, queries, reports, forms, and other things that Access 2000 helps you create to manage and work with your stuff. Instead of storing all those items *individually* on the disk drive, where they can become lost, misplaced, or accidentally erased, they're grouped into a single collective file.

- ✔ dBASE and FoxPro call this a *catalog.* Conceptually, catalogs are like databases, except that the catalog is a separate file that just lists files that you claim are related. In Access 2000, a database file actually *contains* the tables, reports, and such, so it's doing much more than merely organizing them.

- ✔ Paradox doesn't have anything like an Access 2000 database file. The closest you can come is a subdirectory that contains all the tables, queries, reports, and forms.

Frolicking through the Fields

A *field,* you remember, is the place where your data lives; one field holds one piece of data. If you're storing information about a book collection, your database file may use fields like Title, Author, Copyright Date, Publisher, Edition, Price, and so on. Each one of those items is a unique *field*.

Because there are so many different kinds of stuff in the world, Access 2000 offers a variety of field types for *stuff storage.* In fact, Access 2000 puts 10 different field types at your disposal. At first blush, 10 choices may not seem like much flexibility, but believe me — it is. And if that weren't enough to satisfy the database connoisseur extraordinaire, Access 2000 provides a field by using the Lookup Wizard where you can define the possible contents the field. Thanks to the field options, you also can customize the fields to suit your needs precisely. All this and it makes popcorn too — well maybe Microsoft engineers are working on that one.

Each field offers a number of options to make customizing incredibly useful. You can ask for some information, test the entry to see whether it's what you're looking for, and then automatically format the field just the way you want. Everything you need to know about this cool stuff awaits your attention in Chapter 7.

All the field types appear in the following list. They're in the same order as they appear on-screen in Access 2000. Don't worry if you can't figure out why *anyone* would want to use one type or another. Just focus on the ones you need, make a mental note about the others, and go on with your work.

- ✔ **Text:** This field stores text — letters, numbers, and any combination thereof — up to 255 characters. The thing you need to remember is that numbers in a text field *aren't* numbers anymore; they're just a bunch of digits hanging out together in a field. Be careful of this fact when you design the tables in your database.

  Text fields have one more setting you need to know about: size. When you create a text field, Access 2000 wants to know how many characters the field holds. That's the field *size.* If you create a field called First Name and make its size 6, *Joseph* fits into the field, but not *Jennifer.* This could be a problem. A good rule of thumb is to make the field a little larger than you think you actually need. It's easy to make the field even larger if you need to, but it's very dangerous to make it smaller. By the way, performing surgery on fields is covered in Chapter 9.

- ✔ **Memo:** This is a really *big* text field. It's great for general notes, detailed descriptions, and anything else that requires a lot of space. Memo fields hold up to 64,000 characters of information — that's almost 18 pages of text.

✔ **Number:** As you probably guessed, this field holds real for-sure numbers. You can add, subtract, and calculate your way to fame and fortune with these fields. *Currency* fields are a specific kind of number field. If you're working with dollars and cents (or pounds and pence), use a currency field. For your other numeric needs, try a number field.

✔ **Date/Time:** Time waits for no one (and if you're too late, your dates won't, either). Use a Date/Time field to track the whens of life. These fields store time, date, or a combination of the two, depending on which format you use. Pretty versatile, eh?

✔ **Currency:** In an Access 2000 database, the bucks stop here. For that matter, so do the lira, marks, and yen. Use this field to track money, prices, invoice amounts, and so on. If you're in the mood for some *other* kind of number, check out the *number* field.

✔ **AutoNumber:** If I have to name one thing that makes Access 2000 a truly cool product, this is it. The AutoNumber field does just what it says: It fills itself with an automatically generated number every time you make a new record. Just think — when you add a customer to your table, Access 2000 generates the customer number *automatically!* This field type is an absolute boon for people like you and me because making an automatically numbered field used to require a programming degree. With Access 2000, it just takes a mouse click.

✔ **Yes/No:** When you need a simple *yes* or *no,* this is the field to use. Depending on the format you choose, this field type holds Yes/No, True/False, and On/Off.

✔ **OLE object:** You probably won't ever use this type of field. It falls under the heading of *technoweenie features in Access 2000.* OLE (pronounced O-Lay) stands for Object Linking and Embedding, a very powerful, very nerdy technology. If you simply *must* learn more about the OLE object field, consult the Office Assistant or pick up a copy of *Access 2000 Bible* by Cary Prague and Michael Irwin.

✔ **Hyperlink:** If you use Access 2000 on your company's network or use the Internet extensively, then this field type is for you. Thanks to this field type (and a little bit of Net magic provided by Microsoft Internet Explorer 5.0), Access 2000 now understands and stores the special link language that makes the Internet such a cool place. For more about this new field type, as well as other Access 2000 Internet tricks, see Chapter 21.

✔ **Lookup Wizard:** One of a database program's most powerful features is the *lookup.* It makes data entry go faster (and with fewer errors, I might add) by letting you pick a field's correct value from a preset list. No typing, no worry, no problem — it's quite a helpful trick. In some database programs, adding a lookup to a table is really hard. Luckily, the Access 2000 Lookup Wizard makes the process much less painful. Ask the Office Assistant for all of the details about the Lookup Wizard.

A Smattering of Fields to Get You Started

To give you a head start in the database race, Table 4-1 lists some common fields already starring in databases around the world. Some oldies-but-goodies are in here, plus some examples especially for the new millennium.

Table 4-1	A Field for Every Occasion		
Name	*Type*	*Size*	*Contents*
Title	Text	4	Mr., Ms., Mrs., Mme., Sir
First Name	Text	15	person's first name
Middle Initial	Text	4	person's middle initial; allows for two initials and punctuation
Last Name	Text	20	person's last name
Job	Text	25	job title or position
Company	Text	25	company name
Address 1, Address 2	Text	30	include two fields for address because some corporate locations are pretty complicated these days
City	Text	20	city name
State, Province	Text	4	state or province; apply the name appropriately for the data you're storing
Zip Code, Postal Code	Text	10	zip or postal code; note that this is stored as text characters, not a number
Country	Text	15	not needed if you work within a single country
Office Phone	Text	12	voice telephone number; increase the size to 17 for an extension
Fax Number	Text	12	fax number
Home Phone	Text	12	home telephone number (only necessary for people with lives)
Cellular Phone	Text	12	cell phone or car phone
E-mail address	Text	30	Internet e-mail address
Web site	Hyperlink	*	Web page address; sized automatically
Telex	Text	12	standard Telex number; use size 22 to include answerback service
SSN	Text	11	U.S. Social Security Number, including dashes

Playing the (field) name game

Of all the Windows database programs out there, I think Access 2000 has the simplest field-naming rules. Just remember three things, and your field names will be perfect every time.

✓ First, *start with a letter or number.* After the first character, you're free to use any letter or number. You can include spaces in field names, too!

✓ Second, *make the field name short and easy to understand.* You actually have up to 64 characters for a field name, but don't

even *think* about using all that space. But don't get stingy and create names like N1 or AZ773 unless they mean something particular to your company or organization.

✓ Finally, *just use letters, numbers, and an occasional space in your field names.* Although Access 2000 lets you include all kinds of crazy punctuation marks in field names, don't do it. Keep it simple so that the solution you develop with Access 2000 doesn't turn into a problem on its own.

All these samples are *text* fields, even the ones for phone numbers. That's because Access 2000 sees most of the stuff you want to pack a database with as *text.* Remember that computers think that there's a difference between an actual *number* and a string of digits, such as the string of digits that makes up a phone number or government ID number.

These quick tips should keep you on the right path for creating good fields:

✓ Here's an easy test for when to put a number into a text field instead of a number field. Ask yourself, "Will I ever do *math* with this number?" If so, it goes in a number field. Otherwise, stuff it into a text field.

✓ The Table Wizard is packed with ready-made fields for your tables. Look ahead to "Creating Tables at the Wave of a Wand" later in this chapter for more information.

Flat Files versus Relational Databases: Let the Contest Begin!

Unlike ice cream, cars, and summer days, the tables in your database come in only two basic flavors: *flat* and *relational.* These two escapees from the *Nerd Term of the Month Club* explain how tables store information in your database. And now for the cool part: When you build a new database, *you* get to choose which organizational style your new database uses! Don't let it worry you, though — you're not on your own for the decision. The following paragraphs tell you a little about each kind of organization. (Chapter 5 goes into lots of detail on the subject, too.)

A database is either flat file or relational — it can't be both.

Flat files: Simple answers for simple needs

In a *flat* system (also known as *flat file*), all the data is lumped together into a single table. A phone directory is a good example of a flat file database. Names, addresses, and phone numbers (the data) are crammed into a single place (the database). Some duplication occurs — if one person has three phone lines at home, her name and address are listed three times in the directory — but that's not a big problem. Overall, the database works just fine.

Relational databases: Complex solutions to bigger problems

On the other side of the coin sits the *relational* system (or *relational database*). Relational databases try to use as little storage space as possible by cutting down on the duplicated (the nerds like to call it *redundant)* data in the database. To do this, relational databases split your data into several tables, with each table holding some portion of the total data.

Borrowing the phone book example from above, one table in a relational database may contain the customer name and address information, while another holds the actual phone numbers. Thanks to this new approach, the mythical person with three phone lines only has one entry in the "customer name" table (after all, they're *still* just one customer), but they have three distinct entries in the "phone number" table (one for each phone line). By using a relational database, the system only stores the customer's personal information once, thus saving some space on the computer's disk drive.

The key to this advanced technology is, in fact, called just that: the *key field* (or *linking field*). All of the tables in a relational database system contain this special field. The key field's data links together matching records from different tables. The key field works just like the claim stub you receive when you drop off film for processing at the local store. To join up with your film again, you present the claim check, complete with its little claim number. That number connects (or *links*) you and your film so that the clerk can find it. Likewise, in the phone book example, each customer probably has a unique customer ID. The "phone number" table stores the customer ID with each phone number. To find out who owns a phone number, you look up the customer ID in the "customer name" table. Granted, it takes more steps to find someone's phone number than the plain *flat file* system does, but the relational system saves storage space (no more duplicate names) and reduces the chance for errors at the same time.

If this process seems complicated, don't feel bad. Relational databases *are* complicated! That's why Chapter 5 explains the concept in infinitely more detail, complete with examples of how the process works and warning signs to watch for lest you turn into a full-fledged database nerd. For your own sanity, please be patient with yourself when wrestling with relational databases. There's no shame in asking for some help from your friendly neighborhood computer jockey, either.

So, what does all of this mean to you?

Now you at least have an idea of the difference between flat file and relational databases. But do you care? Yes, you do. Each approach has its unique plusses and minuses for your database:

- ✔ Flat file systems are easy to build and maintain. (A Microsoft Excel spreadsheet is a good example.) They're great for simple things like mailing lists, phone directories, and video collections. Flat systems are simple solutions for simple problems.

- ✔ Relational systems really shine in *big* business problems such as invoicing, accounting, or inventory. If you have a small problem to solve (like a mailing list or membership database), a relational approach may be more solution than you need.

- ✔ Anyone can create a very workable flat database system — and I *do* mean anyone. Developing a solid relational database takes skill and practice (and, in some countries, a nerd license). When in doubt, ask a database jockey for help!

Your company probably has a lot of information stored in relational database systems. Understanding how to *use* relational systems is important for you, so that's covered just about everywhere you turn in this book. Specifically, check out Chapter 5 to find out about dealing with the relationships between tables.

On the other hand, I don't recommend that you set off to *build* a relational database system by yourself. If you're *sure* you need one, enlist either the Database Wizard or a friendly guru to help you bring the database to life. There's a lot to understand about how fields work together to form relations (imagine a cross between Biology 101 and your first computer science class). Get some help the first time and then try it on your own later.

By the way, even though Access 2000 is a relational database program, it does flat systems quite nicely. Whether you choose flat file or relational for your database project, Access 2000 is the right program!

Great Tables Start with Great Designs

You're *almost* ready to start up the computer and run Access 2000. Almost, but not quite. There's one more step: designing the tables for your database. I know this seems like a lot of paperwork, but it's absolutely necessary to build good databases. When I create systems for my clients, this is exactly how I do it. (Well, I left out the *take the afternoon off because design sometimes give me a headache* step, but other than that, this is my method.)

1. **Get out a clean pad of paper and something to write with.**

   Despite the wonders of PCs and Windows, some things still work best on paper. Besides, if the database design work isn't going well, you can always doodle.

2. **Write brief descriptions of the reports, lists, and other things you want to come *out* of the system.**

   At first blush, this method seems kinda backward. Why start with the stuff that comes out? Because these reports and such are the *real* reason you're creating the database. If you can't get the information that you need out of the system, why have the system at all? Also, don't worry about making this a totally perfect and complete list. Settle for an *includes most everything* list, because you can always go back later and add new stuff to it.

3. **On another sheet of paper, sketch some samples of the reports, lists, and other outputs you listed in Step 2.**

   You needn't create detailed report designs at this point — that's not the goal. Right now, you're figuring out what information you need to build the stuff that ultimately comes out of your database (the reports, lists, mailing labels, and everything else). Just get a rough idea of what you want the most important reports to look like and write down the stuff that's on them. This list becomes the road map to your database's fields. (After all, you can't print a mailing label if your database doesn't store addresses somewhere.) Now that you know the big picture of where you're going, it's time to fill in some details.

4. **For each field in your list, write a name, field type, and, for text fields, a specific size.**

   You need to do this step even if you're planning to use the Database Wizard or Table Wizard when you build the table. Although those wizards automatically size and name the fields you create, you can still customize the fields to your liking.

5. **Organize the fields into one or more tables.**

   Look for data that naturally goes together, like name, address, and phone number for a contact database, or product ID, description, distributor, cost, and selling price for an inventory system. If you have a lot of fields or if you run out of ideas for putting them together, get help from your friendly guru.

TIP

The last step is the hardest one, but it gets easier with practice. To build your experience, create some sample databases with the Database Wizard and look at how they fit together. Pick a topic you know about (accounting, event scheduling, or — if you're like me — compact disc collecting) and see how the pros at Microsoft did it.

Open the various tables in Design view (in the database window, right-click on the table name, then select Design from the pop-up menu). Which fields went in each table? Why did they organize things that way? Take a big-picture view of how the tables interact within the database, too. For that, click the Relationships button on the Toolbar (see Figure 4-1). Access 2000 displays the Relationships window, which graphically shows how all of the tables in the database link together. Follow the lines between the tables to unravel the connections.

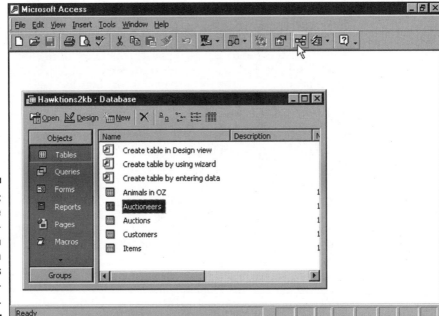

Figure 4-1:
Click the Relation-ships button to view a database's table rela-tionships.

TIP

For more about Design view, see "Building Tables by Hand, Just as in the Old Days" later in this chapter. (The Relationships button is explained and explored in Chapter 5.)

It's Finally Time to Build the Database

After reading page after page of this book, writing reams of notes, and sucking down two or three cans of pop, the moment is finally here — it's time to build the database! Here's where you create the master holding file for your tables, reports, forms, and other stuff. Plus, if you use a Database Wizard, this step *also* creates all the tables, reports, and forms for you — it's one-stop shopping!

If you worked with some *other* database program in the past, then in your mind the term *database* may mean, "where you store the data." Access 2000 calls that a *table*. Tables live *inside* databases, along with all the other sundry stuff you create to get the job done. If the terms still aren't clear, flip back to "Database Terms to Know and Tolerate," earlier in this chapter.

Without further ado, here's how to create a database:

1. **If it's not already running, take a moment to start Access 2000.**

    I know, I know — but I *have* to say it; it's an author thing.

2. **Choose File⇨New from the main menu (see Figure 4-2) or click on the New Object toolbar button.**

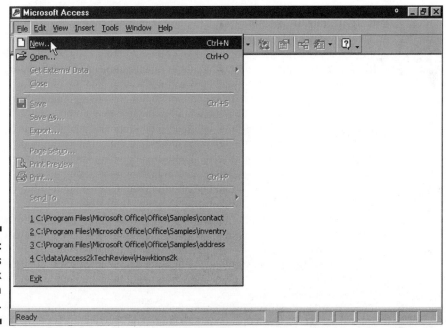

Figure 4-2:
It only takes a quick click to create a database.

3. When the New dialog box appears, click on the Databases tab.

The New Database window appears on-screen, displaying a fine array of
Database Wizard Templates to assist you (see Figure 4-3).

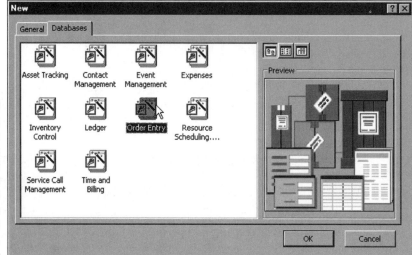

Figure 4-3:
New
Database
window
with so
many wizard
templates
and yet so
little time.

If you just started Access 2000, your screen looks more like Figure 4-4. In that
case, click on the Access database wizards, pages, and projects radio button
and then click on OK to bring up the New Database window to enlist the
help of one of the many fine database wizard templates Access 2000 has to
offer you.

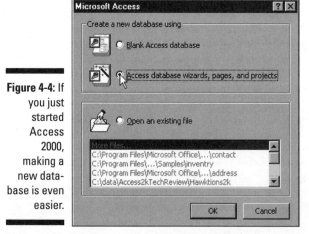

Figure 4-4: If
you just
started
Access
2000,
making a
new data-
base is even
easier.

To create a new database by hand, click on the Blank Access database radio button and then click on OK. Access will ask you for a file name for your database and voilà! One blank database is awaiting your command. Continue with the section "Creating Tables at the Wave of a Wand."

4. **Scroll through the list until you find a Database Wizard template that sounds close to what you want to do and then double-click on it.**

   To create a database by hand, click the General tab of the New Database window and double-click on the Database icon in the upper-left corner of the window.

   Either way, the File New Database dialog box appears.

5. **Type a name for your database and then click on Create (see Figure 4-5).**

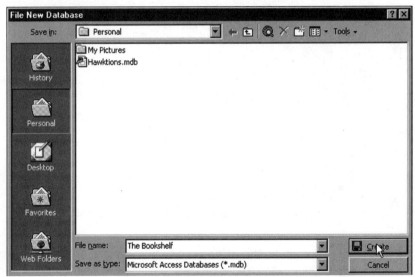

Figure 4-5:
One new database, coming right up!

To store the database somewhere other than the default location (usually the My Documents folder), choose a different folder by clicking on the down arrow next to Save in and working through the directory tree until you find the one you're looking for.

Are you getting a headache from all this talk of folders, directory trees, and such? *Windows 95 For Dummies, Windows 98 For Dummies,* and *Windows NT For Dummies,* all of them by Andy Rathbone, are the perfect remedy. Read once before bedtime and throughout the day as needed.

If a dialog box pops up and asks whether you want to replace an existing file, Access 2000 is saying that a database with the name you entered is already on the disk. If this is news to you, click on No and then come up with a different name for your new database. On the other hand, if you *intended* to replace that old database with a new one, click on Yes and proceed.

6. **Skim over the brief this-is-what-I'm-up-to window to see what the wizard has to say and then click on Next to continue.**

   If you chose the Database option, you see a blank database (see Figure 4-6). To create tables for your new database, skip ahead to the next section in this chapter.

Figure 4-6:
Yup — it's
blank all
right.

7. **If you want to add or remove standard fields from the database that the wizard is building for you, do so in the Fields dialog box (see Figure 4-7) and then click on Next.**

   Unless you're particularly moved to change something, leave this box alone and just click on Next.

8. **Now that the hard part is done, the wizard wants your opinion on some aesthetic questions. First, the wizard wants you to choose a style for the database's on-screen displays. Single-click on the options to see what's available and then double-click on the one you like.**

   Although my wife will accuse me of being bland again, I recommend sticking with the *Standard* option. The others are pretty, but most of them take more time to load. If you simply *must* add some diversity to your database, try the *International, Sumi Painting,* or *Stone* options — they don't slow you down.

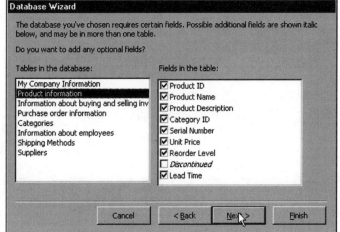

Figure 4-7:
The fields
look good
and fresh
to me.

9. **Pick the style for your reports (at last) and click on Next.**

   As with the previous page, single-click on the options to see what's available. I have no cool recommendations for you here — just pick something you like and move on.

10. **Name your masterpiece and click on Next.**

    The wizard kindly offers his own name, but you're free to change it by simply typing something new in the box at the top of the window.

11. **If you're really into graphics, tell the Database Wizard to add a picture to your reports.**

    To pick an image, click the *Yes I'd like to include a picture* check box and then click on the Picture button to choose the graphic you want to feature on the database's reports.

12. **Click on Finish to build the database.**

    The wizard clunks and thunks for a while, giving you constant updates on how it's doing (see Figure 4-8).

The Database Wizard lets you create a friendly switchboard screen, something like the one I use to keep track of my book collection (see Figure 4-9).

Now that the database is ready, flip through Chapters 6 and 7 for information on entering data, customizing the tables, and getting comfy with your new addition.

Figure 4-8:
The wizard
at work —
your data-
base is
moments
away.

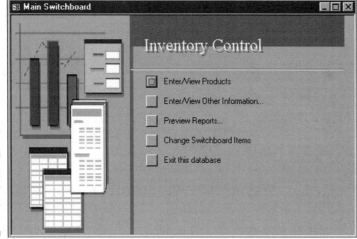

Figure 4-9:
Whoa —
instant
database.

Creating Tables at the Wave of a Wand

Adding a new table to an existing database is easy with the Access 2000 Table Wizard. The Table Wizard offers a variety of ready-made fields to choose from, plus it does all the dirty work of table creation behind the scenes, so you can focus on important stuff (like wondering when you can go home for the day).

With the Table Wizard, you don't so much *build* a table as *assemble* it. The wizard brings lots of pieces and parts — you pick out what you want and go from there.

This approach is helpful when you're completely new at building tables. Instead of worrying about details like field types and sizes, you get to worry about bigger stuff, like field names and purposes. After building a few tables, though, you probably won't use the Table Wizard anymore. Instead of help-ing, he starts getting in the way because you already know what fields you want and how to make them.

As of this writing, the Table Wizard still has some rough edges. Hopefully, the Great Ones Who Write Software will smooth things out before Access 2000 hits the shelves at your local retailer. Because I can't be sure that they really *will* fix the problems, though, the following steps include notes to protect your digital knees from scrapes and scratches on the trouble spots.

Without further ado, here's how to ask the wizard to help you build a table:

1. **Choose File⇨Open or click on the Open Database button on the Toolbar to open the database file that needs a new table.**

   The database pops into its on-screen window.

   If you see a fancy form instead of the database window in Figure 4-10, click on the Windows Close button to close the form and then click on the Restore button (third from the right) on the database window that's hiding in the lower-left corner of the screen. *Now* your database window is ready and waiting.

Figure 4-10:
Get rid
of the
switchboard
and then
view the
database.

2. **Click the Tables tab under the Objects bar of the Database window and then double-click on Create table by using wizard to start the creation process.**

   If everything works right, the Table Wizard dialog box in Figure 4-11 pops onto the screen. If some other bizarre window appears, just close that window and then do this step again.

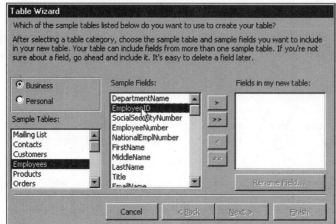

Figure 4-11:
All hail the
mighty Table
Wizard!

3. **Click on a sample table to display the available fields.**

Remember those "rough spots" I mentioned? The Sample Tables list is a big one — it's a *mess*. The tables are jumbled together on the list in no particular order, plus the list includes no descriptions of the fields and what they do. If you look up the term *user friendly* in the dictionary, this dialog box would *not* be listed as an example. To make your life with this dialog box a little easier, check out the upcoming "Highlights from the sample tables" sidebar. It contains some tips to guide you through this seething data morass.

The Table Wizard offers you all kinds of ready-made fields to assemble into a table.

4. **Double-click on the fields you want for the table.**

When you double-click, the field name hops into the Fields in my new table column. Select the fields in the order you want them to appear in the new table. Don't worry if you get one or two out of order — it's easy to fix that later (Chapter 9 tells you how).

If you like *all* the fields from a particular table, click on the > button. That button copies the table's entire set of fields.

To remove a field you chose by accident, click on the field name and then click the < button. To remove *all* the fields and start over with a clean slate, click on the << button.

If you're not happy with the current name of a field in your new table, click on the field name and then click on Rename Field. Type the new field name into the dialog box and click on OK to make the change. Too easy, eh?

5. **Repeat Steps 4 and 5 until your table is populated with fields (see Figure 4-12).**

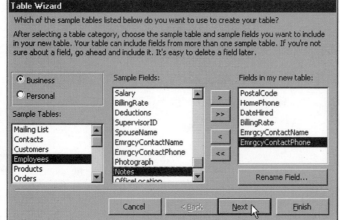

Figure 4-12:
After
reworking
the fields a
bit, it's time
to move on.

6. **When you're done picking fields, click on Next to continue.**

So far, so good — now you're down to the simple stuff. On-screen, the field information runs off to hide as the wizard needs to know some general stuff about the table.

7. **Type a name for the table and click on Next when you're done.**

The table name information vanishes, only to be replaced with the table relationship screen.

Leave the primary key settings alone for now. You can mess with those later (see Chapter 5).

8. **If this table is related to any of the other tables in the database, click on the Relationships button and explain how the tables are involved with each other and then click on Next.**

The Table Wizard is pretty intelligent about this relationship stuff. It checks for fields that may link this new table to the existing ones in your database. The wizard reports its findings in this dialog box.

If you *thought* there would be a relationship but the wizard couldn't find one, click on the related table's entry in the dialog box and then click on Relationships. Follow the on-screen prompts to explain how the link works.

Chapter 5 has more about table relationships. Look in that chapter if you're a little foggy about the hows and whys of linking tables together.

Highlights from the sample tables

In hopes of making the Table Wizard a little more useful, here are some brief descriptions of the sample tables. This list doesn't cover all the sample tables — just the ones that I think are most useful.

Many of these tables link together to form relational databases. For instance, Calls, Contacts, Contact Types, and "To Do's" work together as a single system. Don't bother trying to put the individual pieces together with the Table Wizard. Use the Database Wizard instead — it's a *lot* easier!

✔ **Mailing List:** General information (name, address, and so on) geared toward seminar attendees

✔ **Contacts:** Very full-featured customer information table; stores details about your customers

✔ **Customers:** You guessed it — a customer information list, complete with a field for e-mail address

✔ **Employees:** Solid employee information table; good example of the detail you can include in a single table

✔ **Events:** Great for meeting planners or trainers setting up their own room information

✔ **Orders:** Tracks customer order data

✔ **Order Details:** Covers the line items for each order

✔ **Products:** General product information for a catalog and sales system

✔ **Reservations:** Handles event reservations and pre-paid fees

✔ **Service Records:** Great example of a table that manages call information for a service business

✔ **Tasks:** Tracks to-do items

You're *really* done — click on Finish to complete the task and build the new table.

---

9. **You're *really* done — click on F̲inish to complete the task and build the new table.**

The final window offers a couple of other interesting and timesaving options to consider before whacking that Finish button. To take the table design directly into Design mode after closing the wizard, click the Modify the table design radio button and then click Finish. To have the wizard whip up a quick data entry form, click the long-named *Enter data into the table using a form the wizard creates for me* radio button; then take a few breaths and click Finish.

Whew! You did it. The table proudly takes its place in your database (see Figure 4-13).

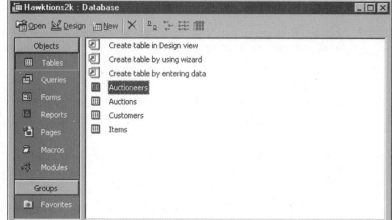

Figure 4-13:
Here's the
new table —
this thing
really
worked!

Building Tables by Hand, Just as in the Old Days

Although automation is a generally great thing, at times it just plain gets in the way. For instance, I appreciate the fact that with the right automatic gizmo, I can clap my hands and turn off the television. This feat becomes a problem when I start keeping time with my favorite song and accidentally drive the TV insane.

Likewise, the Table Wizard makes life easy at first, but soon, you know more about what you want than it does. Don't worry — when you're ready for independence, Access 2000 is there with a straightforward way to build tables by hand.

Actually, you have *two* easy ways to build a table without the Table Wizard. The easiest is *Datasheet view,* where Access 2000 displays a blank datasheet and you just start typing in data. After you're done entering everything, Access 2000 looks at your entries and assigns field types based on the data it sees. The only problem is that Access 2000 frequently misunderstands your data, leaving you to tweak the field types by hand. The bottom line: For anything more complicated than a *really* simple table, don't use Datasheet view. It's a nice thought, but it drives you nuts in the end. Instead, use Design view.

Design view is the formal, almost nerd-like way to build new databases. In this mode, you have full control over the new table's fields. Don't get all weirded out because the screen looks complicated — just go slow, follow the information in the steps, and everything will be fine. (Trust me on this one.)

To create a new table by hand, cruise through these steps:

1. **Choose File⇨Open from the main menu; then double-click on the database that needs a new table.**

   The database file appears on-screen. If a cool-looking form appears in its place, click the Windows Close button in the form's upper-right corner to make the form go away; then click the Restore button on the database window to bring the database front and center on the screen.

   You can also click on the Open Database button on the toolbar, but that's old news by now.

2. **Click the Tables button on the left side of the Databases window and then double-click Create table in Design view.**

   Access 2000 displays a blank table design form that looks a whole heck-uva lot like Figure 4-14.

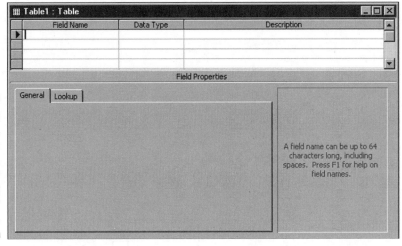

Figure 4-14:
A fresh, clean datasheet, anxiously awaiting your instruction.

Remember the note earlier about creating tables in Datasheet view? If you're heavily into pain, agony, and doing things the hard way, double-click on the Datasheet View option and use it to build the new table. Also, refer to Chapter 8 for lots of cool tips about working with a datasheet (believe me, you need all the help you can get).

3. **Type the field name and then press Tab to move on.**

   The cursor moves to the Data Type column. See — this manual stuff isn't so bad, is it?

4. **Click on the down-arrow to list all available field types, click on the field type you want (see Figure 4-15), and then press Tab to continue.**

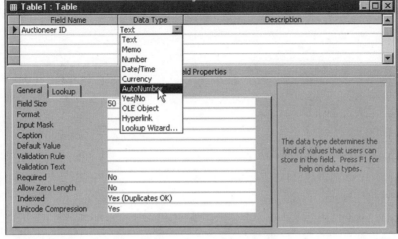

Figure 4-15:
You can
select from
all available
field (data)
types.

The cursor moves into the Description field.

If you create a Text field, you also need to adjust the field size (the default size is 50, which is too much field for almost anyone). Click in the Field Size box in the lower-left side of the screen *before* tabbing elsewhere; then type the correct field size.

5. **Type a clear, concise description of what this field contains and then press Tab once more to move the cursor back into the Field Name column.**

This step is *really* important! The Description information appears in the status bar at the bottom of the screen — it's automatic help text. *Please* take the time to write a quick field description. It makes your tables so much easier to use that you won't believe it.

6. **Repeat Steps 4 through 6 until all the fields are in place (see Figure 4-16).**

What a feeling of achievement! Your new table is almost ready to work.

7. **Select File⇨Save to write the new table to your disk drive or click on the Save button on the Toolbar.**

8. **In the dialog box, type the name you want to use for the table and press Enter.**

Access 2000 may send you a dialog box complaining that There is no primary key defined. This message means that your table won't automatically put itself into any kind of order. Click on Yes in the dialog box to create a key field and then check out Chapter 5 for more about the whole key field thing.

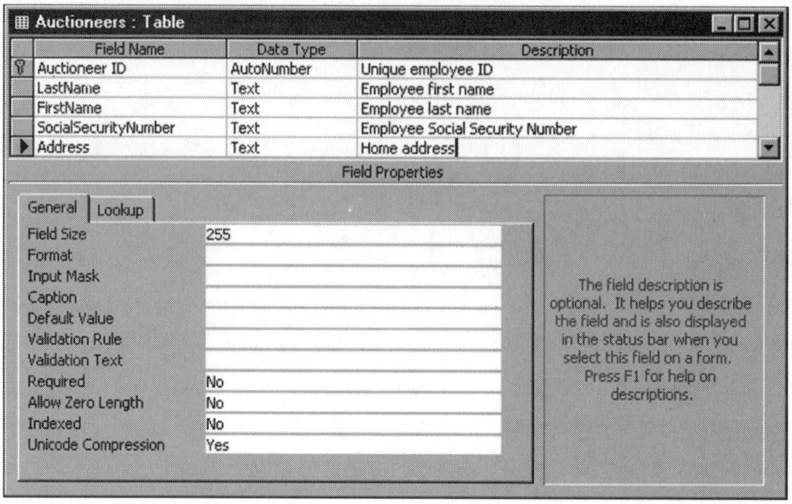

Field Name	Data Type	Description
Auctioneer ID	AutoNumber	Unique employee ID
LastName	Text	Employee first name
FirstName	Text	Employee last name
SocialSecurityNumber	Text	Employee Social Security Number
Address	Text	Home address

Field Properties

General | Lookup

Field Size	255
Format	
Input Mask	
Caption	
Default Value	
Validation Rule	
Validation Text	
Required	No
Allow Zero Length	No
Indexed	No
Unicode Compression	Yes

The field description is optional. It helps you describe the field and is also displayed in the status bar when you select this field on a form. Press F1 for help on descriptions.

Figure 4-16:
The fields are in place . . . time to give it the stress test!

9. Enjoy your new table!

That's not bad for doing the work without automated intervention! Congratulations on a job well-done.

Chapter 5

Relationships, Keys, and Indexes (And Why You Really Do Care)

In This Chapter

▶ Getting organized with a primary key

▶ The scoop about relationships

▶ Building relationships between your tables

▶ Speeding up your life with indexes

*E*very year, it's the same things over and over. Do more with less. Work smarter not harder. They're not problems, they're *opportunities for achievement*. Why do I bring up such wonderful thoughts in a fun book like this? Because this chapter is at least a partial cure for these phrases that afflict you.

You need to get more done in less time, right? If that's you, then check out the index feature in Access 2000. This feature makes your queries fly, your sorts sing, and your hair hold firm in its current position. Are you plagued with *opportunities* because of all the duplicate data infesting your tables? Ferret out the problems with a well-placed key field. A good key ensures that records appear once (and only once) in the table.

And what about the whole *relational database* thing? Can tables *really* have relationships, or do they just spend a lot of platonic time together? Thanks to the wonders of the Relationships tool in Access 2000, your tables work with each other better than ever. Of course, the matchmaking that leads up to a successful relationship isn't any easier with tables than it is with humans, but don't let that worry you. With the tips in this chapter, you'll be a card-carrying *Data Yenta* in no time.

The Joy (And Necessity) of a Primary Key

A table's *primary key* is a special field in your tables. Just about every table you create *should* have a primary key. Why? Because it keeps your data more organized, and because many nerds pitch a snit if you don't (and we don't need any more snit pitching than is absolutely necessary).

You need to know a few things about the primary key before running off to create one:

- First, a table can have only *one* primary key. A single table can have lots of indexes, but only *one* primary key.

- Access 2000 automatically indexes the primary key field (that's one reason that a primary key makes your database work a little faster). For more about indexes and why they're the best thing since individually wrapped cheese food products, see the final section in this chapter, "Indexing Your Way to Fame, Fortune, and Significantly Faster Queries."

- If you create a new table without a primary key, Access 2000 automatically asks whether you want to add one. If you say yes, the program gleefully creates an AutoNumber field at the beginning of your table and sets it as the primary key. If the first field already happens to be an AutoNumber type, Access 2000 anoints it as the primary key without adding anything else to the table. (Yes, this *is* a good reason to put an AutoNumber field first in your table design.)

- Most of the time, the primary key is a single field, but in *very* special circumstances two or more fields can share the job. The technical term for this type of key is a *multifield key.* The big drawback of a multifield key is the simple fact that it's a pain to use. If you ever have the urge to create a multifield key in one of your tables, stop for a moment and try very hard to talk yourself out of it. If you're *still* convinced that a multifield key is the answer to your problems, collar your local database guru and ask for her opinion. Hopefully, she can come up with a better solution for the table.

- Only certain field types can be keys. Text, number, date/time, Currency, Yes/No, and AutoNumber fields all qualify for primary key status. Hyperlink, OLE, and memo fields can't be the primary key.

- The primary key automatically sorts records in the table. This feature is part of the organizational thing I mentioned before — it just keeps things neat and tidy in your table.

- By default, the values in the primary key field *must* be unique. After all, if they aren't unique, how can you hope to find anything?

Unlike many other database programs, Access 2000 doesn't care where the primary key field is in the table design. The key can be the first field, the last field, or some field in the middle. The placement choice is all yours. For your sanity's sake, I recommend putting the key field *first* in a table. In fact, make it a habit (you can thank me later).

✔ All primary keys must have a name, just like the field has a name. This may come as a shock so hold on to your seat, but Access 2000 automatically names all primary keys PrimaryKey. Don't ask me why you would want to name your primary key in the first place. Maybe the programmers at Microsoft were afraid the primary key may begin to develop an identity crisis because the primary key was always being identified by the field's name.

✔ Although the Yes/No field qualifies as a possible contender for primary key status, you would only be able to have a maximum of two records (Yes and No) in your table. Needless to say, you most likely do not want to use a Yes/No field as a primary key in any table.

To nominate a field for the job of primary key, follow these steps:

1. **Open the table in Design view.**

   If you're not familiar with this step, you probably *shouldn't* be messing with the primary key. I recommend spending a little time back in Chapters 1 and 4 before tackling the primary key thing.

Picking the right field is a *key* issue

What makes a good key field? How do you find the right one? Good questions — in fact, they're the two most important questions to ask about a primary key.

The top criteria for a good key field is uniqueness. The values in a key field must be unique. Access 2000 won't tolerate duplicate key values. Each and every entry in the key field must be the only one of its kind. If you see a lot of table creation in your future, then pin the phrase *Think unique* on your office wall.

With the word unique firmly imprinted in your mind, it's time to look for a natural key field in your table. Do you have any fields that always contain unique data? Is there a Customer Number, Stock Keeping Unit, Vehicle ID, or some other field that's different in every record?

If you have a natural key, that's great. Use it! If you don't, create a unique field by adding an AutoNumber field to your table. This field type automatically inserts a new, unique number into each record of your table. AutoNumber even keeps track of numbers that you delete so that Access won't use them again. Best of all, Access takes care of the details so that you don't have to worry about programming or any special tricks to make the program work. The AutoNumber field handles it for you.

2. **Right-click in the button next to the field you've picked for the primary key.**

   One of those cool pop-up menus appears. For some ideas on how to pick the *right* field for a primary key, see the nearby sidebar, "Picking the right field is a *key* issue."

3. **Select Primary Key from the menu (see Figure 5-1).**

   A little key symbol appears in the button. The primary key is set!

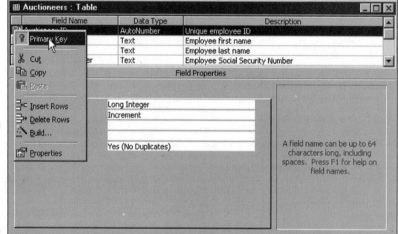

Figure 5-1:
The primary key is created (and the records rejoice).

Divulging the Secrets of a Good Relationship

I introduce the relational thing back in Chapter 4. As a quick recap, databases come in two basic kinds. In a *flat file* system, all the data is lumped into one big file. It's called a flat file because, organizationally speaking, it's flat — like a company with only one job classification.

At the other end of the spectrum are *relational* databases. Here, data is split up among two or more tables. Access 2000 uses a *linking field* to tie related tables together. For example, one table may contain customer names and addresses while another table tracks the customer's payment history. The credit information is tied to the customer's address with a linking field, which, in this example, is probably some kind of customer number.

✔ Usually, the linking field is one table's primary key, but just an average, mild-mannered field in the other table. For instance, the customer table in the example is probably arranged by customer number, while the credit data is likely organized by payment number.

✔ Tables don't magically begin relating to each other just because they're cooped up inside the same database file. You explain the relationships to Access 2000 and it handles the details. Instructions for doing that very thing are in the next section.

✔ Linking fields must be the same data type. Remember, fields of a feather flock together in the weird world of databases. Try repeating that three times quickly.

When you link two tables together, they form one of four possible relationships. Although this information borders on the technical side, Access 2000 is particularly fond of these terms, so please take a minute to check them out.

✔ *One-to-One* relationships are the simplest, but they don't happen often. Here, one record in the first table links to *exactly* one record in the second table. Back in the example, if one customer has one (and only one) store credit account, then the customer and credit tables have a one-to-one link.

✔ *One-to-Many* is a much more common relationship. In this relationship, one record in the first table links to *many* records in the second table. One sample customer may make many purchases at the store, so one customer record is linked to many sales records in the transaction table.

✔ *Many-to-One* relationships are simply the reverse of *one-to-many*. Look at the relationship from the sales record end this time instead of the customer record end. Many sales transactions are linked back to one customer (a customer that *we* want to keep happy).

✔ *Many-to-Many* relationships are very complicated (just like real life). Here, many records in one table link to many records in another. In a given store each sales clerk sells many different products, and each product is sold by many different sales clerks. To have any hope of figuring out what's going on, you need a table in the middle to play traffic cop. In this example, the traffic cop table would contain sale transaction records correlating a sales clerk ID to a product ID. Sound confusing? Trust me, it is. Creating and using tables in a many-to-many relationship is strictly the realm of database professionals (and even *they* don't like it).

The first three relationships are very common, particularly if you're in a corporate environment. If you're a particularly nice individual, lead a good life, and follow the straight and narrow path, you hopefully won't ever come across a many-to-many relationship. If you *do* fall into one, stock up on junk food and put out the word that you're looking for a hungry technoid who knows Access 2000.

Linking Your Tables with the Relationship Builder Thingie

The mechanics of linking tables together in Access 2000 are quite visual. There's none of Paradox's informal sneaking around behind your data's back, nor is it a technical mating dance as in FoxPro. In Access 2000, look at tables, draw lines, and get on with your business. I hate to say this, but linking tables is actually kinda fun. Keep these three limitations in mind:

✔ You can only link tables that are in the same database. Sorry, but that's how life goes in the big city.

✔ Although you can also link queries to tables, that's a little outside the range of normalcy. For more about that, check out *Access 2000 Bible* (IDG Books Worldwide, Inc.).

✔ Unlike Paradox and FoxPro, you need to specifically tell Access 2000 how your tables are related. And you can't tell this stuff to Access on-the-fly — linking tables is a formal process (kinda like ballroom dancing).

When you're ready to arrange some formal relationships among your more impassioned tables, here's how to do it:

1. **From the database window, choose** **Tools**⇨**Relationships or click on the Relationships button on the toolbar.**

   The Relationships window appears, probably looking quite blank at the moment.

   If some tables are already listed in the window, someone (or some-Wizard) has already defined relationships for this database. If you're in a corporate environment, *please* stop at this point and seek assistance from your Information Systems folks before mucking around with this database.

2. **Choose** **Relationships**⇨**Show Table from the menu or click on the Show Table button on the toolbar.**

   The Show Table dialog box appears on-screen, listing the tables in the current database file.

3. **Click on the first table involved in this would-be relationship and then click on** **Add.**

   Repeat the process with the other tables you want to get involved. As you add tables to the layout, a little window appears for each table, listing the fields in that table. You can see these windows next to the Show Table dialog box in Figure 5-2.

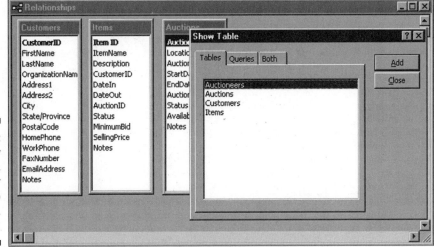

Figure 5-2:
Three of my
four tables,
reporting for
relationship
practice.
Ten, hut!

4. **Click on Close when you're finished adding tables.**

   With the tables present in the window, you're ready to start the relation-ships! (Do you feel like a matchmaker yet?)

5. **Decide which two tables you want to link together. In each table's window, scroll through the field list until the linking fields are both visible on-screen.**

   In Access 2000, you need to *see* the two linking fields on-screen before you can make a relationship.

6. **Put the mouse pointer on one of the fields you want to link and hold the left mouse button down.**

   Did I mention that the same people who developed the old *Twister* game also designed the relationship builder? No? Hmm . . . that must've slipped my mind. Oh well, carry on — you'll discover that soon enough.

7. **While holding down the mouse button, slide the mouse from one link-ing field to the other.**

   The pointer becomes a rectangle. When the rectangle is next to the link-ing field (see Figure 5-3), release the mouse button.

   A dialog box detailing the soon-to-be relationship appears.

   Access 2000 is *very* picky about your aim on this step. You *must* put the tip of the mouse pointer *right next* to the field you're linking to. In Figure 5-3, I want to make a relationship between the AuctionID field in the Auctions table and the field of the same name in Items. I already clicked on AuctionID in the Auctions table. Then I hold down the mouse button and put the boxy mouse pointer right next to the AuctionID field in Items. At this point, all I need to do is let up on the mouse button and the relationship is made.

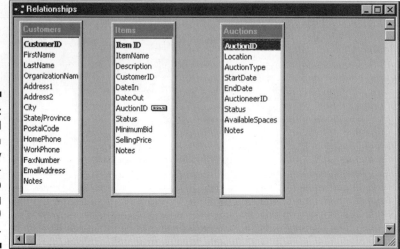

Figure 5-3:
With careful
aim and a
steady
hand, a rela-
tionship
using
Auction ID
begins.

8. **Make sure that the table and field names in the dialog box are correct. When you're confident that the entries are correct, click on
   Create (see Figure 5-4).**

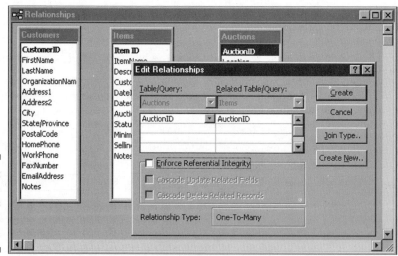

Figure 5-4:
This rela-
tionship is
off to a good
start.

If the table names or field names listed in the dialog box are wrong, just
click on Cancel and try Steps 5 through 7 again.

A line appears to show you that the tables are linked, as you see in
Figure 5-5.

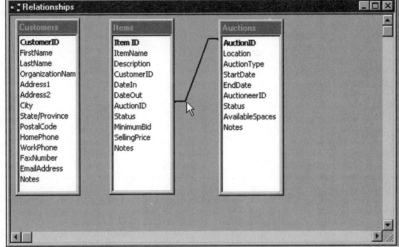

Figure 5-5:
The match is made —
Auctions and Items are together.

9. **To link another pair of tables, go back to Step 4 and begin again.**

When you're done, the Relationships window may look a little messy, as in Figure 5-6. To clean it up, put the mouse pointer on the title bar of a table window and then click and drag the table window to another part of the screen (see Figure 5-7). This process doesn't change the relationship — it just moves the window around. In no time at all, things start looking neat and tidy.

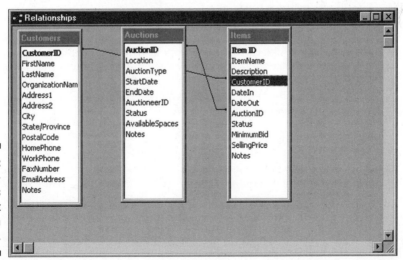

Figure 5-6:
With relationships like this, it could be a soap opera.

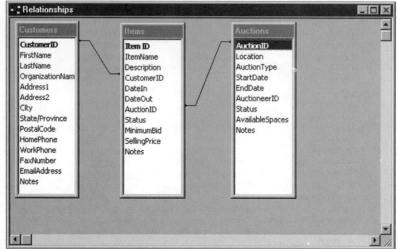

Figure 5-7:
That's much
neater, not
to mention
easier to
understand.

Indexing Your Way to Fame, Fortune, and Significantly Faster Queries

Psst — you with the book. Yeah, you. C'mere for a minute. Want some inside information about your software? I've got a hot tip on a feature that'll blow you away. My tip speeds up your queries, makes sorting a snap, and prevents duplicate records in your tables. Pretty cool, eh? Oh, you *are* interested. Okay, then — here's the scoop.

The cool, semi-secret feature in question is an *index.* An Access 2000 table index works just like the index in a book. When you want to find something in the book, it's quick and easy to flip to the index, discover that the information is on page 731, and then turn immediately to the right page. Using the index is a whole lot faster than flipping page after page in a hopeless search for the correct passage.

An Access 2000 index works just like a book index, but instead of listing page numbers, the index tracks *record* numbers. When you sort or query a table using an indexed field, the index already does most of the work. That's why indexes dramatically speed up queries and sorts — the index lets the query zero in on the information it's looking for without having to sift through the whole table to find it.

Here are a few random thoughts about indexes:

- Most field types (text, number, yes/no, and so on) work just fine with indexes. You *cannot,* however, index a hyperlink, memo, or OLE field.

- Each field in a table can be indexed.

- ✔ Like the primary key, an index may have a unique name that is different from the field name.

- ✔ Primary key fields are indexed automatically. (See the previous section for more about keys and key fields.)

- ✔ Although indexes make queries, searches, and sorts a whole lot faster, building too many indexes in a table actually *slows down* some things. Adding records to a table with several indexes takes a little longer than adding records to an unindexed table. Access 2000 spends the extra time updating all those indexes behind the scenes.

- ✔ Indexes either *allow* duplicate entries in your table or *prevent* them. The choice is yours. How do you choose the right one for your table? Most of the time, you want to *allow* duplicate records. The big exception is with primary key fields. Access 2000 always indexes primary key fields as *No duplicates* — after all, you don't want two customers with the same Customer Number. The *No duplicates* setting tells Access 2000 to make sure that no two records have the same values in the indexed field.

- ✔ To list the table's indexes, open the table in Design view and click on the Indexes button on the toolbar.

The programmers at Microsoft made creating an index a pretty straightforward operation. Here's how it works:

1. **With the table open in Design view, click on the name of the field you want to index.**

   The blinking toothpick cursor lands in the field name.

2. **Click on the Indexed box in the General tab of Field Properties.**

   The toothpick cursor, always eager to please, hops into the Indexed box. A down arrow appears on the right end of the box as well.

   If the *Indexed* display has no entry, then this particular field type doesn't work with indexes. No matter how much you want to, you can't index hyperlink, memo, or OLE fields.

3. **Click on the down arrow at the end of the box to list your index options. Select the kind of index you want from the list (see Figure 5-8).**

   Most of the time, choose Yes (Duplicates OK). In special cases when you want every record to have a unique value in this field (like Customer Numbers in your Customer table), select Yes (No Duplicates).

4. **Click on the Save toolbar button or choose File➪Save to make the change permanent.**

   Depending on the size of your table, it may take a few moments of effort to create the index. Don't be surprised if you have to wait a few moments before Access 2000 is done.

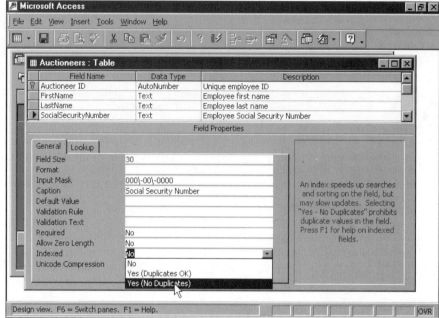

Figure 5-8:
Building an
index is a
one-click
operation.

To remove an index, follow the preceding steps. In Step 3, choose No on the pull-down menu. Access 2000 wordlessly deletes the field's index.

Chapter 6

New Data, Old Data, and Data in Need of Repair

In This Chapter

▶ Opening databases and tables

▶ Adding new records

▶ Changing an existing record

▶ Deleting the pointless ones

▶ What to do after saying, "oops!"

Maintenance is a substantial cost involving anything worth keeping around this planet. No matter what you're talking about — house, car, stereo, television, child, pet, significant other — keeping valuables in good working order always costs more than we think when we first obtain the item.

Your data, however, is an exception to the rule. Thanks to the tools in Access 2000, data maintenance is easy, relatively painless, and costs less than you expect. In fact, keeping your data up to date is one of the program's main goals.

This chapter covers basic data upkeep: adding new records, deleting old ones, and fixing the ones that are broken. If you're looking for table maintenance hints (such as adding new columns, renaming fields, and so on), check out Chapter 9.

Dragging Your Table into the Digital Workshop

Because records cluster together in tables, you need to open a table before worrying about records. Tables prefer company, too. They hang out inside databases. Databases don't care a whit about anything other than them-selves, so you may find them lounging in a folder, sulking on a diskette, or holding forth on a network drive.

That fancy buildup simply means that the first step on the road to record maintenance is opening a database. You have several different ways to open a database, but they all ultimately work the same way.

If you just opened Access 2000, the program displays a massive dialog box (see Figure 6-1) that offers the opportunity to create a new database, reopen one you worked on recently, or wander off into another dialog box to open whatever database strikes your fancy right now.

Figure 6-1:
Is this too
handy or
what?

- To use one of the databases listed at the bottom of the dialog box, double-click on its name. Access 2000 automatically opens the database.

- If the database you want isn't on the list, double-click on the More Files option to bring up the Open dialog box. This dialog box gives you access to all the table files in the current file folder.

- What? The database you want isn't there either? In that case, check out the nearby sidebar, "Bo Peep needed the Find File option," for some tips about the fortuitous file-finding features located under the Tools menu of the Open dialog box.

- If you're in the mood to create a new table, you need to be in a different chapter. Flip to Chapter 4, where all the create-a-table stuff is.

These hints are all well and good if Access 2000 just came roaring to life, but what if it's already running? In that case, you've got a whole different way to open up your database. Here's how it works:

1. **Choose File⇨Open Database or click on the Open Database button on the toolbar.**

The Open dialog box pops onto the screen (see Figure 6-2).

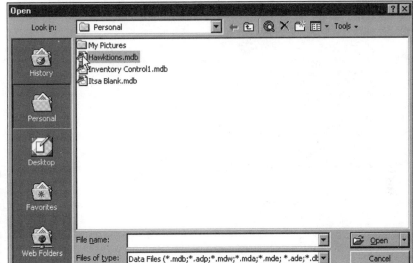

Figure 6-2:
Here's the database I was looking for.

2. **Scroll through the list until you find the database you're looking for.**

If the database you want isn't on this list, it's probably in another folder, on another disk drive, or out on your network. To search for it, click on the Down arrow in the Look in box (along the top of the Open dialog box) to see a list of your local and network disk drives. Click on the drive you want to search. Access 2000 displays a list of all databases and file folders in the current directory of that drive.

 To make things *really* easy, add a few shortcuts to your Favorites list. Include your most commonly used network areas, directories on your hard drive, or wherever you (or the data nerds in your company) store Access files. For more about shortcuts, check out Andy Rathbone's *Windows 95 For Dummies,* 2nd Edition, *Windows 98 For Dummies,* or *Windows NT 4 For Dummies* (from IDG Books Worldwide, Inc.).

3. **When you find the database, open it by double-clicking on its name.**

The database file opens with a flourish, as shown in Figure 6-3. This window shows how a normal, well-mannered database file acts in polite company. The rest of this chapter assumes that your database behaves this way.

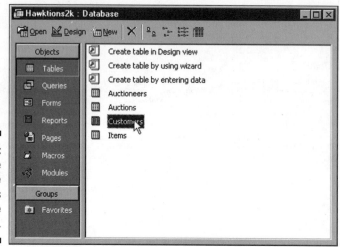

Figure 6-3:
An average
database
file opens
onto the
screen.

An introductory screen of some kind (known as a *switchboard*) may appear instead of the tabbed dialog box. Access is telling you that your database either contains some custom programming or was created by the Database Wizard. You probably have some special forms that help you interact with the information in your database. Unfortunately, I can't tell you much more than that, because the possibilities are endless. The best suggestion I can offer is to look for instructions from your favorite local database nerd.

4. **If it's not already selected, click on the Tables button under the Objects bar.**

   The Objects bar Tables button lists the tables in your database.

5. **Double-click on the table you want to edit.**

   The screen fills with your data, displayed eloquently in Datasheet view.

Adding a Little Something to the Mix

Few tasks are more frustrating than packing your car for vacation and then suddenly discovering the one thing you forgot to put in (and it's always something big). In the real world, this discovery is a repacking nightmare, but in the digital world of Access 2000, adding one or one hundred extra items to your database is easy.

In fact, adding another record to a table takes only a couple of steps. The following instructions assume that you have already opened the database file and selected the table you want to work on. (If you haven't, follow the instructions in the preceding section.) Here's how to add a new record to your table:

1. **Choose Insert⇨New Record or click on the New Record button at the bottom of the datasheet window.**

    Access 2000 responds by opening a blank record in your table and moving the toothpick cursor there (see Figure 6-4).

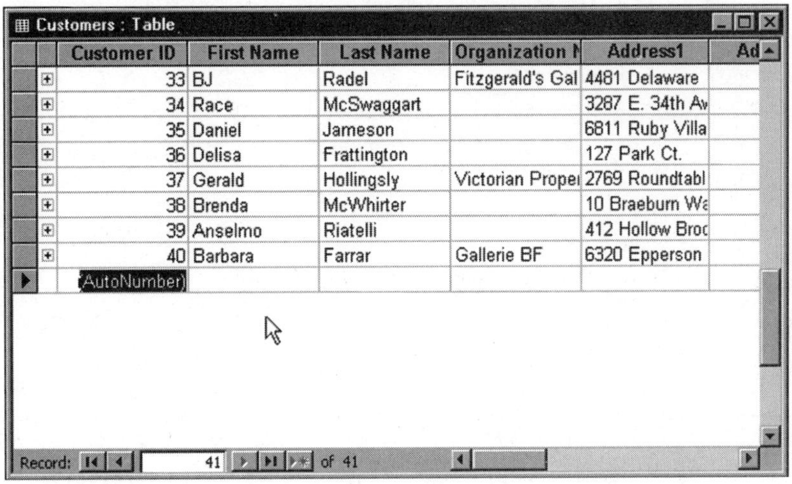

Customer ID	First Name	Last Name	Organization N	Address1	Ad
33	BJ	Radel	Fitzgerald's Gal	4481 Delaware	
34	Race	McSwaggart		3287 E. 34th Av	
35	Daniel	Jameson		6811 Ruby Villa	
36	Delisa	Frattington		127 Park Ct.	
37	Gerald	Hollingsly	Victorian Proper	2769 Roundtabl	
38	Brenda	McWhirter		10 Braeburn Wa	
39	Anselmo	Riatelli		412 Hollow Broc	
40	Barbara	Farrar	Gallerie BF	6320 Epperson	
(AutoNumber)					

Customers : Table

Record: ◄ ◄ 41 ► ►► ►* of 41

Figure 6-4:
A new record is born.

The first field in many databases is an AutoNumber type field, because this field does such a good job of assigning unique customer numbers, part numbers, or whatever kind of number you have in mind. At this point in the process, it's normal for an AutoNumber field to just sit there and stare at you. The AutoNumber field doesn't start working until the next step.

2. **Begin typing your information.**

    If the first field is an AutoNumber type, press Tab and begin typing in the second field. As soon as you start typing, the AutoNumber field generates a new number and displays it in the field.

    Don't panic if the AutoNumber field seems to skip a number when it creates an entry for your new record (see Figure 6-5). The field remembers the last number it assigned and automatically inserts the next sequential number. When an AutoNumber field skips a number, it means that you probably entered (or at least started to enter) a record and then deleted it.

3. **When you're done, either press Tab to add another record or, if you just wanted to add one record, simply go on about your business.**

    Because Access 2000 automatically saves the new record while you're typing it, you have nothing more to do. Pretty cool!

Figure 6-5:
The record takes shape, despite its odd numbering.

Bo Peep needed the Find File option

In terms of job responsibility, Bo Peep had it easy. All she needed to do was keep an eye on a few animals and make sure that they stayed in roughly the same geographic spot. Now fast forward to the 1990s, as Ms. Peep rides herd over databases scattered across a hard drive or network. Imagine the havoc!

The friendly folks who created Access 2000 know that databases, like errant sheep, tend to run off and get lost from time to time. That's why they included the Find File option on the Tools menu at the top of the Open dialog box. Choosing Tools⇨Find brings forth the Find dialog box, which contains a wealth of cool search options. Of the many options available, the File Name search is the most useful. (Apparently the Microsoft programmers thought so, too, because they made this kind of search the default.)

If you know at least part of the database's file-name, type it into the Value box on the lower-right corner of the window. Access 2000 lists all databases in the current folder that match your search text. To make Access 2000 work a little harder (and help you a lot more), tell it to search the subfolders in the current folder, as well. Do that by clicking the Search Subfolders check box just below the Value box. Access 2000 immediately scours the current folder and all folders underneath it, seeking your misplaced database.

The real power of the Find File system comes when you tell Access 2000 to search a disk drive. Click on the Down arrow in the Look in box (in the lower-left corner of the Find window) and choose a local or network disk drive from the pull-down menu. Almost immediately, your computer starts churning through the folders in the disk drive, looking here, there, and everywhere for files that match your specifications.

If you change your mind and want to kill the new addition, choose Edit➪Undo Saved Record or press Ctrl+Z and then click on Yes when Access 2000 asks about deleting the record. If the Undo Saved Record menu choice isn't available, click in the record you just added and then choose Edit➪Delete Record. As before, click on Yes when asked whether you're sure about the deletion.

Changing What's Already There

Even though your stuff is safely tucked away inside a table, you can easily reach in and make changes. In fact, editing your data is so easy that I'm not sure whether this is a good feature or a bad one.

Whenever you're browsing through a table, please be careful! Access 2000 doesn't warn you before saving changes to a record — even if the changes are accidental. (If I were one of those preachy authors, I'd probably make a big, guilt-laden point about how this "feature" of Access 2000 makes doing regular backups all the more important. Luckily, I'm not that kind of guy, so I'm not even going to bring the subject up.)

To change something inside a record, scroll through the table until you find the record that needs some adjusting. Click in the field you want to change, and the blinking toothpick cursor pops into the field.

If you have the Microsoft IntelliMouse, use the wheel button to quickly spin through the table. For such a small innovation, that wheel is a big time-saver! Check out Chapter 8 for more details about browsing your data with Microsoft's answer to the Big Wheel — the IntelliMouse.

What you do next depends on what kind of change you want to make to the field:

✔ To replace the entire field, press F2 to highlight the data and then type the new information. The new entry replaces the old one cleanly.

✔ To repair a portion of the data in a field, click in the field and then use the right- and left-arrow keys to position the toothpick cursor exactly where you want to make the change. Press Backspace to remove characters to the left of the cursor; press Delete to remove them to the right. Insert new characters by typing.

✔ If you're in a time/date field and want to insert the current date, press Ctrl+; (semicolon). To insert the current time, press Ctrl+: (colon).

When you're done with the record, press Enter to save your changes. If you change your mind and want to restore the original data, press Esc or Ctrl+Z to cancel your edits. If you're on a rotary-dial phone, please wait for operator assistance (hmm — perhaps I've been making too many phone calls lately).

Don't press Enter until you're positively sure about the changes you typed. After you save them, the old data is gone — you can't go back.

Kicking Out Unwanted Records

There's no sense mourning over unneeded records. When the time comes to bid them adieu, do it quickly and painlessly. Here's how:

1. **With the table open, right-click on the button to the left of the record you want to delete.**

   The standard I-right-clicked-on-something pop-up menu appears.

   Be sure that you click on the correct record before going on to the next step! Discovering the mistake now is much less painful than finding it in just a moment.

2. **Choose Delete Record from the pop-up menu.**

   Access 2000 does a truly cool screen-effect and visually swallows the old record.

3. **When Access 2000 displays the dialog box in Figure 6-6, pause and reflect once more about deleting the record.**

Figure 6-6: Access 2000 asks the fateful question: Are you sure?

If you're sure, click on Yes and banish the record to oblivion.

If you're the slightest bit unsure, click on No and do some more thinking before exercising the Delete Record command on anything else in your table.

Instead of the Are you sure dialog box, Access 2000 may display the box in Figure 6-7. This message means you can't delete that record, no matter how much you may want to. In this case, you're working with a table that's related to another one. Access 2000 won't let you remove the record because records in another table are linked to the one you want to kill. Sorry — you can't get out of this one. If you still want to delete the record, ask a data hit man (or your local computer jockey) to do the dirty work for you, because there's more to this problem than meets the eye.

Figure 6-7:
Oops — this
record is
going
nowhere.

Recovering from a Baaaad Edit

I have only two suggestions for picking up the pieces from a bad edit. Unfortunately, neither is a super-cool elixir that magically restores your lost data. I wish I had better news to close the chapter with, but I'm fresh out of headlines.

First, double-check any change you make before saving it. If the change is important, triple-check it. When you're sure that it's right, press Enter and commit the change to the table. If you're not sure about the data, don't save the changes. Instead, get your questions answered first and then feel free to edit the record.

Second, keep a good backup so that you can quickly recover missing data and get on with your work. Good backups have no substitute. If you make good backups, the chance of losing data is greatly reduced, your boss will promote you, your significant other will unswervingly devote his or her life to you, and you may even win the lottery. (Truth be told, backups do only one of those things, but it's the thought that counts.)

Chapter 7

Making Your Table Think with Formats, Masks, and Validations

In This Chapter

▶ Finding where the settings live

▶ Better formatting for prettier data

▶ Keeping bad data out with input masks

▶ Performing detailed testing through validations

Scientists have incredibly detailed, long-winded explanations of what it means to "think," but my definition is much simpler. If you see dragons in the clouds, marvel at a child's playtime adventures, or wonder what makes flowers grow, you're thinking.

Whether you use my definition or one from the experts, one thing is for sure: Access 2000 tables *don't* think. If you have nightmarish visions of reading this chapter and then accidentally unleashing The Table That Ate Microsoft's Competitors, have no fear; it's not going to happen. (After all, if such a scenario *could* happen, don't you think Microsoft would have arranged it by now?)

This chapter explains how to enlist your table's help to spot and prevent bad data from getting into your table. The chapter focuses on three different tools: *formats, masks,* and *validation rules.* These three tools may sound kinda technical, but you can handle them (trust me).

Each tool has its own section, so if you're looking for specific information, feel free to jump ahead. (And pay no attention to those computers discussing philosophy in the corner.)

Finding the Place to Make a Change

The first bit of knowledge you need is *where* to make all these cool changes to your table. Luckily, all three options are in the same place: the General tab of the Table Design window.

Use the following steps to put your table into Design view, and then flip to the appropriate section of the chapter for the details on applying a format, input mask, or validation to a field in your table.

1. **With the database file open, click on the table you want to adjust and then click <u>D</u>esign (see Figure 7-1).**

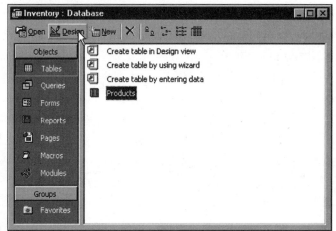

Figure 7-1:
Prepare for
some seri-
ous design
work.

The table flips into Design view, showing its nerdish underbelly to the world.

By the way, if the table you want is already on-screen in Datasheet view, just click on the Design button on the far left side of the toolbar to get into Design view.

2. **Click on the name of the field you want to work on.**

The General tab in the Field Properties section (the bottom half of the window) displays the details of the current field, as shown in Figure 7-2. You're ready to do your stuff!

3. **Click in the appropriate box in the Field Properties section (along the bottom of the window) and type in your changes.**

Format, Input Mask, and Validation Rule each have a box. (The Validation Text has a box too, but you have to look in the validations section later in this chapter to find out more about it — it's a secret for now.)

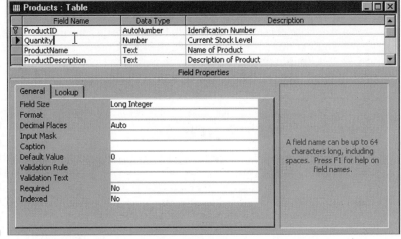

Figure 7-2:
Get ready
for some
work on the
Quantity
field.

4. **If you want to work on other fields, go back to Step 2 and repeat the process.**

You can add one, two, or all three pieces of intelligence to a field at once. Access 2000 automatically saves your changes when you click another field.

5. **When you're through, close the table to save your changes.**

Granted, using formats, masks, and validations involves many more details, but the steps to get started are the same no matter which tool you apply. The following sections tackle each tool individually, so continue on for full discussions of the tools' finer points.

To Format, Perchance to Better See

Formats only change the way you *see* your data on-screen, not how your data is actually stored in the table. Although formats don't directly catch errors, they *do* make your information look simply marvelous (and that's gotta be worth something these days).

Each field type has its own set of formats. Pay close attention to the type of field you're working with. Applying the wrong format to a field is both pointless and frustrating (and goodness knows there are *enough* pointless and frustrating aspects of your computer without actively courting another one) because your data won't *ever* look right, regardless of how hard you try.

To prevent exactly that error, the following formatting information is organized by field type. Check the field type you're working with and then refer to the appropriate section for the available formatting options. By the way, if your format command doesn't work the first time — that happens to me, too — just double-check the field type and then review the format commands. In no time at all, you ferret out the problem.

Text and memo fields

You have four possibilities here. Unfortunately, no ready-made examples are built into the Format text box, unlike the other field types. I guess that means text and memo fields are tough and don't need the help.

Here are your four text and memo formatting options:

- ✔ The *greater than symbol* (>) makes all the text in that field appear in uppercase, regardless of how the text was entered. Although Access 2000 stores the data *just as it was typed,* the data appears in uppercase only. To use this option, put a single greater than symbol in the Format text box.

- ✔ The *less than symbol* (<) does just the opposite of the greater than symbol. The less than symbol shows all that field's text in lowercase. If you entered the data in mixed case, Access 2000 displays the data as lowercase. As with the greater than symbol, only the display is changed to protect the innocent, otherwise the data is still stored as mixed case. Apply this format by putting a single less than symbol in the Format text box.

- ✔ The *at sign* (@) forces Access 2000 to display either a character or a space in the field. If the field data is smaller than the format, Access 2000 adds extra spaces to fill up the format. For example, if a field uses @@@@@@ as its format but the field's data is only three characters long (such as *Tim* or *now*), Access 2000 displays three spaces and *then* the data. If the field data is four characters long, the format pads the beginning of the entry with two spaces. See how the at sign works? (Kinda odd, isn't it?)

- ✔ The *ampersand* (&) is the default format. It means "display a character if there's one to display; otherwise don't do anything." Why create a special format for this option when it's what Access 2000 does by default? I don't know . . . for now, it remains a mystery to me.

  By the way, you include one at sign or ampersand *for each character* in the field, unlike the greater than and less than symbols, which require only one symbol for the whole field.

TIP

Hey Access, save my place!

This tip is a certified Nerd Trick, but it's so useful I had to take the chance and tell you about it. When entering data, sometimes you need to skip a text field because you don't have that particular information at hand. Wouldn't it be great if Access 2000 automatically marked the field as blank as a reminder for you to come back and fill in the info later?

Access 2000 can create such a custom text format for you, and you don't even have to be a master magician to pull off this trick. Here's how

to do it: Type @;"**Unknown**"[**Red**] into the field's Format text box.

This peculiar notation displays the word *Unknown* in red print if the field does not contain a value. You *must* type the command *exactly* like the example (quotation marks, square brackets, and all), or it doesn't work. Feel free to substitute your own word for *Unknown*, though — the command doesn't care what you put between the quotation marks.

Number and currency fields

The friendly folks at Microsoft did all the hard work for you on the number and currency field types. They built the six most common formats into a pull-down menu right in the Format text box. To set a number or currency field format, click in the Format text box and then click on the down arrow that appears at the right side of the box. Figure 7-3 shows the pull-down menu, laden with your choices.

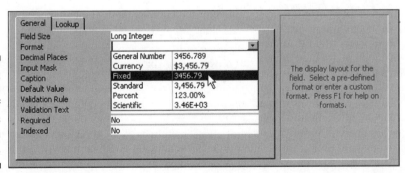

Figure 7-3:
Choose the
format of
your dreams
right from
the menu.

Each format's given name is on the left side of the menu. The other side shows a sample of how the format works. Here's a quick rundown of the most common choices:

✔ **General Number:** This format is the Access 2000 default. It merely displays whatever you put into the field without making any editorial adjustments to it.

✔ **Currency:** This format makes a standard number field look just like a currency field. It shows the data with two decimal places, substituting zeros if decimals aren't present to begin with. Currency format also adds the appropriate currency sign and punctuation, according to the Regional Settings in the Windows Control Panel.

✔ **Fixed:** This format locks the field's data into a specific number of decimal places. By default, this format rounds to two decimal places. To specify a different number of decimal places, use the Decimal Places setting right below the Format setting.

✔ **Standard:** This format does the same thing as Fixed but adds a thousands separator as well. Adjust the number of decimals by changing the Decimal Places setting.

✔ **Percent:** This format is especially for the percentages of life. It turns a simple decimal percentage such as .97 into the much prettier 97%. Remember to enter the data as a decimal (.97 instead of 97); otherwise Access 2000 displays some truly awesome percentages! If your percentages display only as 0.00% or 1.00%, see the next paragraph for a solution.

If your entries automatically round to the nearest whole number and always display zeros in the decimal places, change the Field Size setting (right above Format) from Long Integer to Single. This setting tells Access 2000 to remember the decimal part of the number. By default, Access 2000 rounds the number to an integer as you enter it. (Stupid computers.)

Date/time fields

Like the Number and Currency format options, date/time fields have a ready-to-use set of formats available in a pull-down menu. Click in the Format text box and then click on the down arrow that appears on the box's right side, and the menu in Figure 7-4 dutifully pops down to serve you.

The choices are pretty self-explanatory, but I do have a couple of tips for you:

✔ When using one of the larger formats such as General Date or Long Date, make sure that the datasheet column is wide enough to display the whole date. Otherwise, the cool-looking date doesn't make sense because a major portion of it is missing.

✔ If more than one person uses the database, choosing a format that provides *more* information rather than one that provides less is much better. My favorite is the Medium Date format, because it spells out the month and day. Otherwise, dates such as 3/7/99 may cause confusion, because people in different countries interpret that format differently.

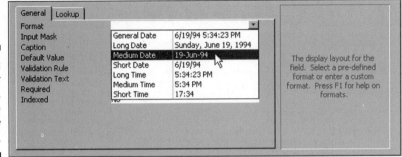

Figure 7-4:
A format for
every date,
and a date
for every
format.

Yes/No fields

You can only say so much about a field with three options. Your preset formatting choices are somewhat limited, as Figure 7-5 shows. By default,
Yes/No fields are set to the Yes/No formatting (programmers are *so* clever,
sometimes). Feel free to experiment with the other options, particularly if
they make more sense in your table than Yes and No.

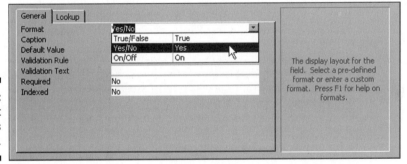

Figure 7-5:
The format
cupboard is
pretty bare.

To display your *own* choices instead of a boring Yes and No, you have to type
a customized format. This procedure works very much like the custom text
format earlier in this chapter. A good example format is something like this:
;"In stock"[Green];"REORDER"[Red]. If an item is in stock, the text *In
stock* appears in green. Otherwise, *REORDER* screams a warning in bright red.
Substitute your own words for mine if you like, because Access 2000 displays
whatever you put between the quotes without making any editorial decisions
about the content. Make certain that the Display Control under the Lookup
tab (next to the General tab) is set to Text Box otherwise you might have
check boxes in your field.

What Is That Masked Data?

Although they have a funny name, *input masks* are filters that allow you to enter only certain data into a field. When they're paired with validations (covered later in this chapter), the fields in your table are *very* well protected against bad information.

An input mask is just a series of characters that tells Access 2000 what kind of data to expect in this field. If you want a field to contain all numbers and no letters, an input mask can do the job. It can also do the reverse (all letters and no numbers) and almost any combination in between. Input masks are stored in the Input Mask area of the field's General tab, along with everything else described in this chapter.

More than half the fields in an Access 2000 table can have their own input mask. Before creating the mask, you have to know *exactly* what the field's data looks like. Creating a mask that allows only letters into a field doesn't do any good if your goal is to store street addresses. Know your data intimately *before* messing around with input masks.

Input masks work best with *short, highly consistent* data. Numbers and number/letter combinations that all look alike are excellent candidates. Part numbers, stock-keeping units, postal codes, phone numbers, and social security numbers beg for input masks to ensure that the right data gets into the field.

You create an input mask in one of two ways: You can either type in the mask manually or ask the Input Mask Wizard for some help. As luck would have it, the Input Mask Wizard isn't terribly bright — it only knows about text and date fields. And even then, the Input Mask Wizard offers just a few options to make your life easier. To accomplish anything more means cracking your knuckles and doing it by hand.

Using the Input Mask Wizard

The Input Mask Wizard gleefully helps if you're making a mask for a phone number, social security number, United States zip code, or simple date and time field. Beyond those fields, the Input Mask Wizard is clueless, so don't look for its help with anything other than text or time/date type fields.

To ask the wizard's help, go through these steps:

1. **With the database file open, click on the table you want to work with and then click on <u>D</u>esign.**

   The table flips into Design view.

2. Click on the name of the field you want to adjust.

The General tab in the Field Properties section (the bottom half of the window) displays the details of the current field.

3. Click on the Input Mask box.

The cursor hops into the Input Mask box. To the right of the box, a small button with three dots appears. That's the Build button, which comes into play in the next step.

 4. Click on the Build button at the right side of the Input Mask text box.

The wizard appears, making a glorious entrance just like in Figure 7-6.

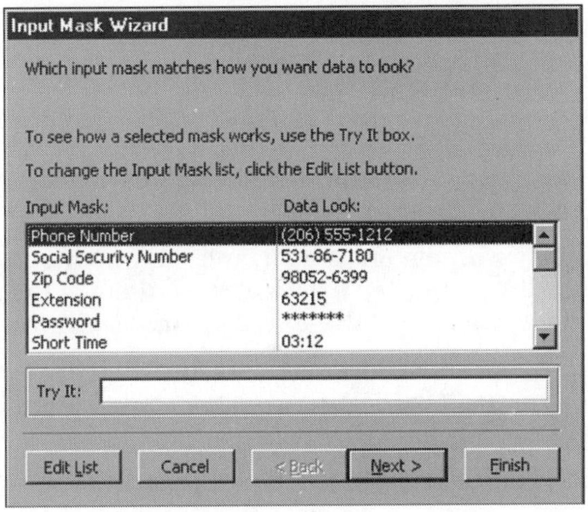

Input Mask Wizard

Which input mask matches how you want data to look?

To see how a selected mask works, use the Try It box.

To change the Input Mask list, click the Edit List button.

Input Mask:	Data Look:
Phone Number	(206) 555-1212
Social Security Number	531-86-7180
Zip Code	98052-6399
Extension	63215
Password	*******
Short Time	03:12

Try It:

Edit List   Cancel   < Back   Next >   Finish

Figure 7-6:
The Input Mask Wizard doesn't do much, but it tries hard.

You can use the wizard only with text and date fields. Don't tempt the wizard's wrath by rousing it to work with another kind of field.

If Access 2000 complains that the wizard isn't installed, you didn't include the proper wizard options while installing Access 2000 (don't fret if you get this error message — I did, too). To fix the problem, get out your original Access 2000 or Office 2000 CD-ROM and put it in your CD-ROM drive. Close Access 2000 and then choose Start⇨Settings⇨ Control Panel. In the Control Panel window, double-click Add/Remove Programs. Follow the prompts to install the Access 2000 developer tools. If you're in a corporate environment and don't have the original master CD-ROM, contact your computer support folks for help.

5. Scroll through the list of available input masks to find what you want. Click on your choice and then click on Next.

The dialog box displays the sordid code behind the mask, plus some other information (see Figure 7-7).

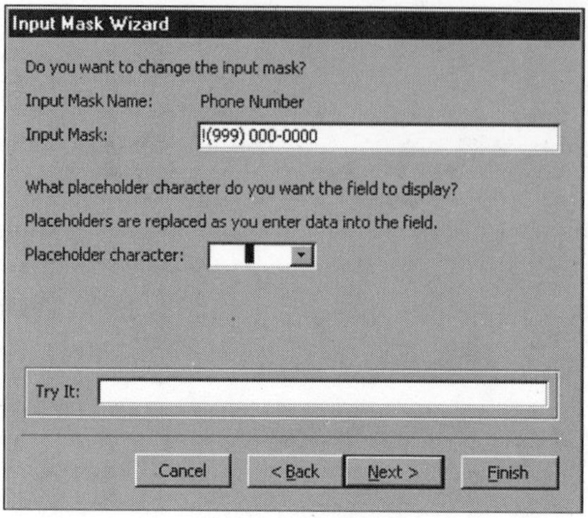

Input Mask Wizard

Do you want to change the input mask?

Input Mask Name: Phone Number

Input Mask: !(999) 000-0000

What placeholder character do you want the field to display?

Placeholders are replaced as you enter data into the field.

Placeholder character:

Try It:

Cancel   < Back   Next >   Finish

Figure 7-7:
Here's what
the wizard
says you
need.

If you choose the Password option (refer to Figure 7-6), nothing is left for you to do, so click on Finish.

6. **If you want to play with the input mask and see whether it _really_ does what you want, click in the Try It area at the bottom of the dialog box. When you're done, click on Finish to use the mask with your field.**

The chosen mask appears in the Input Mask area on the table design screen. (You can click on Cancel to call off the sordid mask affair and make the wizard go away.)

If you click on Next instead of Finish, the wizard offers you an arcane choice about storing characters along with your data. The wizard wants to know whether you want the dashes, slashes, and parentheses that the input mask displays to be stored in your table along with the data you typed. The default is No, which I recommend sticking with. Click on Finish to complete the process.

Making a mask by hand

Few projects are more gratifying than making something yourself. Building an input mask with your bare hands, raw nerve, and these instructions _may_ give you that same feeling of accomplishment. (If so, please seek professional help soon — you're in danger of becoming a technoid.)

✔ The stuff that input masks _do_ isn't terribly complicated, but a finished mask often _looks_ complicated. Don't worry, though. After you get the hang of it, building powerful input masks is easy.

✔ My friends told me the same thing about water skiing, but during my first lesson, I suspected that they were really trying to drown me and make it look like an innocent water sports accident. You have my word that building input masks in Access 2000 isn't anything like that. (Besides, how can you drown in front of a computer?)

With that confidence-building introduction behind you, get ready to roll up your sleeves and plunge your hands in the alphabetic goop of input masks. Designing and using an input mask takes just a few steps:

1. **On a piece of paper, write an example of the data that the mask is supposed to let into the table.**

   As I mention earlier in the chapter, knowing your data really *is* the first step in the input mask process.

   If the information you're storing has subtle variations (such as part numbers that end in either a letter/number or letter/letter combination), include examples of the various possibilities so that your input mask accepts them all.

2. **Write a simple description of the data, including which elements are required and which are optional.**

   If your sample is a part number that looks like 728816ABC7, write six numbers, three letters, one number; all parts are required. Remember to allow for the variations, if you have any. The difference between *one number* and *one letter or number* can be crucial.

   Required information must be entered into the field (such as a phone number). *Optional* elements are just that — optional (such as an area code or extension number). Access 2000 uses different codes for required and optional data, so you need to note the difference.

3. **Using the codes in Table 7-1, create an input mask for your data.**

   Because you know what kind of data you're storing (numbers, letters, or either one), how many characters you need, and whether each one is required or optional, working through the table and creating the mask is easy.

   To include a dash, slash, or parenthesis in your mask, put a backslash (\) in front of it. To include more than one character, put quote marks around them. For example, the mask for a phone number with an area code is !\(999") "000\-0000. This mask uses both the backslash and quote mark to put parentheses around the area code plus a space between the area code and phone number. (See the sidebar "The exclamation point: To know it is to love it" to find out why I included an exclamation point in this example.)

Here's a pop quiz, just to see whether you're paying attention. In the example, is the area code optional or required? What about the phone number itself? Why? Write a long, detailed answer on a very small piece of paper; then rip it to shreds and throw it like confetti into the air. Wasn't that fun?

4. **If your field includes letters and you want them to always be upper-case, add a greater than symbol (>) to the beginning of your mask.**

   To make the letters lowercase, use a less than symbol (<) instead.

   You're ready to tell Access 2000 about your input mask.

5. **Follow the steps at the beginning of the chapter ("Finding the Place to Make a Change"); when you get to Step 3, click in the Input Mask box.**

   The blinking toothpick cursor hops into the box, ready for action.

6. **Carefully type your finished mask into the Input Mask area of Field Properties (see Figure 7-8).**

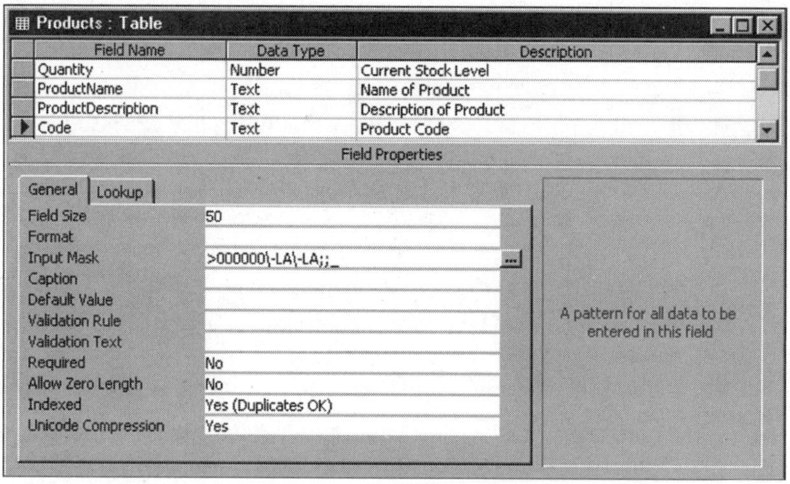

Field Name	Data Type	Description
Quantity	Number	Current Stock Level
ProductName	Text	Name of Product
ProductDescription	Text	Description of Product
▶ Code	Text	Product Code

Field Properties

General | Lookup

Field Size	50
Format	
Input Mask	>000000\-LA\-LA;;_
Caption	
Default Value	
Validation Rule	
Validation Text	
Required	No
Allow Zero Length	No
Indexed	Yes (Duplicates OK)
Unicode Compression	Yes

A pattern for all data to be entered in this field

Figure 7-8:
Putting a mask on the Code field.

Don't worry if the mask looks like a text version of the Frankenstein monster. Beauty is optional in the world of technology.

7. **At the end of the mask, add ;;_ (two semicolons and an underscore character).**

   These three characters tell Access 2000 to display an underscore where you want each letter to appear. This step isn't required, but I think that input masks make more sense with this option. Your mileage may vary.

8. **Click on the Table View button on the toolbar to check out your handiwork.**

Try typing something into the now-masked field. The input mask should prevent you from entering something incorrectly. If it doesn't work, take the table back into Design view (click on the Design View button on the left side of the toolbar) and make some repairs.

If you're adding a mask to an existing table, the mask doesn't ferret out incorrect data that's *already* in the table. You have to click on each entry in the masked field (yes, that means clicking on this field in *every* record of the table) in order to check it. If something is wrong, Access 2000 tells you, but not until you click.

Table 7-1	Codes for the Input Mask	
Kind of Characters	*Required Code*	*Optional Code*
Digits (0 to 9) only	0 (zero)	9
Digits and +/- signs	(not available)	# (U.S. pound sign)
Letters (A to Z) only	L	? (question mark)
Letters or digits only	A	a (must be lowercase)
Any character or space	& (ampersand)	C

TIP

The exclamation point: To know it is to love it

Getting to know the exclamation point took me a while. After all, my input masks seemed very happy without it. Even the explanation in the Access 2000 online Help file didn't change my mind. (I suppose that if the Help file's explanation had made sense, it might have had a better chance.)

While playing with the phone number example, I finally realized what the exclamation point does and why it's so useful. The exclamation point tells Access 2000 to fill up the field from the right instead of the left. Although this notion may sound like the unintelligible ramblings of an over-caffeinated nerd, it really is an important point. Let me show you why.

In the phone number example, the area code is optional, but the number itself is required. If I leave the exclamation point out of the input mask, Access 2000 lets me skip the area code and type a phone number into the phone number spaces. Everything looks fine until I press Enter. Then my seven-digit phone number displays as (555) 121-2. Eeww — not exactly what I had in mind. That's because Access 2000 filled the mask from the left, starting with the optional numbers in the area code (the numbers I didn't enter).

By adding the exclamation point to the input mask, Access 2000 takes my data and fills the mask from the right. This time, the phone number appears on-screen as ( ) 555-1212, which is what I wanted all along.

By the way, the exclamation point can go anywhere in the input mask, but try to get into the habit of putting it either at the beginning or the end. I suggest making the exclamation point the first character in the mask, simply because you won't overlook it in that position.

Validations: The Digital Breathalyzer Test

Your third (and, arguably, most powerful) tool in the War Against Bad Data is the *validation*. With a validation, Access 2000 actually tests the incoming data to make sure that it's what you want in the table. If the data isn't right, the validation displays an error message (you get to choose what it says!) and makes you try the entry again.

Like the other options in this chapter, validations are stored in the General tab of the Field Properties area. Two spaces relate to validations: Validation Rule and Validation Text. The rule is the actual validation itself. The text is the error message you want Access 2000 to display when some data that violates the validation rule wanders in.

Validations work best with number, currency, and date fields. Creating a validation for a text field is possible, but the validations usually get *very* complicated *very* fast. In the name of protecting your sanity and hairline, Table 7-2 contains some ready-to-use validations that cover the most common needs. They're organized by field type, so finding the validation rule that suits your purpose is easy.

I include different kinds of examples to show off the power of the logical operators that validations use. Feel free to mix and match with the operators. Play around and see what you can come up with!

- When using AND, remember that both sides of the validation rule must be true before the rule is met.

- With OR, only one side of the rule needs to be true for the whole rule to be true.

- Be careful when combining >= and <= examples. Accidentally coming up with one that won't ever be true (such as <= 0 AND >= 100) is too easy!

Table 7-2	Validations for Many Occasions	
Field Type	**Validation Rule**	**Definition**
Number	> 0	Must be greater than zero
Number	<> 0	Cannot be zero
Number	> 0 AND < 100	Must be between 0 and 100 (noninclusive)
Number	>= 0 AND <= 100	Must be between 0 and 100 (inclusive)

Field Type	Validation Rule	Definition
Number	<= 0 OR >= 100	Must be less than 0 or greater than 100 (inclusive)
Date	>= Date ()	Must be today's date or later
Date	>= Date () OR Is Null	Must be today's date, later, or blank
Date	< Date ()	Must be earlier than today's date
Date	>= #1/1/90# AND <= Date ()	Must be between January 1, 1990, and today (inclusive)

Chapter 8

Making Your Datasheets Dance

In This Chapter

▶ Wandering around your datasheet

▶ Adjusting column width, row height, and more

▶ Seeing the datasheet in a whole new font

▶ Changing the background

*H*aving your new datasheet look and act just like every *other* datasheet is pretty boring. Where's the creativity in that? Where's the individuality? Where's the life, liberty, and pursuit of ultimate coolness?

Granted, Access 2000 *is* a database program, and databases aren't generally known for being the life of the party. But that doesn't mean you're trapped in a monotonous world of look-alike datasheets. This chapter explores the tools at your disposal to turn even the most dreary datasheet into a slick-looking, easy-to-navigate presentation of your data.

The following pages focus on datasheet tricks — things to do when you're working with information in a datasheet. These tricks work with datasheets from both tables and dynasets, so use them to amble through and spruce up every datasheet in sight. If you haven't heard about dynasets yet, don't worry. They're covered in Part III.

Wandering Here, There, and Everywhere

When a table appears in Datasheet view, Access 2000 presents you with a window to your data. That window displays a certain number of rows and columns, but (unless you have a really small table) what's shown certainly isn't the whole enchilada. To see more, you need to move through the table — which means moving your window around to see what else is out there.

Access 2000 offers several ways to hike through a datasheet. Which method you choose depends on how far you want to go:

- ✔ **To move from field to field:** Use the right- and left-arrow keys (→ ←). Clicking on the arrows on either end of the horizontal scroll bar does the same thing with the mouse.

- ✔ **To move between records:** Try the up- and down-arrow keys (↑ ↓). If you're a mouse-oriented person, click in the arrows at the ends of the vertical scroll bar.

- ✔ **To display a new page of data:** The PgUp and PgDn keys come in handy (depending on your keyboard, these may be called Page Up and Page Down, instead). PgUp and PgDn scroll vertically through the datasheet; Ctrl+PgUp and Ctrl+PgDn scroll horizontally. Clicking in either scroll bar does the same thing.

Table 8-1 looks at the process from a keystroke-by-keystroke point of view. Between the preceding movement tips and the following table, you now know just about every possible way to move through an Access 2000 datasheet.

Table 8-1	Moving through a Table
Keystroke or Control	*What It Does*
Ctrl+End	Jumps to the last field in the last record of the table
Ctrl+Home	Jumps to the first field in the first record of the table
Ctrl+PgDn	Scrolls one screen to the right
Ctrl+PgUp	Scrolls one screen to the left
↓	Moves down one record in the table
End	Goes to the last field in the current record
Home	Goes to the first field in the current record
Horizontal scroll bar	Scrolls right or left one window at a time through the table
←	Moves one field to the left in the current record
IntelliMouse wheel	Turn the wheel to scroll up or down three records at a time through the table (only available with IntelliPoint mouse and driver software)
IntelliMouse wheel button	Press the wheel like a button and it becomes a super-arrow key; scroll one row or column at a time through the table (only available with IntelliPoint mouse and driver software)
PgDn	Scrolls one screen down

Keystroke or Control	What It Does
PgUp	Scrolls one screen up
→	Moves one field to the right in the current record
↑	Moves up one record in the table
Vertical scroll bar	Scrolls up or down one window at a time through the table

Seeing More (Or Less) of Your Data

First on the datasheet tune-up list is fiddling with the look of your datasheet. You have plenty to fiddle with, too. At first blush, your datasheet looks pretty mundane, much like Figure 8-1. To perk it up a bit, you can change the column width, row height, and column order, and you can lock a column in place while the others scroll around it. Heck, you can even make columns temporarily disappear.

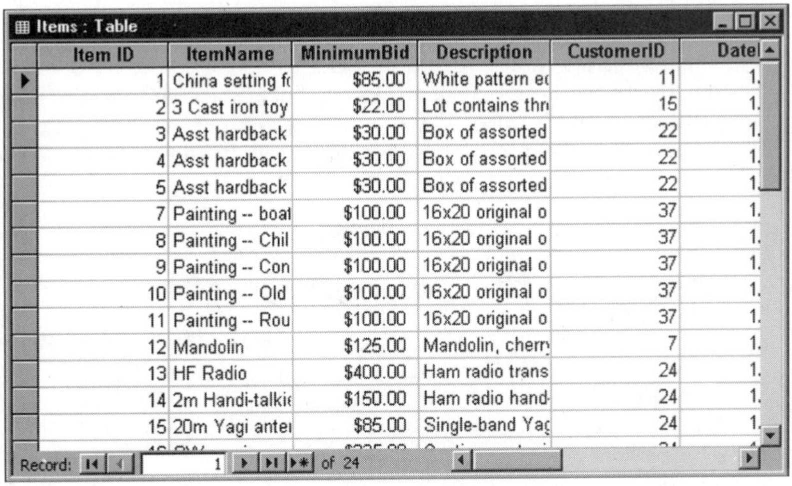

Figure 8-1: Both the ItemName and Description columns are brutally clipped.

Item ID	ItemName	MinimumBid	Description	CustomerID	Date
1	China setting f(	$85.00	White pattern e(	11	1.
2	3 Cast iron toy	$22.00	Lot contains thr(	15	1.
3	Asst hardback	$30.00	Box of assorted	22	1.
4	Asst hardback	$30.00	Box of assorted	22	1.
5	Asst hardback	$30.00	Box of assorted	22	1.
7	Painting -- boat	$100.00	16x20 original o	37	1.
8	Painting -- Chil	$100.00	16x20 original o	37	1.
9	Painting -- Con	$100.00	16x20 original o	37	1.
10	Painting -- Old	$100.00	16x20 original o	37	1.
11	Painting -- Rou	$100.00	16x20 original o	37	1.
12	Mandolin	$125.00	Mandolin, cherry	7	1.
13	HF Radio	$400.00	Ham radio trans	24	1.
14	2m Handi-talkie	$150.00	Ham radio hand-	24	1.
15	20m Yagi anter	$85.00	Single-band Yag	24	1.

Record: 1 of 24

Each of the following sections explores one technique for changing the way your data looks. You can use one option (such as changing the column width) or a number of options — you make the call. Each adjustment is independent of the others. Plus, these changes don't affect your actual data at all — they just make the data appear differently on-screen.

Most of the commands work from the mouse, but some of them send you back to the menu bar. If a command is in both places, it works the same either way.

IntelliMouse: A new way to get around

If you're blessed with a new Microsoft IntelliMouse and its special IntelliPoint driver software, you have an extra tool for moving through your Access 2000 datasheets. Between the two regular mouse buttons, the IntelliMouse sports a wheel that acts as a third button.

✔ Rolling the wheel scrolls up and down through your datasheet three lines at a time.

✔ Clicking and dragging with the wheel button moves the window around the datasheet in whichever direction you move the mouse.

(This maneuver works just like a normal click and drag, except that you're using the wheel button instead of the left mouse button.)

If you spend a great deal of time with Access 2000 or jumping among the Office 2000 applications, I suggest you take the new mouse for a test drive. Each program applies the wheel button a little differently, but *all* the programs (and even Windows itself) use it to make your life a little easier.

After making any of these adjustments to your table, be sure to tell Access 2000 to save the table's formatting changes, or all your hard work is lost forever. To notify Access 2000, either choose File⇨Save from the menu bar or simply close the window. If any unsaved changes are in the table when you try to close the window, Access 2000 automatically prompts you to save the new formatting.

Changing the column width

Even though Access 2000 is pretty smart, it has trouble figuring out how wide to make a column. In fact, it usually just gives up and sets all the column widths identically, leaving some far too wide and others way too narrow. Pretty wimpy solution for a powerful program, if you ask me.

Setting a new column width is a quick operation. Here's what to do:

1. **With your table in Datasheet view, put the mouse pointer on the vertical bar to the right of the field name (see Figure 8-2).**

   The mouse pointer changes into a bar with arrows sticking out of each side.

2. **Click and hold the left mouse button while moving the mouse appropriately.**

   To make the column wider, move the mouse to the right. To make it smaller, move the mouse left.

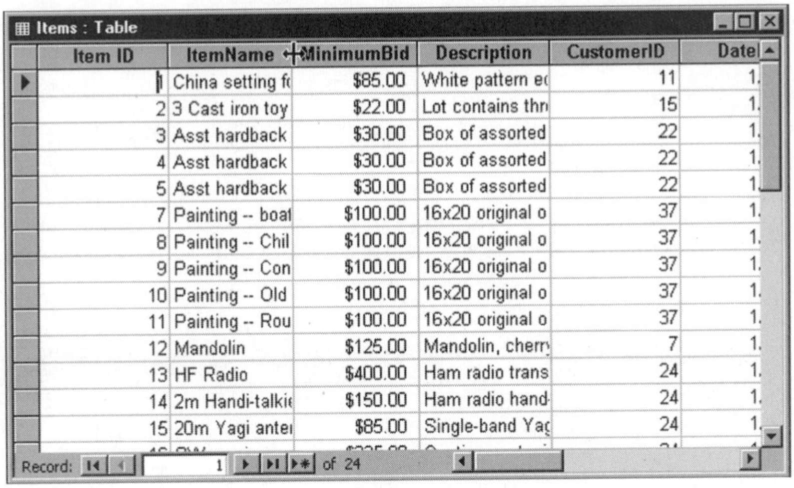

Figure 8-2:
Ready to
widen the
column.

3. **When the width is just right, let up on the mouse button.**

The column is locked into its new size, as Figure 8-3 shows.

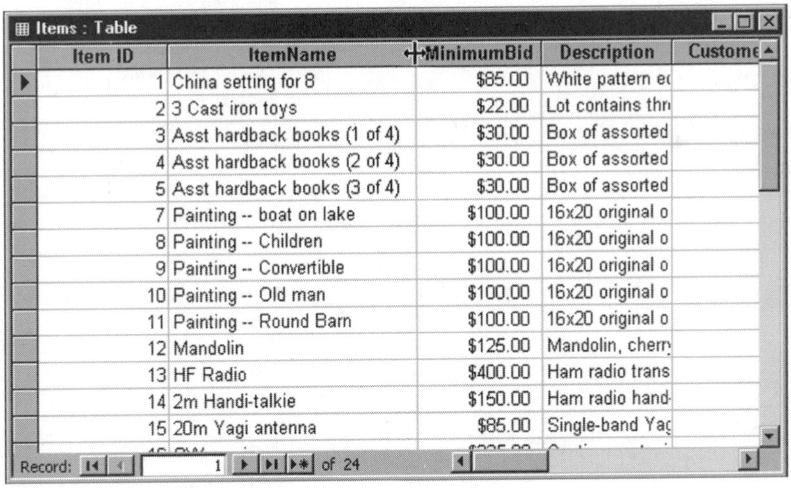

Figure 8-3:
That looks
much better.

Changing the row height

Access 2000 does a little better in the row height department than it does with column widths. It automatically leaves enough room to separate the rows while displaying plenty of information on-screen. Access 2000 still has room for improvement, though, because you can't see all the data in your table's longest fields. Changing the row height fixes this problem by showing more data in each field while displaying the same number of columns on-screen.

Like changing column width, adjusting the row height takes only a couple of mouse clicks:

1. **While viewing your table in Datasheet view, put the mouse pointer in the far left side of the window on the line between any two rows in your spreadsheet (see Figure 8-4).**

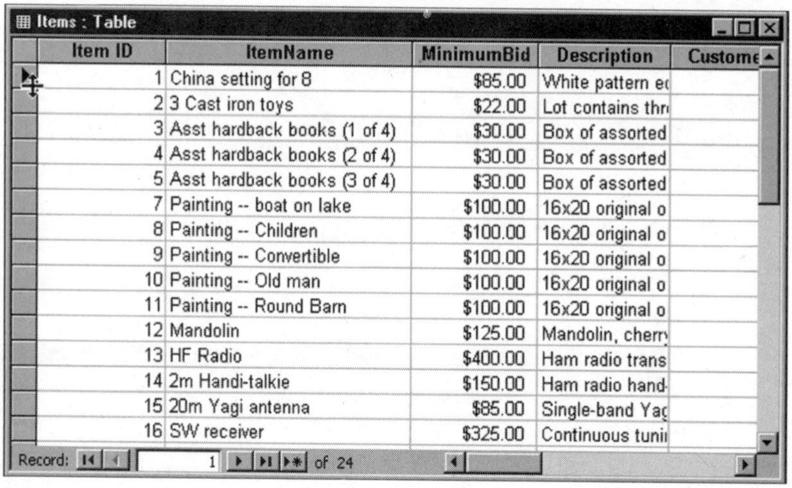

Items : Table				
Item ID	**ItemName**	**MinimumBid**	**Description**	**Custome**
1	China setting for 8	$85.00	White pattern ec	
2	3 Cast iron toys	$22.00	Lot contains thre	
3	Asst hardback books (1 of 4)	$30.00	Box of assorted	
4	Asst hardback books (2 of 4)	$30.00	Box of assorted	
5	Asst hardback books (3 of 4)	$30.00	Box of assorted	
7	Painting -- boat on lake	$100.00	16x20 original o	
8	Painting -- Children	$100.00	16x20 original o	
9	Painting -- Convertible	$100.00	16x20 original o	
10	Painting -- Old man	$100.00	16x20 original o	
11	Painting -- Round Barn	$100.00	16x20 original o	
12	Mandolin	$125.00	Mandolin, cherry	
13	HF Radio	$400.00	Ham radio trans	
14	2m Handi-talkie	$150.00	Ham radio hand-	
15	20m Yagi antenna	$85.00	Single-band Yag	
16	SW receiver	$325.00	Continuous tunii	

Record: 1 of 24

Figure 8-4: One taller row, coming right up (or is that down?).

The mouse pointer changes into a horizontal bar with arrows sticking out vertically.

2. **Click and hold the left mouse button; then move the mouse to change the row height.**

Move the mouse down to make the row higher. Move it up to squash the row and put the squeeze on your data.

3. **When the row height is where you want it, release the mouse button.**

Access 2000 redisplays the table with its new row height (see Figure 8-5).

Reorganizing the columns

When you laid out the table, you put quite a bit of thought into which field came after which other field. Most of the time, your data looks just the way you want it on-screen, but occasionally you need to stir things up a bit.

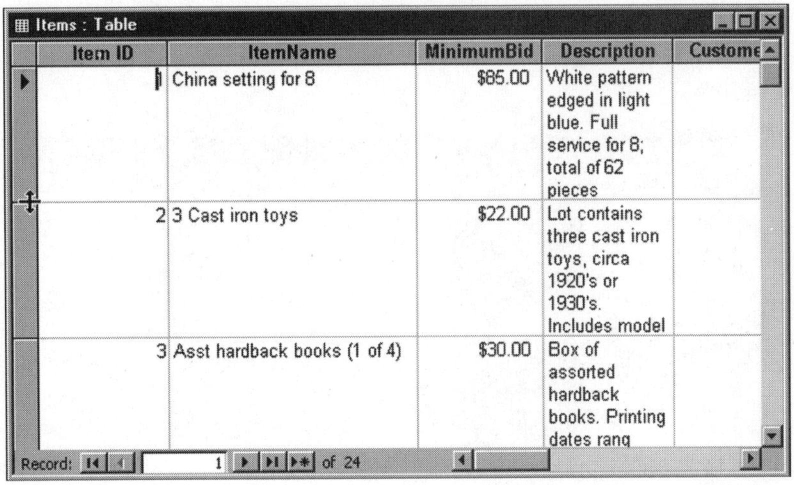

Figure 8-5:
The data automatically fills the new field space.

To move a field to a different place on the datasheet, use these steps:

1. **Click on the field name of the column you want to move; then click and hold the left mouse button.**

   The whole column darkens, and the mouse pointer changes to an arrow with a smaller box at the base of the mouse pointer (see Figure 8-6).

2. **Drag the column to its new destination.**

   As you move the mouse, a dark bar moves between the columns, showing you where the column will land when you release the mouse button. If you accidentally let go of the button before the dark bar appears, Access 2000 doesn't move the column. In that case, start again with Step 1 (and keep a tight grip on that mouse).

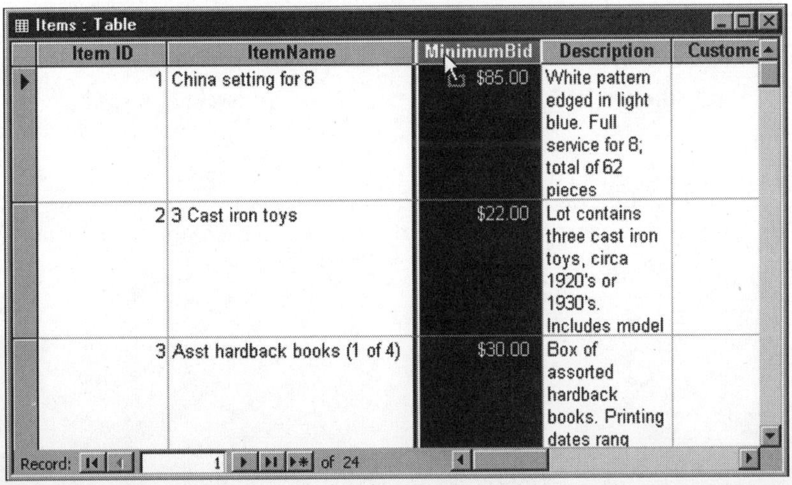

Figure 8-6:
You're ready to move that column.

3. **When the column is in place, let up on the mouse button.**

   The column, data and all, moves to the new spot (see Figure 8-7).

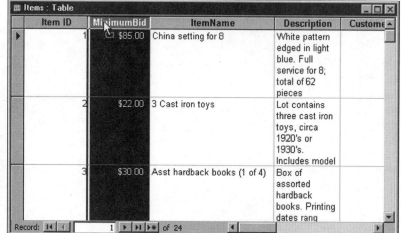

Figure 8-7:
Bringing the
column in
for a nice,
soft landing.

Hiding a column

Hiding a column is one of those features that seem totally unimportant until
the moment you need them, and then they're worth their weight in gold. If you
want to temporarily not display a particular column, just hide the little fellow.
The data is still in the table, but it doesn't appear on-screen. Too cool, eh?

To hide a column, follow these steps:

1. **With your table in Datasheet view, right-click on the name of the
   column to hide.**

   The whole column goes dark, and a pop-up menu appears.

2. **Choose Hide Columns from the menu (see Figure 8-8).**

   {Poof!} The column vanishes.

To hide more than one column at a time, click and drag across the names of
the columns you want to squirrel away and then choose Format⇨Hide
Columns.

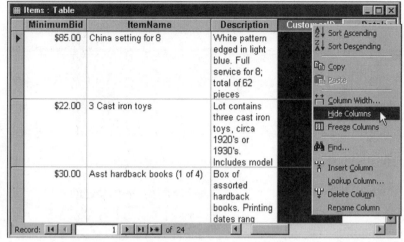

Figure 8-8:
Playing
hide-and-
seek with
the
columns.

When you're ready to bring back the temporarily indisposed column, do this:

1. **Choose Format⇨Unhide Columns.**

   Up pops a small dialog box listing all the fields in the current table. The fields with a check mark in the box next to them are already displayed.

2. **Click in any of the unchecked check boxes next to the respective column that you want to see on-screen again, and then click on the Close button (see Figure 8-9).**

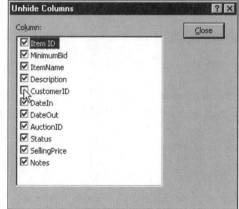

Figure 8-9:
Aha — I
found its
hiding
place!

Depending on the number of fields in the list, you may have to scroll around to find all the fields.

Making design changes in Datasheet view — danger, Will Robinson!

So far, everything in this chapter changes the look of the datasheet without doing anything to the table underneath it. Moving or hiding columns, changing column widths, adjusting row heights — all these are innocuous settings that simply make your digital world a prettier place.

The story changes with the Rename Column, Insert Column, Lookup Column, and Delete Column options that appear on the right-click pop-up menu. These choices actually change the structure of your table, so go slow and treat them carefully!

Rename Column changes the field name. Insert Column adds a new column on the datasheet, which translates into a new field in the table. Lookup Column starts the Lookup Wizard and helps you insert a column for data pulled in from another table. Delete Column is pretty self-explanatory (remember that Access 2000 undoes only the last action you took, so don't delete anything until you're sure that it's the right thing to kill).

You alter the table's structure with these options. Have a look through Chapter 9 for more about these options and how to use them safely. (It's that important.)

Freezing a column

If you have many fields in a table, they don't all fit in the window. As you scroll from one side of the table to the other, fields are constantly appearing on one side of the window and disappearing from the other. What if you want to keep looking at a column way over on one side of the table *while* looking at fields from the other side?

The secret is to *freeze* the column in place. This action locks a column into the left side of the window so that it just sits there while you scroll merrily back and forth through the table. Of course, an *unfreeze* step goes along with it — you don't want your tables catching cold, do you?

Here are the steps to freezing a column:

1. **Right-click on the name of the column you want to freeze.**

   The column turns dark, and the ever-anticipated pop-up menu appears.

2. **Choose Free̲ze Columns from the pop-up menu.**

   The column is now locked in place. You can now scroll back and forth through your table with impunity (and you don't have any restrictions, either).

If you want to freeze more than one column, select the columns by holding down the Shift key and clicking on the column names. Holding down the Shift key and clicking on the column names forms the boundary of the columns that you desire to freeze. Click on the first column's name, hold the shift key down, and then click on the second column's name to highlight all the columns in between. When all the columns you want to freeze are highlighted, choose Format➪Freeze Columns from the menu bar. All highlighted columns are immediately frozen in place.

When you want to thaw out the columns, choose Format➪Unfreeze All Columns.

Fonting Around with Your Table

Being your basic, business-oriented program, Access 2000 displays your table in a basic, business-oriented font. You're not stuck with that font choice forever, though (a good thing, too, because that font is boring). You have control over the font, style, and even the *color* that your data appears in. The decision is up to you, so why not live on the edge and try a new look on your table?

These settings apply to the *entire table,* not just a particular row or column.

To change the font, style, or color of your table, follow these steps:

1. **With the table in Datasheet view, choose Format➪Font.**

   The font dialog box elbows its way onto the screen.

2. **Click on your choice from the Font list on the left side of the box (see Figure 8-10).**

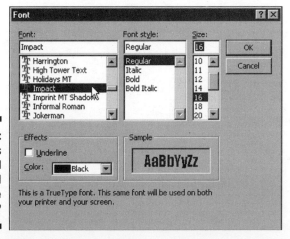

Figure 8-10:
This font is cool, but will it look good on the table?

Access 2000 previews the font in the Sample box on the right side of the dialog box.

Picking a TrueType font instead of the other options is best. TrueType fonts have the little double-T symbol next to them in the list.

3. Click on the preferred style in the Font style list.

Some fonts may not have all the common style options (normal, bold, italic, and bold italic). Exactly which options you have depends on how the fonts were loaded onto your system. For more about fonts and font files, check out *Windows 95 For Dummies,* 2nd Edition, *Windows 98 For Dummies,* or *Windows NT 4 For Dummies,* by Andy Rathbone (IDG Books Worldwide, Inc.).

4. To select a different size, click on a number in the Size list.

As with style, not every font is available in all sizes.

- If you chose a TrueType font back in Step 2, sizing isn't a problem because TrueType fonts are scaleable (Windows simply makes them whatever size it needs).

- If you clicked on a printer font in Step 2 (the ones with a picture of a printer next to them), you may be limited to just a few size options.

The moral of the story is to use TrueType fonts as much as possible.

5. If you want a new color, click on the arrow next to the Color box and pick your favorite from the drop-down menu.

You're almost done — now's a good time to look at the Sample box and see whether your choices look good together. If they don't, click Cancel and start over with Step 1.

6. Click on OK to apply your font selections.

The datasheet now displays your table in its new finery (see Figure 8-11).

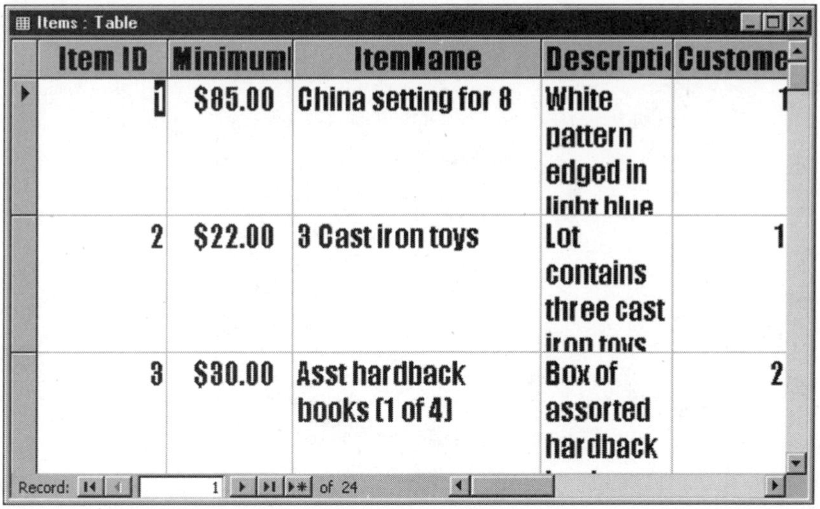

Items : Table				
Item ID	**Minimum**	**ItemName**	**Descripti**	**Custome**
1	$85.00	China setting for 8	White pattern edged in light blue	1
2	$22.00	3 Cast iron toys	Lot contains three cast iron toys	1
3	$30.00	Asst hardback books (1 of 4)	Box of assorted hardback	2

Record: 14 ◄ | 1 | ► ►1 ►* of 24

Figure 8-11:
Eeww...
back to the
font drawing
board.

Giving Your Data the 3-D Look

This final change is purely cosmetic, but even tables like to feel good about how they look. Access 2000 gives you a couple of cool looking, three-dimensional options for your datasheet. If a solution to the problem of boring-looking datasheets exists, 3-D must be it (because 3-D options serve no other purpose).

To turn your datasheet into a cool work of art, follow these steps:

1. **Choose Format➪Datasheet from the menu bar.**

   The Datasheet Formatting dialog box pops onto the screen.

2. **For a cool 3-D look, click on either the Raised or Sunken radio buttons in the Cell Effect area (see Figure 8-12).**

   The Sample box previews your selection. (I think that Raised looks cool and is easy to work with, but that's personal preference.)

   If you don't want the *gridlines* (the lines separating the rows and columns) cluttering up your datasheet, leave Cell Effect set to Flat and click in the Gridlines Shown check boxes so that they're blank.

3. **Click on OK when you're done.**

   The datasheet changes according to your selections, just like Figure 8-13.

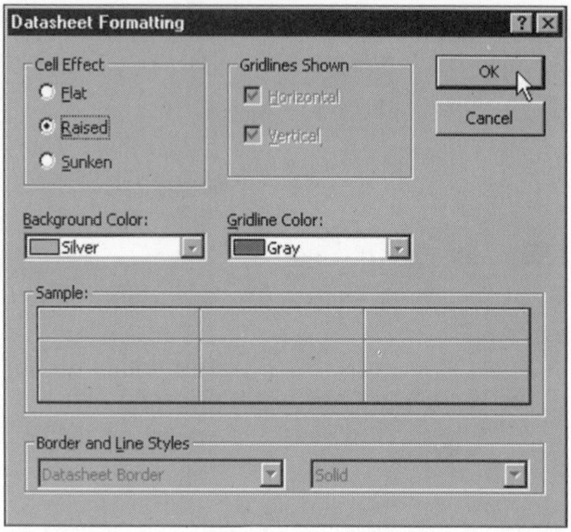

Datasheet Formatting

Cell Effect
○ Flat
● Raised
○ Sunken

Gridlines Shown
☑ Horizontal
☑ Vertical

OK
Cancel

Background Color:
Silver

Gridline Color:
Gray

Sample:

Border and Line Styles
Datasheet Border   Solid

Figure 8-12:
The choice
is made —
let's see
how I did.

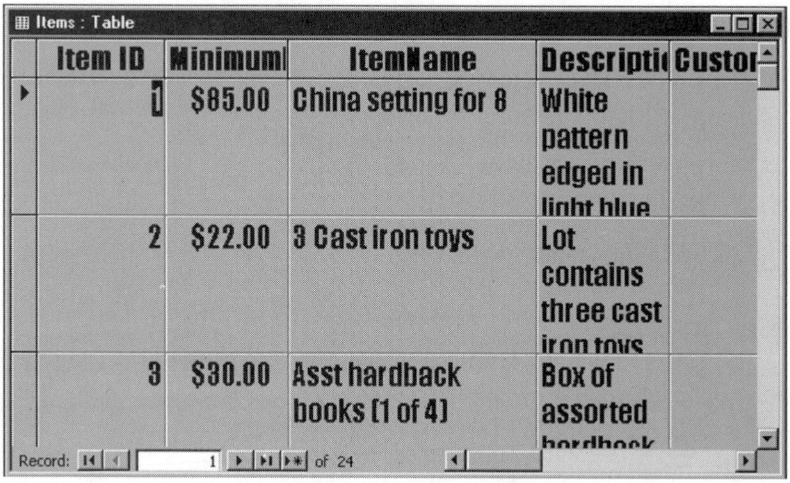

Items : Table

	Item ID	Minimum	ItemName	Descriptio	Custor
▶	1	$85.00	China setting for 8	White pattern edged in light blue	
	2	$22.00	3 Cast iron toys	Lot contains three cast iron toys	
	3	$30.00	Asst hardback books (1 of 4)	Box of assorted hardback	

Record: ◀◀ ◀ 1 ▶ ▶◀ ▶* of 24

Figure 8-13:
That works
for me!

Unless you're really good with color combinations, leave the color settings alone. Because I regularly attempt to wear stripes and plaid
together, I let Access 2000 handle this option on its own.

Chapter 9

Table Remodeling Tips for the Do-It-Yourselfer

In This Chapter

▶ The standard "worried author" disclaimer

▶ Adding a field to your table

▶ Removing a field you don't need

▶ Changing a field's name

*R*emodeling is a part of life — at least it is if you're a homeowner. A touch of paint here, a new wall there, and pretty soon your entire house is a mess, because the jobs never *quite* get finished. For example, my wife has given up hope on updating the electrical outlets in our old house. I worked on the job for three years or so, and I ended with eight outlets done, eight outlets to go, and nobody left on base. I fixed about one outlet per quarter, usually spurred to action because I needed to plug in something that didn't work with the old outlet.

My databases, on the other hand, are a completely different story. There, I'm a digital Bob Vila, with everything organized and up-to-date. When I start changing a table, I finish the job right then and there. My wife says the difference has to do with my aversion to physical labor, but the real reason is the tools that Access 2000 provides for the job. (That and the fact that hammers simply don't like me.)

Whether you're adding a new field, removing an old one, or making some other subtle changes to your table and the data therein, this chapter guides you through the process. Be sure to read the chapter's first section before attempting any serious surgery on your tables. Some grim pitfalls await you out there, and I want you to miss them cleanly.

Even though you can do some of the tasks in this chapter (specifically, add and delete whole columns in your table) through Datasheet view, I don't generally recommend that approach. One simple change in Datasheet view quickly turns into a full-fledged data disaster if anything goes wrong. Instead, make your changes through Design view, where you're in full control of the process. The steps in this chapter walk you through making such changes in Design view.

This Chapter Can Be Hazardous to Your Table's Design

I'm all for starting on a pleasant note, but *now* isn't the time.

To properly set this chapter's mood, I wanted to begin with big, full-color pictures of items that have a natural *don't touch* sign on them — such as snapping alligators, roaring lions, and the *I dare you to audit me* box on your income tax form. My editor suggested that I use a warning icon instead. In the name of compromise (and because finding good editors is so hard these days), I agreed.

Please tread lightly in this chapter. You're tinkering with the infrastructure of your entire database system. A mistake (particularly of the *delete* kind) can cause massive hair loss, intense frustration, and large-scale data corruption. Put simply, it's bad.

Putting a New Field Next to the Piano

No matter how well you plan, sometimes you just forget to include a field in your table design. Or, after using the table for a while, you discover some unforeseen data that needs a home. Regardless of the circumstances, Access 2000 doesn't make a big deal out of adding a new field.

Dropping a new field into your table takes only a moment. Before starting this project, make sure that you know the following bits of information. This makes a good paper and pencil project, so grab your tools and figure out the following items:

- ✔ Typical examples of the data that the field will hold
- ✔ The field type (text, number, yes/no, and so on)
- ✔ The size the field needs to be to hold the data, if applicable
- ✔ What you plan to call the field
- ✔ Where the field fits in the table design

Is it a column or a field?

The answer to this lyrical question — is it a column or a field — is *yes*. In Access 2000 lingo, *columns* and *fields* are really the same critters. When you insert a column into a table in Datasheet view, you actually add a new field to every record. If you build a field in Design view, you create a new column for the datasheet. Either way you say (or do) it, you get the same result.

So when is a field different from a column? It's different when you edit the data in a particular record. If you change one person's postal code in an address table, you aren't changing the whole column. Instead, you're changing the value of the field in that record.

Here's a tip to help you keep the two terms straight: When Access 2000 talks about columns, it means a certain field in every record of the table. When the program refers to a field, it means the data in one part of a particular record.

With that information in hand, you're ready to make a new field. To add the field in Design view, follow these steps:

1. **With the database file open, right-click on the table you want to work with and then choose Design View from the pop-up menu.**

   The table structure appears in Design view.

2. **Highlight the row where you want to insert your new field by clicking on the row button to the left of the Field Name column.**

   Some things are easy when you see them, but confusing to explain — and this step is one of them. On that note, take a gander at Figure 9-1 for help making sense of this maneuver.

   Just one little click highlights the entire row. Pretty cool, eh?

3. **Choose Insert⇨Rows from the main menu.**

   Access 2000 inserts a nice, blank row right where you clicked. Everything below that row moves down one row to make room for the new arrival.

   Don't worry about your data — Access 2000 takes good care of your work. Inserting a new row doesn't hurt anything in the table. *Deleting* a row (covered in the next section of this chapter) is another story, but more about that later.

4. **Click in the Field Name area of the new row and then type the name of your new field.**

   The field name flows smoothly into the text area.

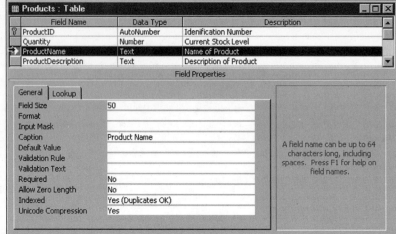

Figure 9-1:
Click on the
button on
the left to
highlight an
entire row.

5. **Press Tab to move into the Data Type column and then click on the down arrow to pick the field's data type from the pull-down list (see Figure 9-2).**

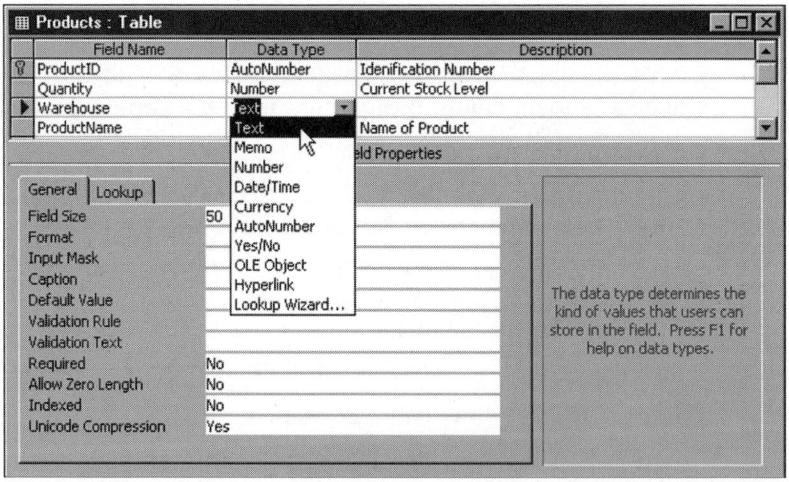

Figure 9-2:
Pick a data
type from
the list.

If you're uncertain which data type works best for this field, flip back to Chapter 4.

6. **Press Tab to hop into the Description area. Type a short description of the stuff that this field contains.**

Although this step is optional, I *highly* recommend adding a description. Trust me on this one!

7. **Save your changes by choosing File⇨Save or by clicking on the Save button on the toolbar.**

Congratulations — I knew you could do it.

Saying Good-bye to a Field (And All Its Data)

Times change, and so do your data storage needs. When one of your fields is past its prime, send it to that Great Table in the Sky by deleting it from your design. Getting rid of the field *also* throws out all the data *in* the field. You probably know that already, but the point is important enough that I want to make sure.

✔ Killing a field *erases all data* in the field. Proceed with caution!

✔ If the data in a table is important to you, make a back-up copy before deleting any of the table's fields. Backing up the data *before* you delete it is always easier. When it's gone, it's gone.

✔ If the data in a field *isn't* important, then why bother with this step at all? Go do something fun instead!

Here's how to delete a field from your table:

1. **With the database file open, right-click on the table you plan to change and then choose Design View from the pop-up menu.**

The Design window pops onto the screen, filled to overflowing with your table design.

2. **Click on the gray button on the left side of the Field Name that you intend to delete.**

This step highlights the doomed field so that all the other fields know what's about to happen and who the victim is.

3. **Choose Edit⇨Delete Rows from the main menu.**

The Dialog of Doom appears, asking whether you really want to do the deed (see Figure 9-3). If the Office Assistant is busily assisting you with Access 2000, it offers a slightly friendlier version of the Dialog of Doom, but the question remains the same.

4. **Click on Yes to delete the field; click on No if you're having second thoughts.**

If you delete the field and immediately wish you hadn't, press Ctrl+Z or choose Edit⇨Undo Delete (see Figure 9-4). Your field instantly comes back from beyond.

Figure 9-3:
Don't click
that button
unless
you're posi-
tively sure!

Figure 9-4:
Change your
mind? Click
here to
restore the
field.

5. **Make the deletion permanent by choosing <u>F</u>ile⇨<u>S</u>ave or by clicking on the Save button on the toolbar.**

   The key word in this step is *permanent,* as in *never to be seen or heard from again.* You can't undo this step — when it's gone, it's gone.

A Field by Any Other Name Still Holds the Same Stuff

Access 2000 really doesn't care what you name the fields in a table. Granted, it has some technical rules for what a legal field name looks like, but editorially speaking, it leaves all the choices up to you. Field names are really a human element, after all (silly humans, we're always running around naming stuff).

Access 2000 offers two ways to change the name of a field:

✔ Retyping the name of the field in Design view (the *official* way, according to Nerds That Know)

✔ Right-click on the field name in Datasheet view (the intuitive way)

This section explains both methods. Go with whichever method makes the most sense to you.

Changing a field name in Design view

Here's how to change a field name using Design view, the Access 2000 version of a digital tune-up bay for your tables:

1. **Right-click on the table you want to change and then choose <u>D</u>esign View from the pop-up menu.**

   The table appears, hoisted up for repair in Design view. (Granted, every step sequence in the chapter opens with this step, but you have to start somewhere.)

2. **Click on the field you plan to rename and then press F2 to highlight it (see Figure 9-5).**

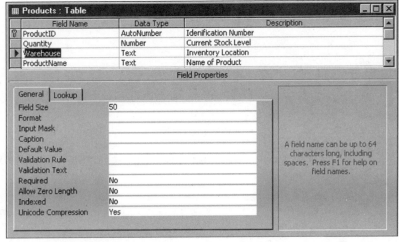

Figure 9-5: The field name is highlighted and ready for the change.

   The name of the field quivers in anticipation at the prospect of your next step.

3. **Type a new name for the field.**

   Because you highlighted the field name before typing, Access 2000 automatically overwrites the old name with the new one, just like in Figure 9-6.

4. **To save the change, choose <u>F</u>ile⇨<u>S</u>ave or click on the Save button on the toolbar.**

   The process is complete!

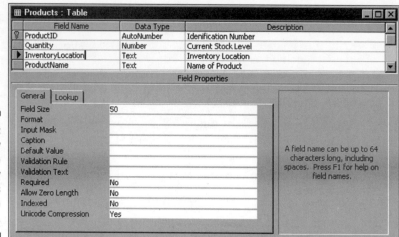

Figure 9-6:
The new
name
gracefully
takes its
place in the
table.

Changing a field name in Datasheet view

Renaming a field in Datasheet view takes about the same number of steps, but some people think that this method is easier. In the name of diversity, here's how to change a field name in Datasheet view:

1. **With your database file open, double-click on the table that you want to change.**

   Surprise — the first step here is *different* than all the other steps! After surviving the shock of a new set of instructions, notice that the table is on-screen in Datasheet view.

2. **Right-click on the field name (at the top of the Datasheet window) that you want to change.**

   The column dons a snappy highlight, and a pop-up menu appears.

3. **Choose Rename Column from the pop-up menu (see Figure 9-7).**

   The name of the column lights up, bracing for the impending change.

4. **Type the new name and then press Enter.**

   Even though you made the change in Datasheet view, Access 2000 actually changes the table's design.

5. **To make the change permanent, click on Save on the toolbar or choose File⇨Save.**

   And another field finds happiness and meaning in a stylish new name. Congratulations — you're done!

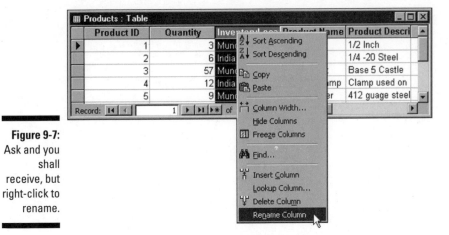

Figure 9-7:
Ask and you
shall
receive, but
right-click to
rename.

Part III

Finding the Ultimate Answer to Everything (Well, Not Everything)

The 5th Wave   By Rich Tennant

Well, obviously one of the fields in the navigational table is corrupt.

In this part . . .

Electronically collecting the data together in one place is nice, but if you're just stacking it on the hard disk instead of piling it around your office, what did you gain (apart from a less cluttered office)?

At the risk of sounding like a marketing brochure, the capability to interact with your data is one of the truly cool features of Access 2000. Because this is a computer product, you can't just say that you're interacting with or questioning the data. No — that would be too easy. In database lingo, you're *querying* the tables.

Even though saying that you're going to query something sounds a lot cooler than saying that you're going to ask a quick question, the basic concept is the same. This part digs into the whole query concept, starting out with simple questions and leading you into progressively more complex prognostications. This is juicy stuff, so work up a good appetite before digging in.

Chapter 10

Quick Searches: Find, Filter, and Sort

. . . .

In This Chapter

▶ Using the Find command

▶ Sorting your database

▶ Filter by selection

▶ Filter by form

. . . .

*Y*ou probably don't need me to tell you what databases do: They help you store and organize the information that's important to your world. That's hardly a new concept, though — 3 x 5 index cards do the same thing (and I bet you never spent $600 upgrading your index-card box). To justify all the time, trauma, and accelerated hair loss associated with them, databases have to do something that a simple stack of paper products just can't match — something like sifting through an imposing mound of data in the merest blink of an eye and immediately finding that one elusive piece of data.

Thanks to the magic of the Find, Sort, and Filter commands, Access 2000 tracks and reorganizes the stuff in your tables faster than ever. When you need a quick answer to a simple question, these three commands are ready to help. This chapter covers the commands in order, starting with the speedy Find, moving along to the flexible Filter, and ending with the organizational Sort.

Find, Filter, and Sort do a great job with *small* questions (things like "Who's that customer in Tucumcari?"). Answering big, hairy questions (such as "How many people from Seattle bought wool sweaters on weekends during last year?") still takes a full-fledged Access 2000 query. Don't let that threat worry you, because the next chapter explains the whole query thing in light and winsome detail (okay, maybe it's really *weight-challenged and vaguely morose detail,* but I promise that it's still fun).

Finding Stuff in Your Tables

When you want to track down a particular record *right now,* creating a whole query for the job is overkill. Fortunately, Access 2000 has a quick-and-dirty way to find one specific piece of data within your project's tables and forms — the Find command.

Find is available both on the toolbar and through the main menu (choose Edit➪Find or, for the keyboard-oriented folks out there, press Ctrl+F). Access 2000 doesn't care which way you fire up the Find command — it works the same from either avenue.

Although the Find command is pretty easy to use on its own, knowing a couple of tricks makes it do its best work. After you know the Find basics (covered in the next section), take a look at the tips for fine-tuning the Find command, in the section called "Tuning a search for speed and accuracy." That section tweaks the Find settings for more detailed search missions.

Finding first things first (and next things after that)

Using the Find command is a pretty straightforward task. Here's how it works:

1. **Open the table or form you want to search.**

   Yes, Find works in both Datasheet view and with Access forms. For more about forms, flip ahead to Chapter 22.

2. **Click in the field that you want to search.**

   The Find command searches the *current* field in all the records of the table, so make sure that you click in the right field before starting the Find process. Access 2000 doesn't care which record you click on — as long as you hit the right field, Access is happy (and remember, it's important to keep your software happy!).

3. **Start the Find command by either clicking on the Find toolbar button (the one with the binoculars on it) or choosing Edit➪Find.**

   The Find dialog box pops into action.

4. **Type the text you're looking for into the Fi̲nd What box, as shown in Figure 10-1.**

   Take a moment to check your spelling before starting the search. Access 2000 isn't bright enough to figure out that you actually mean *hero* when you type *zero*.

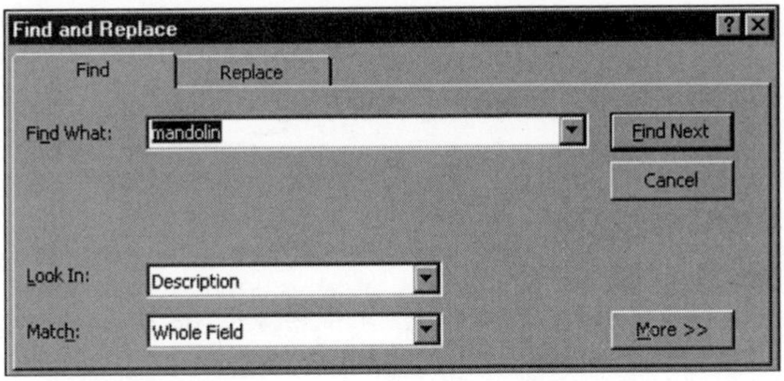

Find and Replace ? ✕

| Find | Replace |

Fi**n**d What: mandolin ▾   **Find Next**

  Cancel

Look In: Description ▾

Mat**c**h: Whole Field ▾   M**o**re >>

Figure 10-1:
The Find
dialog box
gets ready
for a musi-
cal search.

5. Click on F̲ind Next to begin your search.

Before you can count to one by eighths, the Find command tracks down
the record you want, moves the cursor there, and highlights the matching text.

If Find doesn't locate anything, it laments its failure in a small dialog box.
In that case, click on OK to make the dialog box go away, and then make
sure that you clicked in the correct field and spelled everything correctly in the Find What box. You may also want to check the special Find
options covered in the next section to see whether one of them is messing up your search.

What if the first record that Access finds isn't exactly the one you're looking
for? Suppose that you wanted the second, third, or the fourteenth *John Smith*
in the table? No problem — that's why the Find dialog box has a Find Next
button. Keep clicking Find Next until Access 2000 either works its way down
to the record you want or tells you that it's giving up the search.

Tuning a search for speed and accuracy

Sometimes, just providing the information in the Find What box isn't enough.
Either you find too many records or the ones that you match aren't really the
ones that you want. The best way to reduce the number of wrong matches is
to add more details to your search. As a bonus, precise adjustment makes the
pursuit faster, too.

Access 2000 offers several different tools for fine-tuning a Find. Here's a quick
list of the various options and how to use them. All these descriptions
assume that you have already opened the Find dialog by either clicking on
the Find toolbar button or choosing E̲dit⇨F̲ind. The first two settings discussed below (Look In and Match) live on the Find dialog box itself. The
other settings (Search, Match Case, and Search Fields as Formatted) are
hidden from view by default, tucked away in an unseen corner of the dialog
box. To see them, click the More button at the bottom of the Find dialog box.

✔ **Look In:** By default, Access 2000 looks for matches only in the *current* field — whichever field you clicked in before starting the Find command. To have Access 2000 search the entire table instead, change the Look In setting from *field* to *table,* as in Figure 10-2.

✔ **Match:** Access 2000 makes a few silly assumptions, and this option is a good example. By default, Match is set to Whole Field, which assumes that you want to find only fields that *completely match* your search text. The Whole Field setting means that searching for *Sam* would *not* find a field containing *Samuel, Samantha,* or *Mosam.* Not too bright for such an expensive program, is it? Change this behavior by adjusting the Match option to Any Part of Field, which allows a match anywhere in a field (finding both *Samuel* and *new sample product*), or to Start of Field, which recognizes only a match that starts from the beginning of the field. To change this setting, click the down-arrow next to the option and then pick your choice from the drop-down menu, as shown in Figure 10-3.

✔ **Search:** If you're finding too many matches, try limiting your search to one particular portion of the table with the Search option. Search tells the Find command to look at All the records in the table (the default setting) or to merely search Up or Down from the current record. Clicking on a record halfway through the table and then telling Access 2000 to search Down from there confines your search to the bottom part of the table. To see the Search option, click the More button on the Find dialog box. Tune your Search settings by clicking the down-arrow next to the Search box and picking the appropriate choice from the drop-down menu.

✔ **Match Case:** This setting is for the true power-mongers in the audience. Of all the options, Match Case is by far the most restrictive. Not only does the value in question have to meet the criteria in the preceding options, but it also has to *identically* match the search text's case as well. With this option turned on, a search for *McNally* would *not* match *Mcnally* or *MCNALLY.* This setting lives in the secret bottom area of the dialog box, so click More to make Match Case available. To turn this setting on, click in the Match Case check box. A second click turns it off. Multiple clicks make the checkbox look really indecisive and are kinda relaxing to do in the middle of the afternoon.

✔ **Search Fields as Formatted:** Most of the time, this option doesn't make much difference in your life. In fact, the only time you probably care about this Find option is when (or if) you search many highly formatted fields. Search Fields as Formatted instructs Access 2000 to look at the formatted version of the field *instead* of the actual data you typed. Limiting the search in this way is handy when searching dates, stock-keeping unit IDs, or any other field with quite a bit of specialized formatting. View the setting by clicking the More button at the bottom of the Find dialog box. Turn Search Fields as Formatted on by clicking the check box next to it. This setting doesn't work with Match Case, so if Match Case is checked, Search Fields as Formatted is grayed out. In that case, uncheck Match Case to bring back Search Fields as Formatted.

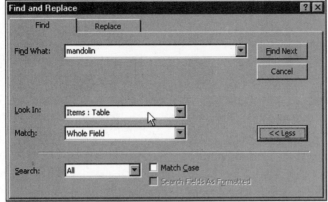

Figure 10-2:
For a quick
look through
the whole
table,
change
the Look
In setting.

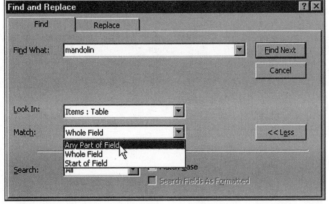

Figure 10-3:
Find a
match any-
where in the
field by
changing
the Match
option.

If your Find command isn't working the way you think that it should, check the options in the preceding list. Odds are that one or more of these options aren't set quite right!

Sorting Out Life on the Planet

Very few databases are already organized into nice, convenient alphabetical lists. So what do you do when your boss wants the world neatly sorted and on her desk within the hour?

The solution, of course, is the Sort command, which is *really* easy to use! The Sort command is on the Records menu, plus two buttons on the toolbar (Sort Ascending and Sort Descending) do the job as well.

✔ Sort Ascending sorts your records alphabetically from top to bottom, so records that begin with A are at the beginning, and records that begin with Z are at the end.

✔ Sort Descending does just the opposite; records that begin with Z are at the top, and A is at the bottom of the list.

The Sort command handles dates and numbers with equal ease. Sort Ascending organizes numbers from smallest to largest and dates from oldest to most recent. Sort Descending puts the largest numbers or most recent dates at the start of the list.

To use the Sort command, click on the field that you want to sort by and then click on either the Sort Ascending or the Sort Descending button. Your records change their order to organize the field you have selected in alphabetical or numeric order. Figure 10-4 shows the auction customer list, sorted by Last Name.

		Customer ID	First Name	Last Name	Organization N	Address1	Ad
▶	⊞	15	Edward	Anderson		431 Brentwood	
	⊞	6	Oslo	Bergenman		4278 Eden Ct.	
	⊞	11	Travis	Cooksey		5807 Layman A	
	⊞	16	King	Daniels	Baystorm, Inc.	9 Graceland Pl.	
	⊞	12	Kevin	Davis		5646 Candelite	
	⊞	36	Delisa	Frattington		127 Park Ct.	
	⊞	22	Sam	Gregory	Whimseco	1620 Edmondsc	
	⊞	24	Gretchen	Hankla	Daisyfield Shop	227 Daisyfield D	
	⊞	4	Gary	Holko		2557 Fisher Driv	
	⊞	37	Gerald	Hollingsly	Victorian Proper	2769 Roundtabl	
	⊞	35	Daniel	Jameson		6811 Ruby Villa	
	⊞	25	Byron	Jiles		1122 Belden Dr.	
	⊞	1	Aan	Kermit		17757 S. Lyons	
	⊞	7	Anistasia	Kimmerly		6774 Wildernes	Apt. 1
	⊞	5	Christopher	Klayton	Tanbara, Inc.	4662 Jefferson F	

Record: ◄ ◄ 1 ► ►► ►* of 37

Figure 10-4:
If you want to organize your data by a certain category, click on that category before you start.

Anything that's *this* useful simply must include an odd behavior or two to keep life interesting. True to form, Sort has its own peculiarity when working with numbers inside a text field. When sorting a field that has numbers mixed in with spaces and letters (such as street addresses), Access 2000 ranks the numbers as if they were *letters,* not actual numbers. Unfortunately, this behavior means that Access 2000 puts "10608 W. Vermont" before "119 Spring Mill." (The 0 in the second position comes before the 1 in the second position.) Oh well, I suppose that you can only expect so much from a program. Such is life in the digital lane.

Filtering Records with Something in Common

Sometimes, you need to see a group of records that share a common value in one field — they all list a particular city, a certain job title, or the same genre of books. Ever the willing helper, Access 2000 includes a special tool for this very purpose — the Filter command.

Filter uses your criteria and displays all the matching records, creating a little mini-table of only the records that meet your requirements. It's like an instant query, without all the extra work, hassle, and overhead (and, of course, without a *lot* of the power).

The Filter commands live on the Records menu and the toolbar. Access 2000 offers four unique filter commands: Filter by Selection, Filter by Form, Filter Excluding Selection, and Advanced Filter/Sort. Each command performs the same basic function, but in a different way and with different bells and whistles attached. The following sections cover the first three options. For details of the Advanced Filter/Sort, flip to Chapter 11.

Filters work in tables, forms, and queries. Although you *can* apply a filter to a report, doing so is really a different kind of beast (and not a very friendly beast, at that). Each section below focuses on applying filters to tables, but the same concepts apply when you're working with queries and forms.

Filter by Selection

The Filter by Selection command is the easiest of the three filter commands to use. It assumes that you have already found one record that matches your criteria. Using Filter by Selection is much like grabbing someone in a crowd and shouting: "Okay, everybody who's like him, line up over there."

To use Filter by Selection, click in the field that has the information you want to match. For example, suppose that you're looking at the items for sale at the auction and decide that you need to look only at those items that have a minimum bid of exactly $30.00 (no more, no less — filters don't understand concepts like *greater than*). When you find one item that meets that criteria, click in the item's MinimumBid field (or whatever the field is called) and then click the Filter by Selection toolbar button. Access 2000 immediately displays a table containing only the items with a minimum bid of exactly $30.00 (see Figure 10-5). Of course, you can select Records⇨Filter⇨Filter by Selection from the main menu instead of using the toolbar button, but the toolbar button works a little faster in this case.

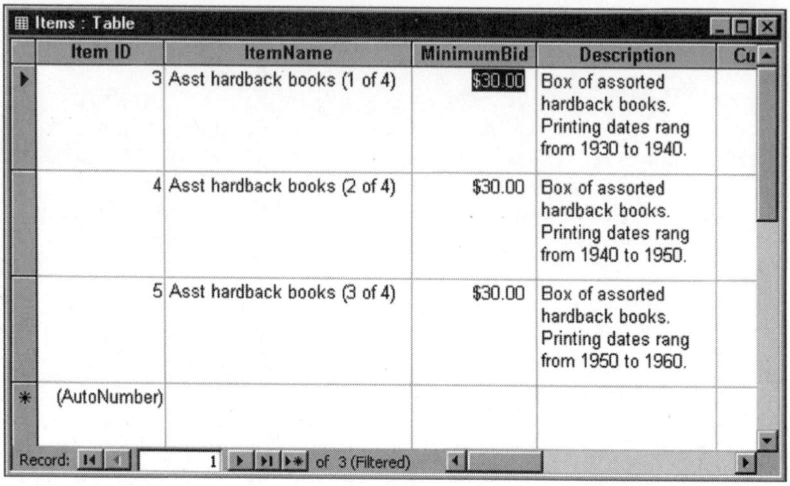

Item ID	ItemName	MinimumBid	Description	Cu
3	Asst hardback books (1 of 4)	$30.00	Box of assorted hardback books. Printing dates rang from 1930 to 1940.	
4	Asst hardback books (2 of 4)	$30.00	Box of assorted hardback books. Printing dates rang from 1940 to 1950.	
5	Asst hardback books (3 of 4)	$30.00	Box of assorted hardback books. Printing dates rang from 1950 to 1960.	
*	(AutoNumber)			

Record: 1 of 3 (Filtered)

Figure 10-5:
Filter by
Selection
finds the
records that
match high-
lighted
criteria.

When you finish using the filter, click the Remove Filter toolbar button to return your table or form to its regular display.

At this stage of the game, you may want to save a list of everything that matches your filter. Unfortunately, you can't — Filter's simplicity and ease of use now comes back to haunt you. To permanently record your filtered search, you need to create a query (see Chapter 11).

Filter by Form

You can tighten a search by using additional filters to weed out undesirable matches, but doing so takes a ton of extra effort. For an easier way to isolate a group of records based on the values in more than one field, turn to the Filter by Form feature (try saying that three times fast!).

Filter by Form uses more than one criteria to sift through records. (In some ways, it's like a simple query. It's so similar, in fact, that you can even save your Filter by Form criteria *as* a full-fledged query!) Say, for example, that you need a list of all the customers at your auction who came from Illinois or Indiana. Well, you can do two Filter by Selection searches and write down the results of each to get your list, or you can do just *one* search with Filter by Form and see all the records in a single step.

To use Filter by Form, either choose Records⇨Filter⇨Filter by Form or click on the Filter by Form toolbar button. An empty replica of your table fills the screen, just like the one shown in Figure 10-6.

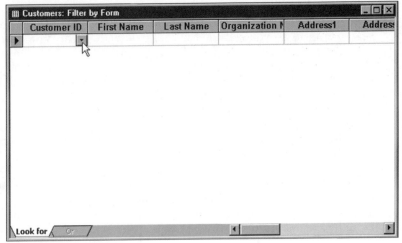

Figure 10-6:
The Filter by
Form table
lets you give
detailed
instructions
on what to
look for in
your data.

Notice in Figure 10-6 that an arrow button is in the CustomerID field of the
table. That arrow button is there because that field was active when the Filter
by Form command was selected. The arrow is useful if you want to filter by
customer ID number, but you're going to look at states of residence. Scroll
right and click in the State/Province column — the little arrow obligingly
jumps to that column. You can then click on the arrow to open a list box
showing all the entries for that field in your open database, as displayed in
Figure 10-7.

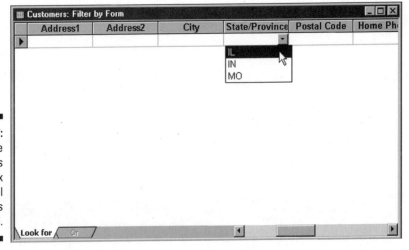

Figure 10-7:
The little
arrow opens
a list box
showing all
the entries
for that field.

In the lower-left corner of the table is a tab labeled Look For. When that tab is highlighted, you can click on an entry to designate that entry as your primary search criteria. So you click on the abbreviation IL in the drop-down list of the State/Province list box, and IL moves into the State/Province column.

But wait! What about the records that have the state entered as "Illinois?" Don't worry — looking for multiple values is what Filter by Form is all about. Look back at the lower-left corner of the table. Next to the Look For tab is another tab labeled Or. Click on Or and then open your list box again. You can click on any other entry (Illinois, for example), and Access 2000 searches for that entry as well as for IL.

Repeat this process as many times as you need and in any field you need. Every time you click on the Or tab, another Or tab poofs into existence so that you can add still more criteria to your search. Figure 10-8 shows how the Filter by Form table looks with an extra Or tab in place.

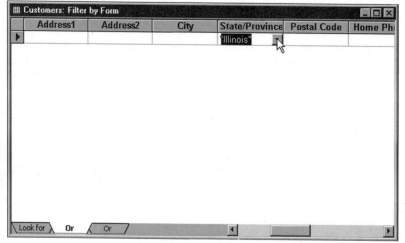

Figure 10-8: You can use as many Or statements as you need to define all the criteria.

When you finish entering all the criteria for the filter, click on the Apply Filter button, and Access 2000 does the rest. Figure 10-9 shows the results.

Figure 10-9: Access 2000 successfully filtered your table just like the form asked.

And now, here are a few final Filter by Form thoughts:

✔ Although you can get fancy by adding Or searches to your heart's content, keeping track of your creation gets tough in no time at all. Before creating *The Filter That Identified Incredibly Detailed Sub-Sets of Manhattan,* remind yourself that queries work better than filters do when the questions get complex. Flip to Chapter 11 for the lowdown on queries.

✔ What if you invest a great deal of time to create an incredibly detailed and mind-blowingly useful filter? Can you turn that work into a real query and press on to greater heights of data manipulation success? Yes, you can do it! (Sorry — I get too excited about this stuff sometimes.) Convert your cool Filter by Form creation into a full-fledged query by clicking the Save As Query button on the toolbar. Access 2000 dutifully remakes your work into a query and then adds it to the Query list in your database.

When you finish fiddling with your filter, click the Remove Filter by Form toolbar button. At that point, your table returns to normal (or at least as normal as data tables ever get).

Removing your mistakes (or when good criteria go bad)

What do you do when you enter criteria by mistake? Or when you decide that you really don't want to include Ohio in your filter right after you click on OH? No problem — the Clear Grid button to the rescue!

When you click on the Clear Grid button, Access 2000 dumps all the entries in the Filter by Form grid and gives you a nice, clean place to start over again.

If you want to get rid of just a single Or tab instead of clearing the whole grid, click on that tab and then choose Edit➪Delete Tab.

Chapter 11

Pose a Simple Query, Get 10,000 Answers

● ●

In This Chapter

▶ Defining a query

▶ Answering easy questions with Advanced Filter/Sort

▶ Digging deeper with queries

▶ Calling the Simple Query Wizard

● ●

Someone infinitely smarter than me once observed that the most interesting things in life spring not from the answers that life gives us, but instead from the questions that we pose along the way. One way or another, *everything* that we know — every shred of information in our minds — springs from questions that we either asked aloud, pondered silently, or whispered furtively to the student at the next desk in hopes that he would take the risk of broaching the subject in class for us.

Databases follow this rule of life pretty well. Gathering your information into a database isn't easy, nor does the simple act of *gathering* really make the data easier to use. (After all, when you're done, all you have is an electronic pile of the same stuff that previously lived in filing cabinets.) The real power of a database flows from the questions you ask of it and the answers that it provides.

Access 2000 (and all databases in general) uses its own terminology for questions posed to your database. Access calls these questions *queries* — and they're the wily technological animals that this chapter covers.

The chapter starts with an introduction to the gentle (and frequently arcane) art of asking questions about the information in your database. Next, the chapter explores the basics of the simplest query in Access 2000, which is *so* simple that the programmers gave this query the confusing name *Advanced*

Filter/Sort just to keep things murky. From there, the chapter guides you deeper into the data jungle where you find the true power of Access 2000, the Select Query.

Don't worry if your first few queries produce odd results. That's how queries start for everybody (myself included). Queries aren't easy to master, but the payoff at the end is huge. Go slowly, be patient with yourself, and take comfort in the fact that others before you trod the same path you now walk — the path called "Hmm, that's not the answer to the question I thought that I asked."

Database Interrogation for Fun and Profit

Of all the cool features in Access 2000, queries take the medals as the true heroes in the ongoing Battle to Enhance Your On-The-Job Performance. Queries help you make sense of all the data that you, your co-workers, and a cast of a thousand others who have slavishly typed over the course of too many hours, days, months, years, biannual bird migrations, and deep space satellite voyages.

Just as tables prepare your data for work by lining all the information up in neat rows and columns, queries make the data start doing something by culling out the irrelevant details and shining light on murky mysteries. When you use queries, your data starts paying a return on all of your labor.

All of this querying sounds great, but it leaves open a simple question: *What the heck is a query?* Simply put, a *query* is a question about the data in one or more of the tables in your database. Queries make lists, count records, and even do calculations based on the data lurking in your database.

Queries discover things like how many spools of purple silk thread sit in your warehouse, which customers bought the most organic cactus face cream (in both non-prickly and extra prickly varieties), and how weather affects carry-out pizza sales. In short, queries put the power behind your Access 2000 data.

Query magic doesn't stop with just answering questions. More advanced queries can add or delete records in your tables, calculate summary figures, perform statistical analyses, and with the right add-ons from Microsoft, probably even wash your dog.

This chapter isn't big enough to hold *everything* about queries, but it gives you a good start. Browse through the other chapters in this part for the full query scoop.

On Your Way with a Simple Query — Advanced Filter/Sort

At first glance, you may wonder why I just spent all this time talking about queries if the first technical thing in the chapter is a *filter*. Trust me — there's a method to my madness (kinda nice for a change, isn't it?).

The folks who created Access 2000 know that different searches require different techniques. For different searches, they include *two* search tools in the software: filters and queries.

Filters, the simpler tool of the two, quickly scan a single table for whatever data you seek. Filters are fast but not terribly smart or flexible. For example, if you want to quickly see a list of all records for people living in Nevada, then a filter works wonderfully. If you want to do *more* than merely *see* the list, then the filter falls short. The previous chapter covers filters in their limited but useful glory.

Queries go far beyond filters. But to get there, queries add more complexity. After all, a bicycle may be easy to ride (at least it is for some people — goodness knows that I had plenty of trouble with it), but a bike won't go as far or as fast as a jumbo jetliner. For all of its power, though, the jet is a *tad* bit more complex to operate than your average two-wheeler. And so it goes with queries as well. Queries work with one or more tables, let you search one or more fields, and even offer the option to save your results for further analysis.

For all of the differences, the most advanced filter is, in reality, a simple query, which makes some kind of perverse sense. Your first step into the world of queries is also your last step from the domain of filters. Welcome to the Advanced Filter/Sort, the super filter of Access 2000, masquerading as a mild-mannered query.

As its name implies, Advanced Filter/Sort is more powerful than a run-of-the-mill filter. The filter is *so* powerful, in fact, that it's really a simple query. You use exactly the same steps to build an Advanced Filter/Sort that you use to create a query — and the results look quite a bit alike, too.

Even though it looks, acts, and behaves like a query, Advanced Filter/Sort is still a filter at heart, while being constrained by a filter's limits. The Advanced Filter/Sort limitations include:

- ✔ Advanced Filter/Sort only works with one table or form in your database at a time, so you can't use it on a bunch of linked tables.

- ✔ You can only ask simple questions with the filter. Real, honest-to-goodness queries do a lot more than that (which is why a whole part in this book is about queries).

✔ The filter displays all of the columns for every matching record in your table. With a query, *you* pick the columns that you want to appear in the results. If you don't want a particular column, leave it out of the query. Filters aren't bright enough to do that.

Even with those limits, though, Advanced Filter/Sort makes a great training ground to practice your query building skills.

Although this section only talks about applying filters to tables, you can also filter a query. Precisely *why* you'd filter a query is a little beyond me, so just let the nerds worry about this feature — it definitely falls under the heading *Features for People with Too Much Time on Their Hands*.

Peering into the filter window

The Filter window is split into two distinct sections. The upper half of the window holds the *field list*, which displays all the fields in the current table or form. For now, don't worry about this portion of the window — the upper half comes more into play when you start working with full queries.

The lower half of the screen contains a blank query grid where the details of your filter go. Even though you're building a *filter*, Access 2000 calls the area at the bottom of the screen a *query* grid. You see almost the exact same grid later in the chapter in the section about building real queries.

To build the filter, you simply fill in the spaces of the query grid at the bottom of the window, as shown in Figure 11-1. Access 2000 even helps you along the way, with pull-down menus and rows that do specific tasks. The following sections cover each portion of the query grid in more detail.

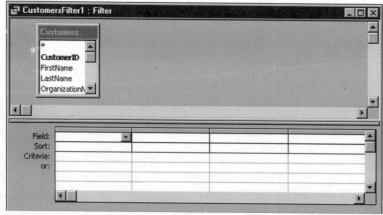

Figure 11-1: The Advanced Filter/Sort window looks a lot like a regular query.

Building a simple query — er, filter

Start your filter adventure by firing up the basic query tool of Access 2000, the Advanced Filter/Sort. Here's what to do:

1. **Open the table that you want to interrogate.**

   With good luck and wind from the East, your table hops into view.

   The Advance Filter/Sort tool also works on forms. If you feel particularly adventuresome (or if you mainly work with your data through some ready-made forms), give the filter a try. Filtering a form works just like filtering a table, so just follow the other steps below.

2. **Decide what question you need to ask and which fields the question involves.**

   You may want a list of products in inventory more than 60 days, customers who live in Munich or Amsterdam, books by your favorite author, or recipes that take less than an hour to cook *and* also contain spinach. Whatever your desire, figure out which field in your table contains the answer to your question, and exactly what your question is.

   Don't worry if your question includes more than one field (such as the recipe problem above) or multiple options (such as the customer city example). Filters — and, of course, queries — can handle multiple-field and multiple-option questions.

3. **Select <u>R</u>ecords⇨<u>F</u>ilter⇨<u>A</u>dvanced Filter/Sort from the main menu.**

   The Filter window (refer to Figure 11-1) appears on-screen, ready to accept your command.

   The Filter window is nothing but a simplified query window. The filter looks, acts, and behaves a lot like a real query. To keep things easier, though, the Filter window offers fewer bells and whistles than the full query window. More about full queries comes later in the chapter, so flip ahead to the next section if that's what you need.

4. **Click in the first box on the Field row and then click on the down-arrow that appears on the right side of the Field box.**

   The drop-down menu lists all of the fields in your table.

5. **Click on the first field you identified back in Step 2.**

   Access 2000 helpfully puts the field name into the Field box on the query grid. So far, so good.

6. **To sort your filter results by this particular field, click the Sort box, and then click the down-arrow that appears. Select either Ascending or Descending from the drop-down menu.**

   If you want to see the results in the same order that your data always appears in, just skip this step entirely.

Ascending order means smallest to largest; *descending* is largest to smallest. (I never *could* keep those straight for some reason.)

7. Click in the Criteria box under your field. Type the question for your filter to answer.

Setting the criteria is the most complex part of building a query — it's the make or break item in the whole process. The criteria is your actual question, formatted in a way that Access 2000 understands. Building a query with the right criteria can involve a lot, but Table 11-1 gives you a quick introduction to the process.

Flip to Chapter 13 for a deeper look into the world of Boolean logic, the language of Access criteria.

Table 11-1	Basic Comparison Operators	
Name	*Symbol*	*What It Means*
Equals	(none)	The filter displays all records that exactly match whatever you type. **Example:** To find all items from customer 37, put 37 into the Criteria row.
Less Than	<	This operator lists all values that are *Less Than* your criteria. **Example:** <30 in the MinimumBid field finds all bids from $29.99 to negative infinity.
Greater Than	>	This operator lists all values in the field that are *Greater Than* the criteria. **Example:** >30 in the MinimumBid field finds all bids that are more than $30 (starting with $30.01).
Greater Than or Equal To	>=	This operator works just like Greater Than, except that it also includes all entries that exactly match the criteria. **Example:** >=30 finds all values from 30 to infinity.
Less Than or Equal To	<=	If you add the = sign to Less Than, your query includes all records that have values below and equal to the criteria value. **Example:** <=30 includes not only those records with values less than 30, but also those with a value of 30.
Not Equal To	<>	This operator finds all entries that do not match the criteria. **Example:** If you want a list of all records except ones with a value of 30, enter <>30.

8. **If your question includes more than one possible value for this field, click in the Or box and type your next criteria.**

   Feel free to include as many Or options as you need. Just keep scrolling down to open up a new row for your criteria.

   If you type a bunch of Or lines, your first entries seem to disappear. Don't worry — you didn't mess up anything. Access 2000 just scrolled the table up a bit to make room for the new criteria. Click on the up arrow on the scroll bar to see your original entries again.

9. **Repeat Steps 4 through 8 if your question involves more than one field.**

   With all the criteria in place, it's time to take your filter for a test drive.

10. **To turn on the filter, select Filter➪Apply Filter/Sort from the menu bar or click on the Apply Filter button on the Toolbar.**

    After a moment of thinking (or whatever Access 2000 does when it's figuring out something), your table view changes and only the records that match your filter are left on display (see Figure 11-2). Pretty cool, eh?

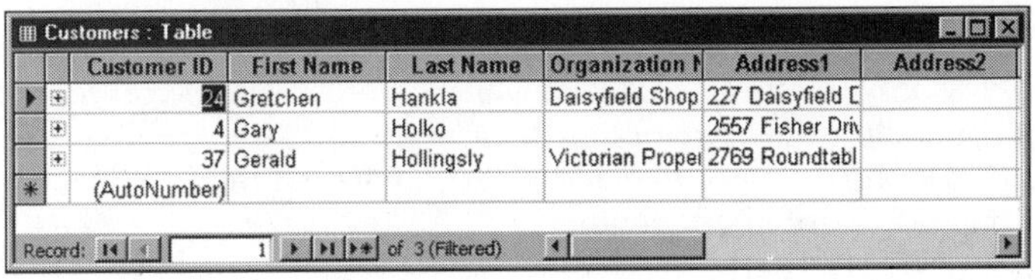

Figure 11-2:
Ta dah! Your
filtered data
marches
proudly
across the
screen.

		Customer ID	First Name	Last Name	Organization N	Address1	Address2
▶	⊞	24	Gretchen	Hankla	Daisyfield Shop	227 Daisyfield D	
	⊞	4	Gary	Holko		2557 Fisher Driv	
	⊞	37	Gerald	Hollingsly	Victorian Proper	2769 Roundtabl	
*		(AutoNumber)					

Record: ◀◀ ◀ 1 ▶ ▶▶ ▶* of 3 (Filtered)

To see all the data again, click the Apply Filter button one more time. The filtered records join their unfiltered brethren in a touching moment of digital homecoming. (Sorry — it's the romantic in me.)

If you *really* love this particular filter and want to use it again in the future, click the Save As Query button on the toolbar (the picture of a disk with a funnel over it). Access 2000 displays a dialog box asking what you want to call the query. Type a name and then click OK. Access carefully saves your filter as a query, including this query with the others of its kind on the Queries page in your database window.

Plagued by Tough Questions? Try an Industrial-Strength Query!

Sometimes, quick and easy information is all that you need — ask the question, get the answer, and then go on with life. At other moments though, you need introspection, analysis, and concerted thought — in other words, your information calls for work. Thanks to the Access 2000 query tools, that work just got easier.

The basic query tool, created to make your life easier, is the Select query. Since developers use all of their creativity while writing programs, they tend to name their creations according to what the software actually does — hence, a Select query. These queries *select* matching records from your database and display the results according to your instructions.

Unlike its simplified predecessor in this chapter, a Select query offers all kinds of helpful and powerful options. These options include:

- ✔ Use more than one table in a query. Because Select queries understand the relational side of Access 2000, this kind of query can pull together data from more than one table.

- ✔ Show only the fields that you want in your results. You don't need every single field from your tables in your answer? No problem! Select queries include the ever-popular *Show* setting, which tells Access which fields you really care about seeing.

- ✔ Put the fields into any order you want in the results. Organize your answers with fields where *you* want them, without changing anything in your original table.

- ✔ List only as many matching entries as you need, thanks to the Select query's Top Value option. If you only need the top five, 25, or 100 records, or even a percentage like 5% or 25%, Access meets your need through the Top Value's setting.

The following section covers the basics of building a single-table Select query, but the other chapters in this part dig into detail on the goodies mentioned in the bullets above.

Build a Better Query and the Answers Beat a Path to Your Monitor

Creating a Select query looks a lot like putting together one of those Advanced Filter/Sort thingies, but the Select query includes a few extra, interesting buttons and levers. The following steps run through the process and toss out some tips about advanced stuff that you don't want to miss:

1. **Open the database that you want to interrogate and then click the Queries button on the left side of the screen.**

   Access lists all of your existing queries (assuming that you have some in there), plus offers a couple of options for query creation.

2. **Decide what question you're asking with the query, which fields you need to answer the question, and which fields you want in your results.**

   Because Select queries let you pick and choose with more detail, you need to think through more options than you did with the Advanced Filter/Sort. The basic step remains the same though. Which fields contain the data you want to know about? Which fields do you need in the solution? Think it through carefully, because these decisions form the major groundwork of your query.

3. **Double-click on Create query in Design view.**

   The screen does a quick change, and you get two new windows: a blank Select Query screen and a smaller Show Table dialog box.

4. **In the Show Table dialog box, click on the table you want to use and then click <u>A</u>dd. Click <u>C</u>lose to get rid of the Show Table dialog box.**

   Access puts a little window listing the table's fields into the top of the Select Query window, as shown in Figure 11-3.

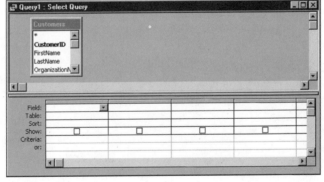

Figure 11-3:
Your table, in fashionable glory, pops into the query window.

5. **Select the first field for your query by clicking the down-arrow in the Field box and then click the name of the field in the drop-down menu.**

   Access automatically puts the name of the table in the Table box and assumes that you want to include the field in your results by putting a checkmark in the Show box.

You can also scroll through the field list in the small table window (the one that's in the upper part of the query window) and double-click on each field that you want in the query. As you double-click, Access fills the field names into the query grid. Personally, I prefer doing it this way, particularly when you start using multiple-table queries, (which is covered in the next chapter).

6. Repeat Step 5 until all of the fields you want are in the query grid.

Now, you're ready to adjust the sorting options.

7. To sort the query results by a particular field, click in that field's Sort box, click the down-arrow, and select Ascending or Descending from the drop-down menu.

Just like Advanced Filter/Sort, Access gives you the little-to-big and big-to-little options you know and love.

If you tell Access to sort with more than one field, Access starts with the field closest to the left of the query grid, and then sorts the other fields when it runs into identical records in the first field. For more about controlling your sorts, see the sidebar "Putting everything in *your* order."

8. If you don't want a field to appear in the results, uncheck the Show box for that field.

Once you narrow down which fields make the cut to the big answer, continue to the criteria step.

9. Enter the criteria for each field that's part of the question.

Select queries use the same rules as the Advanced Filter/Sort, including all of the operators shown in Table 11-1 (earlier in the chapter). If you need some *Or* criteria (such as customers in Indiana or Illinois), use the Or lines in the query grid (as shown in Figure 11-4).

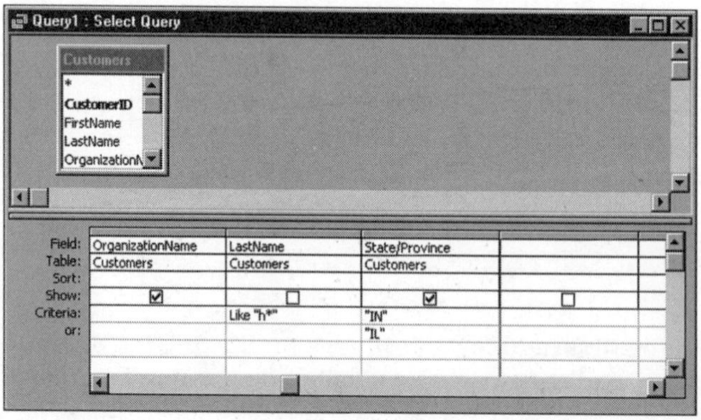

Figure 11-4:
Use the Or line when you need more than one criteria for a single field.

Field:	OrganizationName	LastName	State/Province		
Table:	Customers	Customers	Customers		
Sort:					
Show:	☑	☐	☑	☐	
Criteria:		Like "h*"	"IN"		
or:			"IL"		

Putting everything in *your* order

Access has a nice tool for sorting the results from a query. After all, queries don't get much easier than clicking a little box labeled *Sort,* and then telling the program whether Ascending or Descending is your pick for sort-flavor-of-the-moment.

The only problem with this little arrangement is that Access automatically sorts the results from *left* to *right.* If you only request one sort, then this order is no big deal. But if you request *two* sorts (for example, organize the results by both Customer ID *and* Item ID), then the column that's closest to the *left* side of the query automatically becomes the primary sort, with any other field playing second (or third) fiddle.

Taking control of the sort order isn't hard, but it also isn't very obvious. Because Access looks at the query grid and performs the sorts from left to right, the trick is to *move the column* for the main sorting instruction to the left side of the grid. (Only a computer jockey can come up with a solution like this.)

To move a column in the grid, put the tip of the mouse pointer in the thin gray box just above the field name on the query grid. When the mouse turns into a down-pointing arrow, click once. All of a sudden, the chosen field highlights for you. (Fear not — highlighting the field was the hard part of the process.)

With the mouse pointer aimed at the same little gray area right above the field name, click and drag the field to its new position on the grid. As you move the mouse, a black bar moves through the grid, showing you where the field will land when you let up on the mouse button. When the black bar is in the right place, release the mouse button. The field information pops into view again, safe and happy in its new home.

In addition to changing the sort order of your query, this moving trick *also* changes the order that the fields display in your query results. Feel free to move things here, there, or anywhere, depending on your needs. Is this some *great* flexibility or what?

Thanks to their extra power, Select queries support some special operators in the Criteria section in addition to the ones in the table. Flip ahead to Chapter 13 for more about the super-duper cool operators from Mr. Boole's bag of tricks.

10. **Take one last look at everything, take a deep breath, and click the Run button.**

   After a few (or perhaps *many*) moments of chunking and thunking, your query results pop onto screen, looking like Figure 11-5.

   If what you see *isn't* exactly what you thought you asked for (isn't that just like a computer?), double-check your query instructions. Common problems include mixing up the greater than (>) and less than (<) signs, leaving out an equals sign (=) in your greater-than-or-equal-to statements, or simply misspelling a region name, state, or postal code.

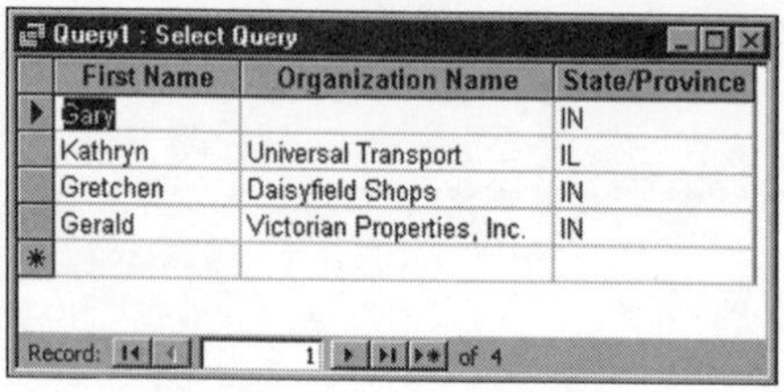

Figure 11-5:
And there
they are —
the results I
wanted!

First Name	Organization Name	State/Province
▶ Sary		IN
Kathryn	Universal Transport	IL
Gretchen	Daisyfield Shops	IN
Gerald	Victorian Properties, Inc.	IN
*		

Record: 1 of 4

If you love this select query (in a friendly and useful kind of way), click the Save button on the toolbar (it looks like a floppy disk). Access pops up a little dialog box asking what you want to call the query. Type a name and then click OK. Access stores the query with the others of its kind in the Queries area of your database.

Toto, Can the Wizard Help?

Besides the Advanced Filter/Sort query and the Select query, you can rely on the Simple Query Wizard. Also, if you know how to build queries by hand with the New Query function, the Simple Query Wizard is a breeze. Like all the other wizards in the land of Access 2000, the Simple Query Wizard takes care of the behind-the-scenes work for you, but you have to enter the sorting and criteria information on your own. (But I can at least dream. . . .)

The next time you click on the New command from the Query tab, choose the Simple Query Wizard instead of New Query. When you do, the wizard appears in a flash of flame and thunder, as shown in Figure 11-6.

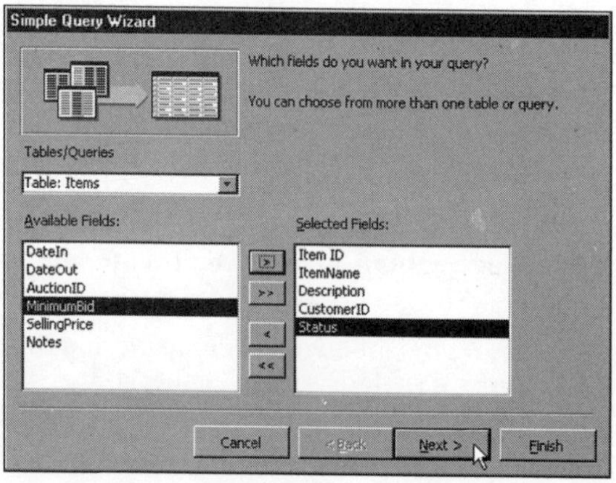

Figure 11-6:
The Simple
Query
Wizard of
Access
arranges
the data you
want into a
single
query.

Simple Query Wizard

Which fields do you want in your query?

You can choose from more than one table or query.

Tables/Queries

Table: Items

Available Fields:
DateIn
DateOut
AuctionID
MinimumBid
SellingPrice
Notes

Selected Fields:
Item ID
ItemName
Description
CustomerID
Status

Cancel   < Back   Next >   Finish

The wizard asks you to provide three bits of information:

✔ The first, Tables/Queries, enables you to select which tables you want to use in this query. Click on the arrow to see the drop-down list and choose from the available choices. Don't worry, the wizard is wise and includes all the queries and tables in the current database.

✔ After selecting the tables to use, the Available Fields box shows the table's available fields. Move these fields to the Selected Fields box by highlighting the fields that you want to use and clicking on the > button. Or, if you know that you want to use all the fields in the database, click on the > button to see everything transfer over.

✔ If you decide that you don't want a field that you've already transferred, highlight that field in the Selected Fields box and click on the < button. If you want to remove all the selected fields, click on the << button.

When you finish telling the wizard which fields to use, click the Next button. The wizard thinks for a moment, and then asks if you want a lot of Detail (to see every field of every record) or if you merely want a Summary (which automatically totals the numeric fields in your table). Pick your option and then click Next.

The final step, shown in Figure 11-7, asks you to name your query. If you want to dress up the query a little and add some cool extras, select the Modify the query design radio button, which tells the wizard to send your newly created query directly into the shop for more work. On the other hand, if you are satisfied with your options at this point, select the Open the query to view information button to see the Datasheet view.

Figure 11-7:
The wizard asks for your query's name and offers more help.

The last check box on this screen (Display Help on working with the query?) automatically opens a Help file that explains how you can customize your query. After you make your selections, you're ready to click Finish to see your handiwork.

Chapter 12

Searching a Slew of Tables

· ·

In This Chapter

▶ Setting up queries with more than one table

▶ Enlisting the Query Wizard's help

▶ Building multiple-table queries in Design view

· ·

Questioning just one table at a time kinda defeats the purpose of a relational database program. After all, relational database programs, which Access 2000 proudly claims to be, spend all of their time and energy encouraging you to organize your data into *multiple*-tables. Why would they do that if they didn't include *some* way to link the various tables together and ask intelligent questions? (Yes, they *may* do it just to be annoying, but let's assume that's not a possibility here.)

In keeping with its membership in the Relational Database Application Club of America, Access 2000 does indeed include tools for querying multiple-tables. Because the process is on the arcane side, the chapter focuses on enlisting the Query Wizard to help you through the process. For the more technically inclined out there, the chapter explains how to build a multiple-table query by hand, too.

There's no shame in using the wizard's help when building a multiple-table query. The process isn't easy — remember, some people go to college to *study* databases — but the Query Wizard covers the hard parts for you.

Some General Thoughts about Multiple-Table Queries

You may need to look at information from a variety of tables to get full use from your data. (In fact, if you're in the corporate world, it's almost a foregone conclusion that you need to blend data from multiple-tables.) Fortunately, Access is specifically called a *relational database* because it enables you to establish *relationships* among the different tables you work with. This feature means that Access queries can look at two or more tables and (with your help and guidance) recognize information that goes together.

In most cases, a multiple-table query works the same as a single-table query. You merely need to let Access 2000 know that you are drawing on information from different tables, and the software does the rest.

Access 2000 maintains links between the tables in your database. Usually you (or your Information Systems department) create this link when you first design the database. When you build the tables and organize them with special *key fields,* you are actually preparing the tables to work with a query.

Key fields are the glue that link Access tables together. Queries use these links to match records in one table with their mates in another. For example, in Figure 12-1, the auction house considers the people who sell items their customers. The auction house, which sells the items for their customers, wants to keep track of the sold items, so they record each sold item in the Items table. The auction house also must keep track of their customers (the sellers) so the auction house knows who to send the money to for each item sold. To keep track of the customers, the auction house creates a Customers table. Because each item also has a seller (or auction house customer), the Items table has a SellerID field which stores a value corresponding to a unique record in the Customers table. The SellerID field in the Items table tells Access 2000 who the customer or seller of the item is.

The SellerID field is not a key field in the Items table because the main goal of the Items table is to keep track of the items that are sold. For the Items table, a key field called ItemID is created. This key field is unique and necessary because after all, the auction house can't sell the same item twice. If more information is needed about the seller, the auction house has the Customers table with the CutomerID that matches the SellerID, found in the Items table. The CustomerID field is a key field in the Customers table, which is unique because the auction house doesn't want a customer's information placed in their Customers table more than once.

Figure 12-1:
In a
multiple-
table query,
the tables
are linked to
share their
data.

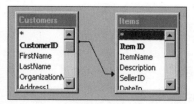

Before building a bunch of multiple-table queries, you *must* understand how the tables in your database work. More specifically, you need to know which fields the tables use to link the data together. If you don't know, then you're begging for trouble (which arrives in the form of queries that don't tell you anything useful). To find out more about relationships in general and how to use the relationship-building tools of Access 2000, flip back to Chapter 5.

Calling on the Query Wizard

The Query Wizard wouldn't be much of a wizard if all it could do were create single-table queries. Luckily, it's one *heckuva* wizard because it comprehends the multiple-table queries details as well.

To create a multiple-table query, follow these steps:

1. **In the database window, click the Queries button below the Objects bar on the left side of the window.**

    The window lists all of the queries currently living in the database.

2. **Double-click on Create query by using wizard to start the Simple Query Wizard.**

    The Simple Query Wizard window appears. Don't be surprised if the window looks familiar — it's the same one you use to make single-table queries. With a twist of the wrist (and a click of the mouse), it *also* builds multiple-table queries!

3. **Click in the down-arrow next to the Tables/Queries box, as shown in Figure 12-2, and then click on the name of the first table to include in this query.**

    The Available Fields list changes and displays the fields available in the table (but you probably guessed that).

4. **Double-click on each field you want to include in the query.**

    If you click on the wrong field, just double-click on it in the Selected Fields list. The field promptly jumps back to the Available Fields side of the window.

5. **When you finish adding fields from this table, repeat Steps 3 and 4 for the next table you want use in the query.**

    After you list all of the fields you want in Selected Fields area, go to the next step.

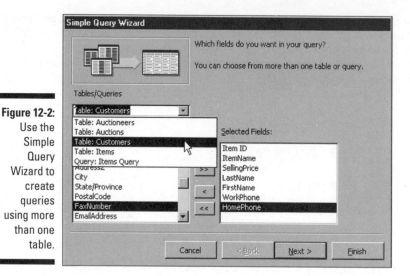

Figure 12-2:
Use the
Simple
Query
Wizard to
create
queries
using more
than one
table.

6. Click on Next to continue building the query.

A screen amazingly similar to Figure 12-3 *may* hop into action, but don't panic if it doesn't. If Access 2000 wants you to name the query instead, skip ahead to Step 8.

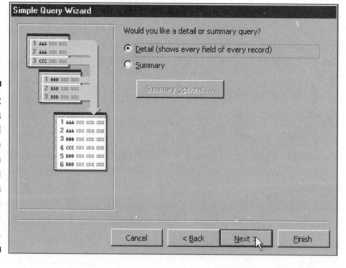

Figure 12-3:
Sometimes
the wizard
needs more
information
from you
when it's
creating a
multiple-
table query.

If you included fields from two tables that aren't related, the Access 2000 Office Assistant leaps into action when you click on Next. Office Assistant reminds you that the tables must be related and suggests that you fix the problem before continuing. Actually, *suggests* isn't quite correct — it politely *demands* that you fix the relationship before trying to create the query. If this error appears, click on the OK button in the Office Assistant's message to go directly to the Relationships window. Repair the relationship and then restart the Query Wizard to try again. Check out Chapters 4 and 5 for more about relationships.

7. **If the wizard asks you to choose between a** <u>D</u>**etail and a** <u>S</u>**ummary query, click on the radio button next to your choice and then click on** <u>N</u>**ext.**

   Detail creates a datasheet that lists all the records that match the query. As the name implies, you get all the details.

   Summary tells the wizard that you aren't interested in seeing every single record; you want to see a summary of the information, instead. If you want to make any special adjustments to the summary, click on Summary Options to display the Summary Options dialog box shown in Figure 12-4. Select your summary options from the list and then click on OK.

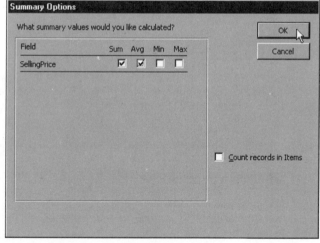

Figure 12-4:
You don't have too many Summary options, but the options you get are helpful.

8. **Type a title for your query into the text box and then click on** <u>F</u>**inish.**

   The query does its thing and Access 2000 displays the results on-screen, as shown in Figure 12-5. Congratulations!

	Last Name	First Name	Work Phone	Home Phone	Sum Of Selling	Avg Of Selling
▶	Cooksey	Travis		(317) 864-7736	$87.00	$87.00
	Anderson	Edward	(317) 388-1842	(317) 783-9195	$45.00	$45.00
	Gregory	Sam	(317) 292-8367		$156.00	$156.00
	Gregory	Sam	(317) 292-8367		$345.00	$345.00
	Gregory	Sam	(317) 292-8367		$70.00	$70.00
	Gregory	Sam	(317) 292-8367		$34.00	$34.00
	Hollingsly	Gerald	(317) 237-7965		$1,050.00	$1,050.00
	Hollingsly	Gerald	(317) 237-7965		$233.00	$233.00
	Hollingsly	Gerald	(317) 237-7965		$560.00	$560.00
	Hollingsly	Gerald	(317) 237-7965		$900.00	$900.00
	Hollingsly	Gerald	(317) 237-7965		$340.00	$340.00
	Kimmerly	Anistasia	(317) 687-0819	(317) 687-4998	$400.00	$400.00
	Hankla	Gretchen	(317) 779-4773		$100.00	$100.00

Record: 1 of 25

Figure 12-5: The Datasheet view of the multiple-table summarized query.

Rolling Up Your Sleeves and Building the Query by Hand

Using a wizard to build your multiple-table queries isn't always the best solution. Maybe the query is too complex or requires some special summaries (or perhaps you just don't feel up to tangling with the Query Wizard at the moment). For those times when creating a query by hand is the best choice, use Design view instead.

Although it sometimes looks a bit complicated, Design view is nothing to be afraid of. After you get the hang of it, you may discover that you *prefer* building queries this way. (What a scary thought!)

TIP

A gaggle of geese, a waggle of wizards

Is there a collective noun for a group of wizards? If not, there should be, because Access 2000 is loaded down with a whole plethora of wizardly assistants. Chapter 11 introduces the Simple Query Wizard, the most useful wizard for your general Access 2000 query needs.

But the wizard corps doesn't stop there. Access 2000 includes three other Query wizards that await your call: the Crosstab Query Wizard, Find Duplicates Query Wizard, and Find Unmatched Query Wizard.

Unfortunately, not all of the wizards are as straightforward as the Simple Query Wizard. Of the remaining four, the Crosstab Wizard is the only one that normal humans are likely to use. For more about the Crosstab Wizard, check out Chapter 14. The remaining two wizards (Find Duplicates Query Wizard and Find Unmatched Query Wizard) are so weird that you don't need to worry about them.

Here are a couple of quick starting thoughts to brighten your day before getting into the details of Design view:

✔ It is not a good idea to build database relationships between your tables until the design and construction of your database is complete. Building your relationships within the queries is typically a much better approach because you can change your table designs in the future without having to delete your database relationships. When your database design and construction is complete, building relationships for the database can be very useful for automating updates between tables. For the scoop about relating tables together, see Chapter 5.

✔ If you know how to build single-table queries, you're already well on your way to creating multiple-table queries, because the process is almost exactly the same.

To build a multiple-table query by hand in Design view (the way Grandma used to make 'em, by golly), follow these steps:

1. **Click the Queries button below the Objects bar on the left side of the database window.**

   The database window lists all of your queries, ready for action.

   Before starting a new multiple-table query, make sure that the tables are related! If you aren't sure about the table relationships, get back to the database window and click the Relationships button on the toolbar. For more about table relationships, see Chapter 5.

2. **Double-click on Create a query in Design view.**

   After a moment, the Show Table dialog box appears. Behind it, you see the blank query window where your query will soon take shape.

3. **Double-click on the name of the first table you want to include in the query.**

   A small window for the table appears in the query window (see Figure 12-6).

4. **Repeat Step 3 for each table you want to add to the query. When you're done, click on Close to make the Show Table dialog box go away.**

   Don't worry if lines appear between your tables in the query window (see Figure 12-7). That's actually a good thing — it shows that Access 2000 knows how to link the two tables.

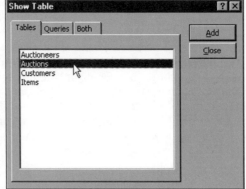

Figure 12-6:
The first
table takes
its place in
the query.

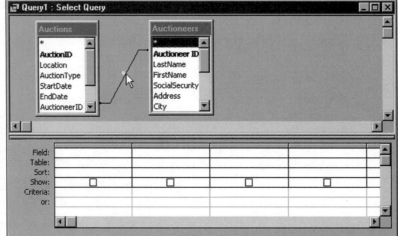

Figure 12-7:
Access 2000
knows how
to link
the Auctions
table to
Auctioneers.

If you're done adding tables to the query but there aren't any lines between the tables, Access is telling you that it doesn't have a clue how to link the tables together. Your best bet at this point is to cancel the query by closing the query window, and then use the Relationships button to build some relationships.

5. **Add fields to the query grid by double-clicking on them in the table dialog boxes (as shown in Figure 12-8). Repeat this step for all of the fields you want to include in the query.**

   Pick your fields in the order you want them to appear in the query results. Feel free to include fields from any or all of the tables at the top of the query window. After all, that's why you included the tables in the query to begin with.

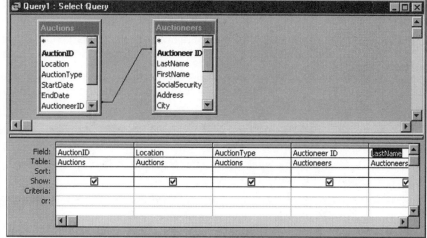

Figure 12-8:
You can mix
and match
fields from
different
tables in a
single
query.

If you accidentally choose the wrong field, you can easily fix your mistake. Click on the field name's entry in the query grid and then select the oddly named Edit⇨Delete Columns option from the menu bar. The incorrect field's entry (its column) is gone.

6. **With your fields in place, take a minute to set the sort order, if you want one. To sort by a particular field, click in the Sort box under the field name and then click on the down arrow that appears at the edge of the Sort box. Click on either Ascending or Descending (see Figure 12-9).**

Repeat this step if you want to sort by more than one field.

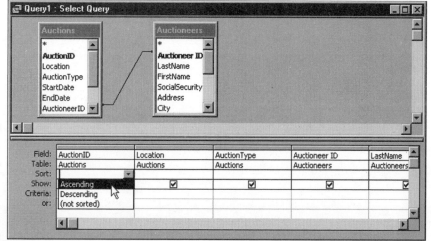

Figure 12-9:
A-sorting
we will
go . . .
ascending,
that is.

7. **In the Criteria box for each field, set up the selection information for the query.**

   Even though this is a multiple-table query, you build criteria in the same way you did for single-table queries. Refer to Chapter 11 for help.

8. **If you want to include a field in the query but you don't want that field to appear in the final results, uncheck the Show entry for that field.**

   Odds are you won't ever need this step, but the nerd in me demands that I mention it.

9. **Review your work one more time. When you're sure it looks good, save the query by choosing File⇨Save.**

10. **In the Save As dialog box, type a name for the query and then click on OK.**

    You don't want to lose all that hard work by not saving your query!

11. **Cross your fingers and then choose Query⇨Run (or click on the Run button) to run your query.**

    How did it work? Did you get the answer you hoped for? If not, take your query back into Design view for some more work.

12. **Choose View⇨Design View (or click on the Design button).**

    Keep at it until you get your query just right. Remember to save your changes with File⇨Save!

Chapter 13

Lions AND Bears OR Tigers? Oh, My!

- -

In This Chapter

▶ The difference between AND and OR

▶ Using the AND function

▶ Using the OR function

▶ Using AND and OR in the same query

- -

*I*t's a fact of life: The longer you work with Access 2000, the more complex are the questions that you ask of your data. Sorting your stuff up, down, right, and left, and filtering it through and through is not enough — now you want it to march in formation while doing animal impressions. (Well, you always did set high goals.)

Access 2000 queries may make your data do tricks, but even queries need some help to complete the most advanced prestidigitation. That's where Dr. Boole and his magic operators enter the picture. By enlisting the unique capabilities of Boolean operators, your queries can scale new heights, perform amazing acrobatics, and generally amuse and astound both you and your coworkers. They may even surprise your boss!

This chapter looks at AND and OR, the two main operators in the world of Access 2000. It explains what the operators do, how they do it, and (most importantly) why you care. Get ready for a wild ride through the world of logic — strap your data in tight!

Comparing AND to OR

AND and OR are the stars of the Boolean sky. In spoken and written language, AND sticks phrases together into a complex whole, while OR describes a bunch of options from which to choose. In the world of databases, they perform much the same duty.

For example, if the woods are full of *lions AND tigers,* you can expect to find both types of animals anticipating your arrival. On the other hand, if the woods are full of *lions OR tigers,* then you know that *one or the other* is out there, but you don't expect to see both. In database terminology, AND means *both,* whereas OR means *either* (egad — this sounds like a grammar class).

Here's an easy rule to keep the two operators straight:

- ✔ AND narrows your query, making it more restrictive.
- ✔ OR opens up your query, so more records match.

If you start looking for an individual with blue eyes AND red hair AND over six feet tall AND male, you have a relatively small group of candidates (and I'm not among them). On the other hand, if you look for people with blue eyes OR red hair OR under six feet tall OR male, the matching group is much, much bigger. In fact, half of the people who worked on the book — including my spitz dog — meet the criteria.

Finding Things between Kansas AND Oz

One of the most common queries involves listing items that fall between two particular values. For example, you may want to find all the records that were entered after January 1, 1999, and before January 1, 2000. To ask this type of question, you use an AND criteria.

Using an AND criteria is pretty easy. Put the two conditions together on the same line and separate them with an AND. Figure 13-1 shows the query screen restricting DateIn in the Items table of the Auction database to sometime during the year 2000. By the way, don't worry about the pound signs — Access puts those in automatically to feel like it contributed something useful to your query. Wait a minute! Since when do we put pound signs around a date? Call it a condition of the drinking water at Redmond that caused the engineers there to come up with this one, but for some reason you must place pound signs around dates only.

Take a close look at the formula in the query. Access 2000 begins processing the query by sifting through the records in the table and asking the first question in the criteria, "Was the record entered *on or after* January 1, 1999?" If the record was entered before this date, Access 2000 ignores it and goes on to the next one. If the record was entered after January 1, 1999, Access 2000 asks the second question, "Was the record entered before January 1, 2000?" If yes, Access 2000 includes the record in the results. If not, the record gets rejected and Access 2000 moves on to the next one. Notice that the comparison uses greater than or equal for the first date (January 1, 1999), because you want to include records written on the first day of the year as well.

This type of "between" instruction works for any type of data. You can list numeric values that fall between two other numbers, names that fall within a range of letters, or dates that fall within a given area of the calendar. Access 2000 doesn't care *what* kind of data you test.

When making a "between" type of query, make sure that you correctly match the greater than and less than operators with the right criteria. If you reverse them, your query won't work at all! For example, no single record could be created both *before* January 1, 1999 and *after* January 1, 2000. The record may fall between those dates as in the example above, but it can't be outside *both* of them. If you change that AND to an OR, though, the query can work, because a single record *can* be created either before one OR after the other.

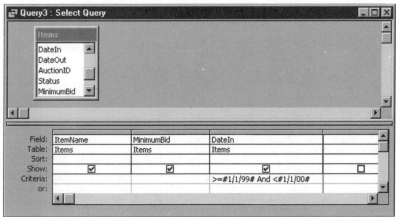

Figure 13-1:
The AND function finds all dates between January 1, 1999, and January 1, 2000.

Multiple ANDs: AND Then What Happened?

One of the best things about Access 2000 (apart from this book) is its flexibility. Overall, Access lets you do whatever you want in a query. For instance, Access doesn't limit you to just *one* criteria in each line of a query — heck, no! You can include as many criteria as you want. Access 2000 treats the criteria as if you typed an AND between each one.

Multiple criteria queries are tricky, though. Each criteria that you add must sit together on the same row. When you run the query, Access 2000 checks each record to make sure that it matches all of the expressions in the given criteria row of the query before putting that record into the result table. Figure 13-2 shows a query that uses three criteria. Because all of the criteria sit together on a single row, Access treats the three criteria as if they were part of a big AND statement. This query only returns records for auctions held at "The Ranch" that included items from customer "Donati" that had a minimum bid of less than $25.

When you have a very large database and you want to restrict your results down to a minimum of records, combining a few criteria together is the most useful way to go.

Need to narrow your results even more? (Wow, your boss *is* demanding!) Because Access 2000 displays the query results in Datasheet view, all of the cool Datasheet view tools work with the query — tools like your old friend, the filter! Just use any of the filter commands (on the Records⇨Filter menu) to limit and massage your query results. If you need a quick refresher about filters, flip back to Chapter 10.

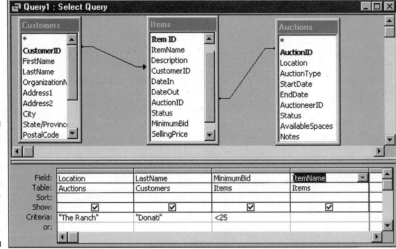

Figure 13-2: Finding the one record that meets all your requirements.

Are You a Good Witch OR a Bad Witch?

Often, you want to find a group of records that match one of several different possibilities, (such as people who live in France OR Belgium OR the United States). This kind of search calls for the OR criteria, the master of multiple options.

Access 2000 makes using an OR criteria almost too easy for words. There's nothing special to type, nothing to buy, and no salesman will call. In fact, the OR option is built right into the Access query dialog box, ready and waiting for your call.

To make a group of criteria work together as a big OR statement, list each criteria on its own line at the bottom of the query. Each line can include criteria for whichever fields you want, even if another line in the query *already* has a criteria in that field. (Trust me, this is easier than it sounds.) The example in Figure 13-3 uses three criteria in the same field, Animals. By putting them on different lines, the query looks for records continuing either with Lions OR Bears OR Tigers.

Figure 13-3:
The built-in OR command lets you find all the scary beasties in the forest.

Field:	Animals	Where?	What they eat		
Table:	Animals in OZ	Animals in OZ	Animals in OZ		
Sort:					
Show:	☑	☑	☑	☐	
Criteria:	"Lions"				
or:	"Tigers"				
	"Bears"				

Of course, you can list the criteria in different columns, too. For example, Figure 13-4 shows the Items table of the Auction database with a request for items that were entered by the Donati family OR which have a MinimumBid of $30 or less.

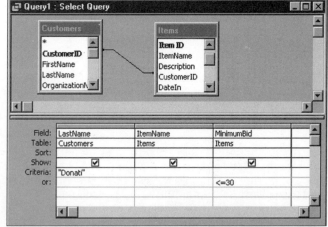

Figure 13-4:
You can create OR criteria from different fields.

Field:	LastName	ItemName	MinimumBid		
Table:	Customers	Items	Items		
Sort:					
Show:	☑	☑	☑		
Criteria:	"Donati"				
or:			<=30		

Notice that each of the criteria is on a separate line. If the criteria were listed on the same line, you would be doing an AND operation, and only those records that matched both rules would appear.

Figure 13-5 shows the results of the query with labels indicating why each record is included. Notice that you have some records that match each of the rules and a few records that actually match both. Had you set this query up as an AND query, you would have gotten only the records that matched both.

Figure 13-5:
Breaking
down the
results of
the query.

LastName	Item Name	Minimum Bid
Ingle	Box of ham radio magazines	$30.00
Donati	Wedding dress	$760.00
Donati	Engagement ring	$550.00
Donati	97 Audio CDs	$20.00
Donati	Miscellaneous men's clothing	$20.00
Haseman	Board games (5)	$10.00
Rosen-Sheid	3 cast iron toys	$22.00
Allen-Brown	Asst hardback books	$30.00
Allen-Brown	Asst hardback books	$30.00
Allen-Brown	Asst hardback books	$30.00
Allen-Brown	Asst hardback books	$30.00

This record is $30.

These records match only the 'Donati' criteria.

These records match both criteria.

These records are $30 or less.

AND and OR? AND or OR?

Sometimes, using the AND and OR operators by themselves isn't enough. You need to ask a question about several different groups. Part of the question involves restricting the groups (with an AND), and other parts require including records based on a different criteria (with an OR).

Be careful with these queries. They get *really* fancy *really* fast. If a query grows to the point that you're losing track of which AND the last OR affected, then you're in over your head. Either start over or seek help from a qualified database nerd.

The most important point to remember is that each OR line (each line within the criteria) is evaluated separately. If you want to combine several different criteria, you need to make sure that each OR line represents one aspect of what you are doing.

For example, in the Auctions database, knowing which items will sell for less than $30 or more than $100 at a single auction site may be useful. Finding the items in those price ranges requires the use of an OR condition. (If you were trying to find items with a MinimumBid *between* $30 and $100, you would use an AND criteria instead.) Using an OR condition means that the criteria go on separate lines.

However, that restriction isn't enough. You only want the items that are for sale at one site (in this example, it's The Ranch). For this query to work, you need to repeat the site information on each OR line. Congratulations — you have a bouncing baby AND/OR combination query.

To set this query up, you need a two criteria line. One criteria asks for those items that are less than $30 AND are for sale at site one; the other criteria calls out items that are over $100 AND are for sale at site one. Because the criteria are on two lines, Access treats them as a big OR statement. Figure 13-6 shows the two ANDs with an OR. (I could try to insert a joke about one line lending an *AND* to the other, but I think it would be a bit much. You can thank me later.)

Figure 13-6:
Any criteria on the same line are AND functions and restrict the search. Criteria on different lines are OR functions and expand the search.

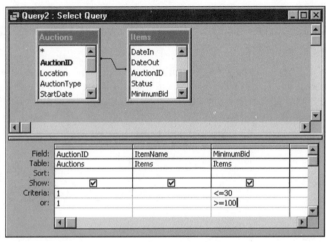

When reviewing your criteria, look at each line separately to make sure that line represents a group that you want included in the final answer. Then check to see that the individual lines work together to distill the answer you're seeking:

- ✔ AND criteria all go on the same line and are evaluated together.

- ✔ OR criteria go on separate lines, and each line is evaluated separately.

- ✔ If you have criteria that you want to use in each of the ORs, they must be repeated on each of the separate lines.

As with other types of queries, you don't have to use the same fields on each OR row. In fact, each row can be entirely separate. For example, Figure 13-7 shows a criteria asking for those items that are being sold by the Donati family at site one OR items that are being sold for less than $100 at site two. Notice that both rows use the site location, but that the items that are combined with them are separate.

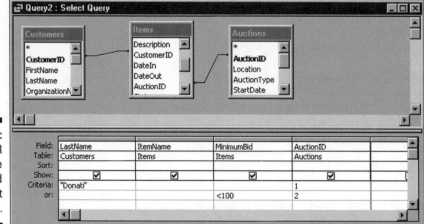

Figure 13-7:
Your OR
rows can be
represented
in different
fields.

To add another OR to the stew, just fill in another row. As soon as you press enter, you can use the scroll bars on the right side of the screen to see additional query rows. The additional rows, even though they are not labeled, all function as separate OR rows.

Chapter 14

Teaching Queries to Think and Count

In This Chapter

▶ Using the Totals row

▶ Grouping entries together

▶ Understanding the Count and Sum functions

▶ Asking crosstab queries

▶ Choosing the top values

▶ Applying more functions

*G*etting quick answers to simple questions about the stuff in your data-base is nice, but there's more to life than finding out precisely how many folks from Montreal or Bombay bought pastel-colored back scratchers between January and May of the previous year. What if you needed to know the total amount of money they spent on back scratchers? Or the number of orders they placed? Or wanted to see which 25 cities purchased the most?

In what's rapidly becoming a recurring theme of the book, Access 2000 comes to the rescue. Well, technically speaking, it's Access 2000 *query calculations* and *counting tools* to the rescue.

Query calculations do simple math, count matching entries, and perform several other tricks, provided you know how to ask for their help. The program's Top Values tool quickly and easily helps you focus on the records that *best* match your criteria. This chapter explains the inner workings of these helpful functions. Read on and put those queries to work!

Totaling Everything in Sight

In addition to just answering questions, Select queries can also perform simple calculations on the data in your tables. For example, if you tell Access to list all the customers from Germany, it can count them at no extra charge. What a deal!

The first step in adding a total to your query is to turn on the Total row in the query grid. (For the sake of keeping queries as simple as possible, Access doesn't display this row by default.) With your query on-screen, select View⇨Totals from the main menu or click on the Totals button. Figure 14-1 shows the Select Query screen with the Total row added.

Figure 14-1:
The Total
row appears
between the
Table row
and the
Sort row.

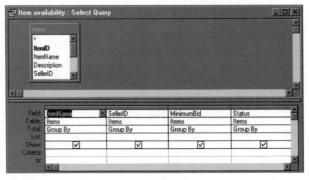

The symbol on the face of the Totals button is the Greek letter *sigma,* meaning *to add everything up.* Mathematicians, engineers, and others with interpersonal communication difficulties use this symbol when they want a total.

To use the Total row, set up an average, normal Select query, just as you usually do. As you add the fields to the grid, the Total row fills in with the Group By entry automatically. The Group By entry tells Access to organize the query results into groups based on that particular field. In addition, the Group By entry eliminates duplicate entries in your results. For example, a normal query that includes only the DateIn field lists all of the dates that items arrived at the auction. If four items arrived on the same date, that date appears in the list four times. By turning on the Group By option, Access generates a *unique* list of all the dates on which new items were added to the auction (as shown in Figure 14-2).

Each date is listed only once, even though several items may have come in that day (which means that several records with that date exist in the database). Without the Group By instruction, the query would list the date each time it appears in the database.

Figure 14-2: The Group By instruction lists each entry in the field only once.

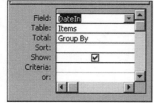

If you have more than one field showing with the Group By instruction, the query results show each unique combination of those two fields. For example, Figure 14-3 shows a query with the Group By instruction in both the Item Name and the DateIn fields. Figure 14-4 lists the results of the query.

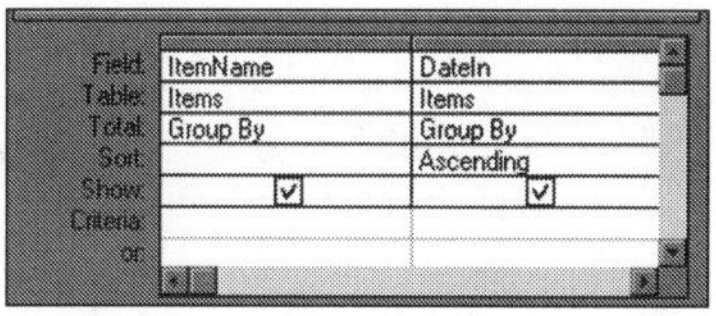

Figure 14-3: The query lists all items and their arrival dates while sorted by date.

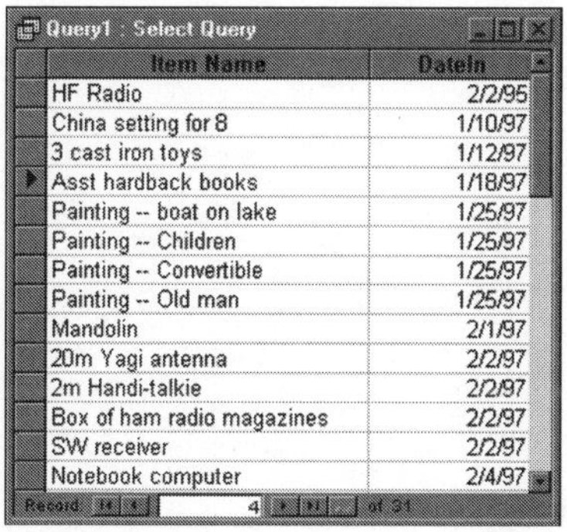
Query1 : Select Query

Item Name	DateIn
HF Radio	2/2/95
China setting for 8	1/10/97
3 cast iron toys	1/12/97
Asst hardback books	1/18/97
Painting -- boat on lake	1/25/97
Painting -- Children	1/25/97
Painting -- Convertible	1/25/97
Painting -- Old man	1/25/97
Mandolin	2/1/97
20m Yagi antenna	2/2/97
2m Handi-talkie	2/2/97
Box of ham radio magazines	2/2/97
SW receiver	2/2/97
Notebook computer	2/4/97

Record: 4 of 31

Figure 14-4: The query lists the items in order by the DateIn field.

In Figure 14-4, each date shows every item added and the date it arrived. Notice that for dates such as February 2, several different items are listed as having come into the auction. On the other hand, when the same type of item was brought in (such as the Asst hardback books that came in on January 18), the item is only listed once because the Item Name was the same for each record.

When you use Group By, tread very carefully. Group By is a very powerful tool, but it's also an easy one to misuse by accident. (I shudder to think of how many times I messed up my results with it!) The more fields that you use with a Total query, the better your results. The results get strange sometimes (such as the note above concerning the hardback books) if you include only two or three fields in the query.

Counting the Good Count

Although listing the unique entries in a field is useful, the Total row can do much more. Another useful option is the *Count* instruction, which as the name implies, counts matching records in your table and displays the total in your query results.

The Count instruction requires at least two entries in your query: one to create the groups (with Group By in the Totals row) and one to count (with Count in the Totals row).

Select the Count function by clicking on the cell in the Total row for the field that you want to count. After you click, a down-arrow button appears. Click on the down-arrow to see a drop-down list of functions, one of which is Count.

The most difficult part of the whole operation is deciding which field to use for counting. If you want to count each record that matches, you must be certain that the field you use has a unique entry for each and every record. For example, Figure 14-5 shows the Query that Dorothy uses to count the number of members in each of the guilds.

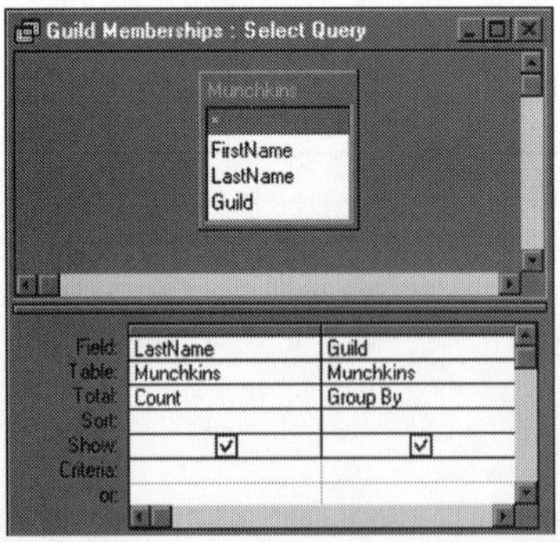

Figure 14-5:
Access calculates the number of members in each guild.

In the Guild field's Total row, Dorothy uses the Group By instruction. For her other field in this query, she uses LastName. To do the arithmetic, she includes a Count instruction in the LastName field's Total row. Group By tells

Access to group the records by the entry in the Guild field, and Count tells Access to count the records in each group (guild), increasing the count by one for each record with a last name. Because all Munchkins have last names, this instruction means that Access counts the number of Munchkins in each guild. Figure 14-6 shows the results of Dorothy's search.

Figure 14-6:
The Great
Guild
Membership
Count is
complete.

Counting with Crosstab

Some types of information naturally lend themselves to being grouped by two categories. For example, polls often use gender (which is traditionally a two-option category) to break down their results for each question. You can do the same kind of breakdown in Access with a crosstab (or *cross tabulation*) query.

Figure 14-7 shows what crosstab results look like. Even though you may not know the name *crosstab,* you more than likely recognize how it works. This crosstab breaks down auction information by the home states of the customers and the location where their items were sold. Each row represents a different state, and each column represents one of the sites. Each box within the table contains the number of customers from that state who sold items at that site. Four states and two sites make eight values in the table.

Figure 14-7:
The
Datasheet
view of a
crosstab
query.

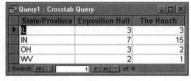

A crosstab query grid includes both the Total and the Crosstab row (as shown in Figure 14-8). Crosstab queries always involve three fields. *Row Heading* is used for the row categories. *Column Heading* tells Access 2000 where to find the column category. The third field explains where the values for the crosstab come from.

Figure 14-8:
In a crosstab query, one field becomes the Row Heading, one the Column Heading, and one the Value.

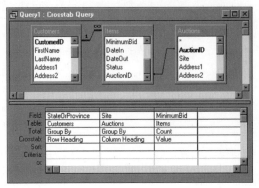

Both of the fields used as headings have a Group By instruction on the Total row. The field used for value has the function (usually Count, Sum, or Avg) that is used for calculating the values for the table.

You can also use one or many criteria to limit which records are included in the summary. As with other queries in this chapter, you do so by adding a criteria to one of the fields already being used. The easiest way to do this is by adding another field to the query, using the Where instruction (so that the field doesn't show up in the results), and then adding the criteria to that field.

Of course, you don't have to do all this stuff by hand. The Crosstab Query Wizard guides you through each of the steps for a basic crosstab query. Take advantage of it; otherwise, the wizard begins to feel lonely. To start the Crosstab Wizard, open your database and then click on the Queries Options Bar button (no surprises there). Click the New button in the database window and then double-click on Crosstab Query Wizard. Follow the wizard's carefully presented path to find crosstab success.

Does It All Add Up?

You can use other functions on the Total row instead of Count, Where, or Group By. One of the most useful is the Sum function, which totals the data in one or more numeric fields of your table.

For example, you can use just the MinimumBid field from the Items table of the Auction database with the Sum function and no other field. To create a query that sums a total, add the MinimumBid field to your query grid and use the Sum instruction on the Total row. Leave the rest of the grid blank. The records are put into one large group and then values in the MinimumBid field are added together to create the sum. By running that query, you get the total amount of all minimum bids, as shown in Figure 14-9.

Figure 14-9:
Total all
the values
in a field
by using
the Sum
function.

As with the Count function, you can combine the Sum function with other instructions on the Total row (or even with criteria). For example, you may want to find out what the total is for each Seller ID number. To do so, you simply add the SellerID field to your query with a Group By instruction, as shown in Figure 14-10.

Figure 14-10:
When you
use the Total
row, each
field must
have an
entry. Here,
I calculate
the mini-
mum bids
total for
each seller.

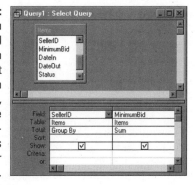

When you run that query, you see the results shown in Figure 14-11. Each Seller ID is listed individually with the total for that seller.

Figure 14-11:
If you
combine
SellerID
with Group
By, you get
the total
value of the
minimum
bids for
each seller.

Seller ID	SumOfMinimumBid
3	120
5	45
6	100
9	750
11	85
12	2375
14	125
15	22
20	1350
21	225
22	120
37	400
41	2245
49	1030

If you want to have the seller's name rather than the ID number, all you need to do is set up a multiple-table query that links to the Customer table by the ID number. To complete the process (for this example), you use the LastName field for your Group By rather than SellerID, as shown in Figure 14-12. When you run the query, the information is organized by last name with the total minimum bid for each individual instead of simply listing the seller number.

Figure 14-12:
Using the
Customer
table, you
can organize
your query
by seller
name rather
than by ID
number.

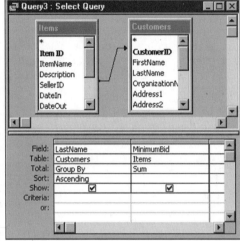

Here's a tidbit from the Because You're Already Here School of Access 2000: You can also activate the Sort function and have the list organized in descending order (largest to smallest) by any field in your query. To do that, put the *Descending* instruction on the Sort line under the field you want to sort with. Figure 14-13 shows the Auction query set up with a descending sort on the MinimumBid field.

The query's results are shown in Figure 14-14.

You can find more about the Sort row in Chapter 11. If you're curious about sorting in general, flip to Chapter 10.

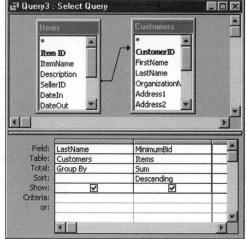

Figure 14-13:
Having
Access 2000
sort the
minimum
bids in
descending
order
is easy.

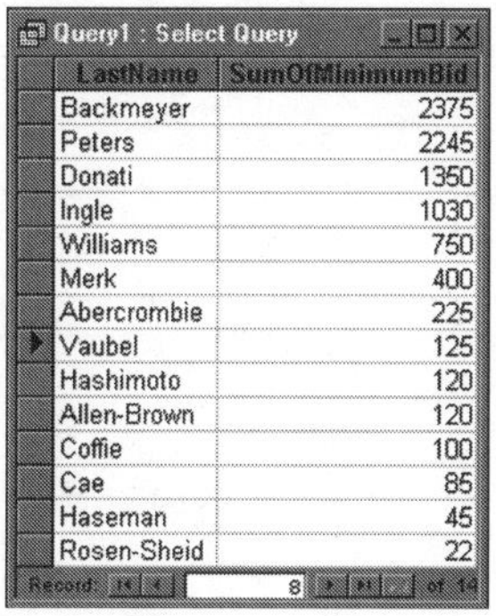

Figure 14-14:
The results
are in —
and in order
from largest
to smallest.

There's More to Life Than Sum and Count

Don't get the idea that the world of queries begins and ends with Sum and Count. Access 2000 includes many other functions to organize, evaluate, and generally figure out what your data is saying. Some of the more popular and useful functions are listed in Table 14-1.

Each entry in the table includes the name of the function and a brief description of what it does. Each function can be selected from the drop-down list on the Total line.

Table 14-1	Access Functions and What They Do
Function	*Purpose*
Group By	Organizes the query results in this field
Sum	Adds up all the values from this field in the query results
Avg	Calculates the average of the values in this field
Min	Tells you the lowest value the query finds
Max	Gives you the highest value the query finds
Count	Tells you the number of records that match the query criteria
First	Returns the first record that Access 2000 stumbles across that meets the query criteria
Last	Returns the last matching record Access 2000 finds or the opposite of First
Expression	Tells Access that you want a calculated field (see Chapter 15 for more information)
Where	Tells Access to use this field as part of the query criteria

Chapter 15

Calculating Your Way to Fame and Fortune

. . . .

In This Chapter

▶ Developing an expression

▶ Performing more complex calculations

▶ Calculating text fields

▶ Using the Expression Builder

. . . .

*O*ne of the big rules in database creation is the decree that a table should contain as few fields as possible. Smaller tables load faster, are easier to document and maintain, and take up less disk space. One extra field isn't much by itself, but it adds up when your table contains several hundred thousand records!

So how do the pros keep their tables small? By storing only what they *really* need and using *calculations* to figure out whatever else they require. For example, if your table contains the wholesale cost and the retail price of an item, then why bother storing the markup percentage? When you need that information, use a *calculated field* to create it on the fly!

A calculated field takes information from another field in the database and performs some arithmetic to come up with new information. In fact, a calculated field can take data from more than one field and combine information to create an entirely new field, if that's what you want.

This chapter shows you how to build all kinds of calculations into queries. From simple sums to complex equations, the info you need is right here.

Although the examples in this chapter deal with calculated fields within queries, the same concept applies to calculated fields within reports. For a few tips about calculating fields and reports, flip ahead to Chapter 20.

A Simple Calculation

When you want to create a calculated field within a query, first figure out which fields you need for the calculation and then find out which tables contain those fields. The query must include all of the tables on your list. If the fields live in one table, just include that one table in the query (see Figure 15-1). If the fields are split among several tables, make sure to include all of the tables containing fields that you want to use in the calculation at the top of the query screen. Otherwise, Access can't do the calculations. (Even with its sometimes amazing antics, Access is *still* merely software — it's not terribly bright, and it gets confused easily.)

Figure 15-1: To calculate the expected price for an item, you just need the MinimumBid and ItemName (so you know which item it is) fields.

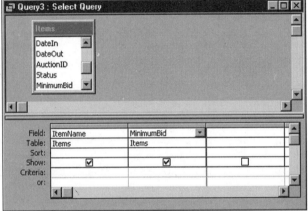

Start building the calculated field by clicking in the empty field name box of the column where you want the results to appear. Instead of selecting an existing field, type the calculation that you want Access 2000 to perform.

As you may suspect, Access uses a special syntax for building calculated fields. You can't just type *add these together and display the result* — that's *way* too simple and understandable. Surprisingly, though, calculating is not much tougher than that.

Basically, you type the calculation just like you enter it into a pocket calculator, except that you substitute field names for at least some of the numbers. The key to the whole process is the square bracket symbol ([ ]). To make Access understand which parts of the calculation are fields, you put square brackets around the field names themselves. Access miraculously recognizes that those entries refer to fields in your table. Anything else Access finds in the calculation (such as numbers, for example), Access treats as constants (which is the math nerd term for *it means whatever it says*).

Using the auction example, suppose that research says that most items sell for 47 percent more than the minimum bid price. To calculate the expected price, you need to add 47 percent to the MinimumBid. One formula to do this is

```
[MinimumBid] + ([MinimumBid] * .47)
```

The square brackets around `MinimumBid` tell Access that MinimumBid is a field in the table, not just a bunch of text in the calculation. Because the `.47` on the end doesn't have any brackets around it, Access assumes that you mean the numeric value .47. Because Access 2000 isn't smart enough to recognize the percent sign, you need to convert percentages to decimals (thus 47% turns into .47).

Calculations go into the Field line anywhere in your query. Figure 15-2 shows the calculation in progress, sitting in the empty Field box next to MinimumBid. Figure 15-3 proudly displays the finished formula.

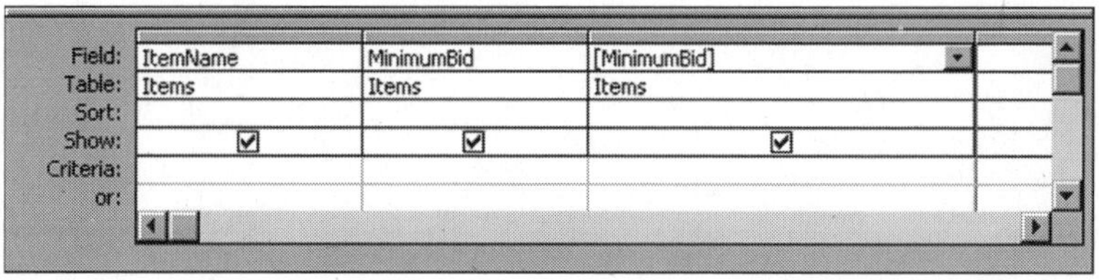

Figure 15-2:
Using
square
brackets
tells Access
that you are
discussing
a field.

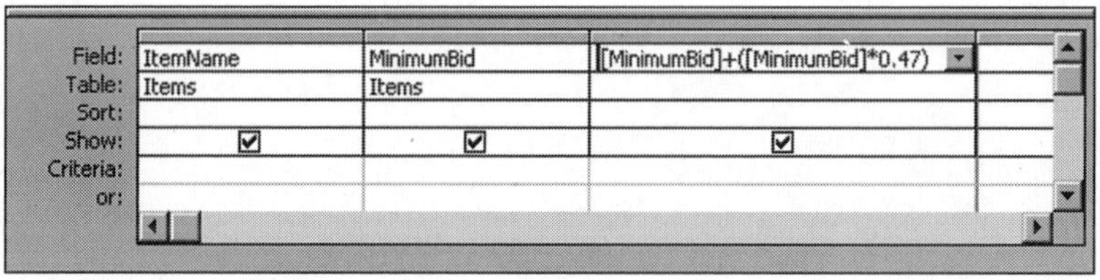

Figure 15-3:
The formula
for the
expected
price of your
sale items.

✔ You have to manually type each field name into your formula — you can't just drag the field name down from the table list. Dragging down the field name adds it as a field itself (which isn't *quite* what you had in mind).

✔ Don't worry if your query grows past the edge of the Field box. Access still remembers everything, even if it doesn't appear on-screen. For a quick tip about adjusting the query grid to make some extra room, see the nearby sidebar "Isn't that box a little small?".

✔ To include fields from more than one table in a single calculation, tell Access the table name for each field in the query. Hang on to your hat — the details get kinda weird. To include the table name with the field in the calculation, type the table name in square brackets, type an exclamation point, and then type the field name in square brackets. Your finished entry looks something like this: `[table]![field]`. Yes, it *does* sound like some kind of odd fraternity ritual.

When you run a query containing a calculation, Access produces a datasheet showing the fields you specified, plus it adds a new column for the calculated field. In Figure 15-4, the datasheet shows the item name, the minimum bid, and the calculated field containing the expected price for each item.

ItemName	MinimumBid	Expr1
China setting for 8	$85.00	124.95
3 Cast iron toys	$22.00	32.34
Box of Ham Radio Magazines	$30.00	44.1
Asst hardback books (2 of 4)	$30.00	44.1
Asst hardback books (3 of 4)	$30.00	44.1
Asst hardback books (4 of 4)	$30.00	44.1
Painting -- boat on lake	$100.00	147
Painting -- Children	$100.00	147
Painting -- Convertible	$100.00	147
Painting -- Old man	$100.00	147
Painting -- Round Barn	$100.00	147
Mandolin	$125.00	183.75
HF Radio	$400.00	588

Record: 1 of 25

Figure 15-4: The calculation actually works!

Isn't that box a little small?

Because the field box in the query grid is kinda small, the grid may not display your entire calculation at once. Isn't that just like a computer? Although the query *stores* your whole calculation, Access may or may not be able to show it all to you.

If that happens, you have two choices: Either keep typing and trust that what you are typing is actually going into the field or enlarge the field so that it is wide enough to display the entire formula. I'm a trusting soul, but because I also like making sure that my query calculations are accurate, I usually vote for resizing the query grid a bit.

To make the field area bigger, move the mouse pointer into the gray box above the field name; then click and drag the line at the right end of the box. Your mouse pointer changes into a funky line bisected with two arrows, which is one of the official Windows resizing cursors. Drag the mouse as far to the right as necessary. The box expands as you go. When the box is big enough, release the mouse button.

Notice that the column for the expected price is labeled a little strangely. Left to its own devices, Access came up with the clever moniker Expr1, which stands for Expression 1. Expr1 is the default name for the first expression (or formula) in a calculation. Changing the expression heading is easy. If you look back at the query grid after creating an expression, you find that Access 2000 inserted the Expr1 default field name and a colon in front of the calculation. To give the field a different name, simply highlight Expr1 and type your replacement (as shown in Figure 15-5).

Figure 15-5:
The words before the expression create the label for the finished calculation.

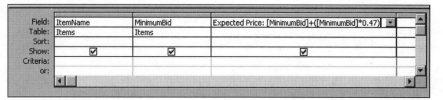

In addition to changing the field name, you may want to change its format. To change the format of the field, right-click on the field in the query grid and select Properties from the pop-up menu. In the Field Properties dialog box (shown in Figure 15-6), click in the Format line and then click on the button that appears on the right end of the field (the one with the downward-pointing arrow).

Figure 15-6:
Use the Field Properties dialog box to change the formatting of your fields.

In the drop-down list that appears, select the type of format that you want to use for the field. For this example, select Currency. Figure 15-7 shows the resulting table after you change the name of the field to Expected Price and use the Currency format for all the values.

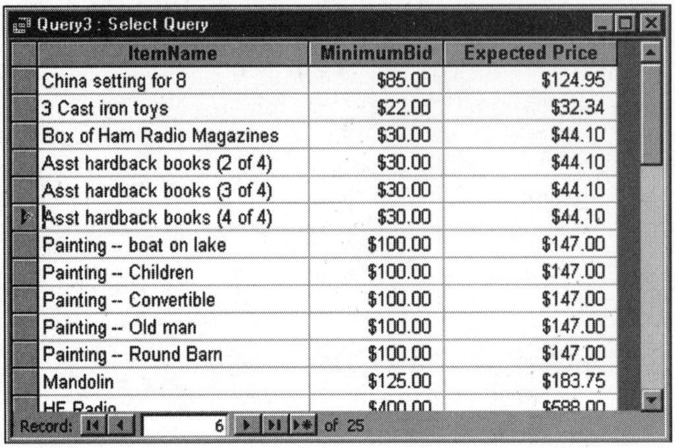

Figure 15-7:
Using the
Format sec-
tion of the
Field
Properties
dialog box,
you can set
a particular
format for
any field.

ItemName	MinimumBid	Expected Price
China setting for 8	$85.00	$124.95
3 Cast iron toys	$22.00	$32.34
Box of Ham Radio Magazines	$30.00	$44.10
Asst hardback books (2 of 4)	$30.00	$44.10
Asst hardback books (3 of 4)	$30.00	$44.10
Asst hardback books (4 of 4)	$30.00	$44.10
Painting -- boat on lake	$100.00	$147.00
Painting -- Children	$100.00	$147.00
Painting -- Convertible	$100.00	$147.00
Painting -- Old man	$100.00	$147.00
Painting -- Round Barn	$100.00	$147.00
Mandolin	$125.00	$183.75
HF Radio	$400.00	$588.00

Query3 : Select Query

Record: 6 of 25

Bigger, Better (And More Complicated) Calculations

After getting the hang of simple calculations, you can easily expand your
repertoire into more powerful operations, such as using multiple calculations
and building expressions that use the values from *other* calculations in the
same query. This stuff really adds to the flexibility and power of queries.

Add another calculation — go ahead, add two!

Access makes it easy to put multiple calculations into a single query. After
building the first calculation, just repeat the process in the next empty Field
box. Keep inserting calculations across the query grid until you just don't
care anymore — Access gleefully lets you keep right on going.

Figure 15-8 shows how multiple calculations look in the query grid. The
query contains three calculations, labeled `Expr1`, `Expr2`, and `Expr3`. Both
Expr2 and Expr3 use the MinimumBid field. (Expr3 also uses the value from
the second calculation, but that's covered in the next section.)

It's perfectly legal to use the same field in several calculations. Access
doesn't mind at all. (In fact, it probably enjoys the process in some twisted
digital way.)

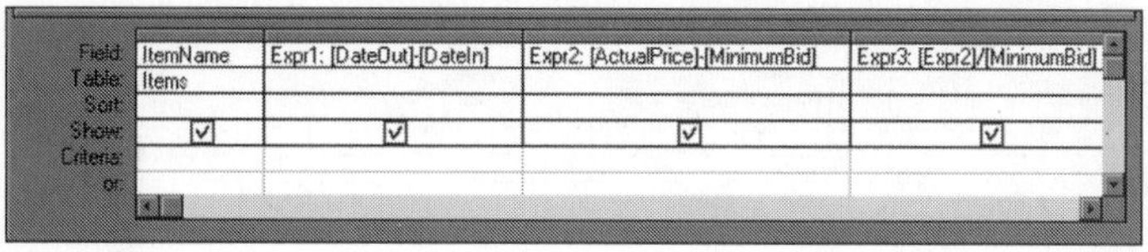

Figure 15-8:
This query
uses three
different
expressions.

Field:	ItemName	Expr1: [DateOut]-[DateIn]	Expr2: [ActualPrice]-[MinimumBid]	Expr3: [Expr2]/[MinimumBid]
Table:	Items			
Sort:				
Show:	☑	☑	☑	☑
Criteria:				
or:				

Using one expression to solve a different question

One of the most powerful calculated field tricks involves using the solution from one calculated field as part of *another* calculation in the same query. Not only does the calculation create a new field in the query results, but the handy calculation also supplies data to other calculations in the same query, just like it's a real field in the table.

Although the details are simple, the technique borders on the realm of true techno-magic. Tread carefully because a small error in one calculation quickly compounds into a huge mistake when other calculations use an accuracy-challenged number.

Each calculation gets a name (the text that sits in front of the calculation in the query grid), whether the name's the default Expr1 or something more colorful, like DaysInStock. To use the results from one calculation as part of another, just include the name of the first calculation in square brackets. In short, treat the first calculation as if it is a field in your table.

The query in Figure 15-8 shows this technique in action. The answer to the second calculation (labeled Expr2) is part of the third calculation (Expr3). Notice that it looks just like any other field in the query — Access doesn't see the field any differently.

Although these formulas produce correct results, the fields would be clearer if they had names that were more descriptive and formatting that was more logical. Figure 15-9 shows the query grid after the names of the fields are changed to DaysToSell, AmountAbove, and Increase. Note that if you change the field name for the second field (the one calculating the difference between the actual sale price and the minimum bid), you need to change the reference to that field in the third formula — in this case, from Expr2 to AmountAbove.

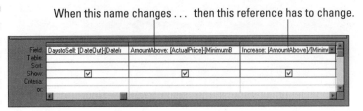

Figure 15-9:
Make sure references match in calculated fields.

When this name changes . . . then this reference has to change.

As with most things, you can build many calculations in more than one way. After looking at the query in Figure 15-9 for a minute, you may realize that displaying the AmountAbove field isn't necessary — you can just include the information for that field directly in the formula for the Increase field. Instead of having AmountAbove above the divisor, your formula would be

```
([ActualPrice]-[MinimumBid])/[MinimumBid]
```

Whichever way you do it is up to you.

Figure 15-10 shows the results of the query using these formulas. Rather than show all the items, the list includes only those items that have been sold (and therefore have ActualPrice and DateOut fields). Setting up such criteria is discussed in Chapter 11, but to refresh your memory — just add the Status field and type **Sold** in the Criteria row.

Figure 15-10:
The results of your calculations for auction items already sold.

Item Name	DaystoSell	AmountAbove	Increase
BW receiver	13	$150.00	46.15%
Portable printer	11	$125.00	71.43%
Wedding dress	0	$440.00	57.89%
Miscellaneous men's clothing	0	$5.00	25.00%
Treadle sewing machine	21	$45.00	56.25%
Box of asst silk thread	6	$5.00	10.00%
50 asst laser disks	2	$50.00	25.00%
Board games (5)	0	$5.00	50.00%
China setting for 8	36	$45.00	52.94%
3 cast iron toys	20	$13.00	59.09%
Asst hardback books	42	$0.00	0.00%
Asst hardback books	14	$10.00	33.33%
Painting -- Children	21	$50.00	50.00%
Painting -- Old man	7	$65.00	65.00%

Record: 1 of 14

Making Access 2000 ask

At times, you may want a value that's not in your database included in a formula. If you already know the value, you can simply type it into the formula, just as you type **.47** for 47 percent (see "A Simple Calculation" earlier in this chapter). But if you'd rather enter that value as you run the query, that's easy to do, too.

Simply create a field name to use within your formula. For example, you may choose to calculate an ExpectedPrice field by using a percentage value that you plan to enter when you run the query. Imagine that this field is called PercentIncrease. You then create your calculated field by using this formula:

```
[MinimumBid]+([MinimumBid]*[PercentIncrease])
```

When you run the query, Access displays a dialog box like the one shown in Figure 15-11. This dialog box lets you enter a value for the increase that you're expecting.

Figure 15-11:
Access asks
you to
provide a
value for
your
calculation.

When the dialog box appears, just enter the value of your expected increase (as a decimal value), and then Access 2000 does the rest. This option means that you can use the same query with different values to see how changing that value affects your results.

Working with words

Number fields aren't the only fields you can use for calculations. In fact, performing the calculation by using a text field is often more useful. Figure 15-12 shows one of the most common database formulas, which is used to combine the FirstName and LastName fields to provide the full name.

Figure 15-12:
You can turn
a name
into a calcu-
lated field.

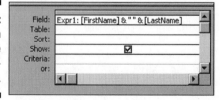

This formula consists of the FirstName field, an ampersand, then a single space inside quotation marks, followed by another ampersand, and then the LastName field:

```
[FirstName]&" "&[LastName]
```

When you run this query, Access 2000 takes the information from the two fields and puts them together, inserting a space in between them. The results of this query are shown in Figure 15-13.

Figure 15-13:
And now the name looks complete once again.

Notice that each individual's name appears as it would on a mailing list label. This kind of text calculation makes taking information from your database and turning it into a more readable format easy.

Expression Builder to the Rescue

Creating calculated fields has two basic problems. First, you have to figure out what the formula should say. And then you have to know how to enter the formula so that Access 2000 can recognize it.

Unfortunately, Access 2000 can't help you with the first problem — but it can help with the second. To get help creating a calculated field the way Access 2000 wants it, click on the Build button and bring out the Expression Builder.

The Expression Builder has several parts to it, as you can see in Figure 15-14. The top part is the area where you actually create the expression, and immediately below that are the operators you can use to work with the information in your expression.

The first group of these operators does simple mathematical operations: addition, subtraction, multiplication, and division. The next operator, the ampersand (&), is similar in that it is used to combine two text fields.

The expressions are put together here.

These are your tools.

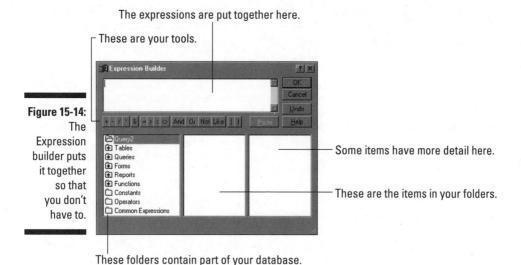

Figure 15-14:
The
Expression
builder puts
it together
so that
you don't
have to.

Some items have more detail here.

These are the items in your folders.

These folders contain part of your database.

The next two groups of operators do logical comparisons. These operators create expressions similar to formulas used in the Criteria field and return a response of True or False. The final two buttons in this collection enable you to enter parentheses. (You can also simply type these symbols directly from your keyboard, which is often much easier.)

The lower half of the dialog box has three windows. The left window contains folders of the various parts of your Access 2000 environment, including all the information in your tables.

To add a field from one of your tables, simply open the Tables folder and then open the folder for the table that you want to use. A list of all the fields in that table appears in the middle window. To add a field to the expression, simply double-click on it. Figure 15-15 shows the Expression Builder with the Items folder open and the MinimumBid item already added to the expression.

Figure 15-15:
You can find
a field in the
lower half of
the builder
and add it
to an
expression
by double-
clicking
on it.

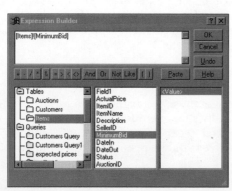

Notice that when you use the Expression Builder to add a field, it includes the table name in front of the field name with an exclamation mark in between the two. The format for this is

```
[Table Name]![Field Name]
```

The other folders listed in the left window often contain much more information. In some cases, this information is organized into categories within the folder. For example, the Functions folder contains a variety of built-in functions, as well as some functions that you or others may have defined in your database. These functions can be used to perform calculations using the information in your database.

To use one of the built-in functions, simply open the Functions folder, select a category of functions from those in the middle window, and then look through the list in the right window until you find the function you want to use. Figure 15-16 shows the Built-In Functions folder open, with the Financial functions displayed in the right window. To select a category of functions, simply click on the category name in the middle window. To select a function, double-click on it in the right window.

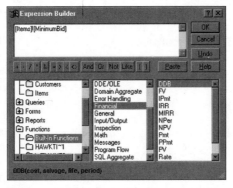

Figure 15-16:
In the lower left, you see a brief synopsis of the function that you've selected.

The other folders contain useful goodies as well. The Constants folder contains constants that are defined for use in comparisons, including True, False, and some that can represent empty fields. The Operators folder contains symbols used for creating expressions.

The Arithmetic category (inside the Operators folder) includes the same four operators that are available as buttons. It also includes the caret (^), which is used for exponents (raising a number to a higher power); MOD, which is used to return the remainder of a division operation; and the backslash, which is used for integer division. With integer division, dividing 5 by 2 (5/2) gives you the answer 2, and 5 MOD 2 gives you the result of 1, the remainder.

Finally, Common Expressions enable you to include various common entries. These entries are most useful for creating a report and are discussed in Chapter 20.

For intimate details about the operations and other sundry doohickeys in the Expression builder, fire up the Office Assistant by clicking Help in the Expression builder window. The Office Assistant offers thoughts, explanations, and samples of most everything the Expression Builder knows how to do.

One of the advantages to using the Expression Builder is that it helps to remind you what you need to do. For example, when you are creating an expression, the Expression Builder won't let you just place two fields, side by side. Figure 15-17 shows what would happen if you double-click on the DateOut and DateIn fields, one after the other.

Figure 15-17:
The
Expression
Builder tells
you when
you need to
add an oper-
ator to an
expression.

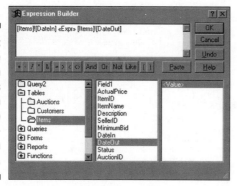

Notice the angle bracket (the two less than signs), Expr, and angle bracket (the two greater than signs)

```
<<Expr>
```

that appear between the two fields. They remind you that you need to insert an expression between the two fields. If you click on the <<Expr> entry, the entire text highlights, and then you can click on one of the operators to insert it between the two fields (for example, the minus sign).

Chapter 16

Automated Editing for Big Changes

- -

In This Chapter

▶ Anguishing over the process

▶ Replacing data

▶ Deleting data

▶ Updating data

- -

*F*ixing an incorrect entry in an Access 2000 table is pretty easy. A couple of clicks, some typing, and {poof!} the problem is gone.

But what if you need to fix 26,281 records? Suddenly, you're talking about a whole bunch of clicking and typing and clicking and typing. Editing an entire table by hand doesn't sound like a {poof!} experience to me — it sounds more like a clean-the-elephant-herd-with-a-toothbrush kind of experience.

Fortunately, Access 2000 has a variety of large-scale housekeeping and editing tools. These tools enable you to make widespread changes to your database without wearing down your fingers in the process. This chapter explores the tools available within Access 2000 and gives you examples of how to use them to make quick work of the elephant herd in your life.

First, This Word from Our Paranoid Sponsor

Please, oh *please* read carefully through this chapter. The queries explained in here are wonderful tools, but they're also incredibly dangerous double-edged swords.

Used correctly, these automated editing queries save incredible amounts of time. Unfortunately, if something goes wrong, they can inflict incredible amounts of damage to your table with a single click. Any time you plan to remove, change, or add to the data in your tables with one of these queries, take a moment and make a backup copy of at least the table, if not the entire database.

To back up a table, open the database file and click the Tables button on the left side. Right-click on the table you plan to edit and then select Copy from the pop-up menu. Next, right-click anywhere on the open space of the database window and select Paste from the pop-up menu. Selecting Paste brings up the Paste Table As dialog box. Fill in a name for the new table (such as Customer table backup), and then click on OK. Don't worry about the other radio buttons in the dialog box — the default settings work just fine.

Quick and Easy Fixes: Replacing Your Mistakes

Automated editing queries have a lot of power. Before hauling out the *really* big guns, here's a technique for small-scale editing. The technique may seem trivial, but is quite handy — don't let its simplicity fool you.

The method in question is the Replace command, which changes a mistake in your table into a new (and hopefully non-mistaken) value. When you open a table in the Datasheet view, you can choose the Replace command from the Edit menu to display the dialog box shown in Figure 16-1.

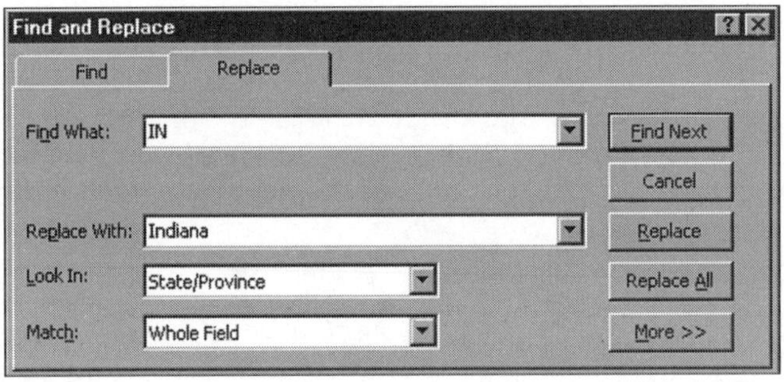

Figure 16-1:
The Replace dialog box lets you correct inaccurate information.

Find and Replace	? ✕
Find	Replace

Find What:	IN ▼	Find Next
		Cancel
Replace With:	Indiana ▼	Replace
Look In:	State/Province ▼	Replace All
Match:	Whole Field ▼	More >>

In this dialog box, you can enter the information that is currently in your database (the wrong word) in the Find What box and enter the proper information into the Replace With box. When you have entered text in both fields, the buttons on the right side become available; you can use these buttons to move through your data, making changes as you go.

If you misspell "munchkin" throughout your data (I *hate* it when I do that) and need to change all its occurrences to the proper spelling, you can simply put the incorrect spelling in Find What, the proper spelling in Replace With, and click on the Replace All button. Your computer goes off and does your bidding, changing each and every instance of the word in the Find What box to the word in the Replace With box.

Access gives you a lot of control over the process. In addition to the options you know and love from the Find command (discussed back in Chapter 10), Replace offers additional options:

- ✔ Clicking the **Match Whole Field** from the drop-down arrow tells Access to only look for cases where the information in the Find What box *completely matches* an entry in the table. If the data in your table includes any additional characters in the field — even a single letter— then Match Whole Field tells Access to skip it.

- ✔ The **Find Next** button highlights the next matching item in your table *without* changing the current selection. Find Next is handy if you need to selectively change some data without bothering anything else.

- ✔ The **Replace** button tells Access to change the current selection and *then* move on to the next match.

- ✔ **Replace All** is the Big Kahuna button in the dialog box. Replace All gives Access a free hand to implement your changes without asking anything else from you.

If your editing goes awry, remember the wonderful Undo option. Just select Edit⇨Undo from the main menu or press Ctrl+Z.

Different Queries for Different Jobs

Although Select queries do most of the work within Access, they aren't alone in the Access universe. Select queries are just one of several types of queries available for your amusement and use. You can change the type of query that you are using by selecting a new choice from the Query menu (found in Query Design View) or by using the Query Type button on the Query Design View toolbar. When you click on the downward-pointing arrow on the right side of the Query Type button, a list of query types drops down, as shown in Figure 16-2.

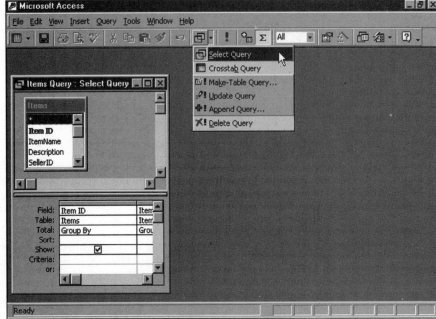

Figure 16-2:
A veritable smorgasbord of query types unfurl from the Query Type button.

 The last four types of queries (Make-Table, Update, Append, and Delete) are pictured with exclamation marks to remind you that these types of queries actually change the way your information is organized. When you work with these four types of queries, you can use the Query View button to preview which records are affected by the query. I strongly recommend that you do a preview before running any of these queries, because previewing is the only way to make sure that the changes you're making are really the ones you intend.

 With most types of queries, the difference between using the Run button and the Query View button is minor. But when you use either the Delete query or the Update query, whether you use the Run or the Query View button makes a BIG difference. When you use the Query View button with these two functions, you see the results without really changing your database. If you use the Run button instead, your information is changed for all time and eternity (well, unless you have a backup — which you *already made,* right?).

You're Outta Here: The Delete Query

The easiest of the editing queries is a Delete query. Unfortunately, the Delete query is also one of the most dangerous queries around. (Why do *easy* and *dangerous* always go together in computer programs?)

Creating a Delete query works just like creating a Select query. In fact, they're identical, except for the query type setting. Before doing a Delete query, create a Select query first to test your criteria and to make sure that the query finds the records you really want. Once you know that the criteria work correctly, change it from a Select query into a Delete query with the Query Type setting mentioned above.

Here's a quick step-by-step run through building a Delete query:

1. **Create a normal Select query.**

2. **Set up your criteria to identify the records you want to delete.**

3. **Run the Select query to make sure that it does, in fact, find *only* the records that you want to work with. If the Select query finds *other* records as well, adjust the criteria so that the extras don't match.**

4. **Return to the Design view and use the Query Type drop-down list to choose a Delete query or choose Delete from the Query menu.**

When you switch to a Delete query, the name in the Title Bar changes and the Sort line changes to a Delete line. Figure 16-3 shows a typical Delete Query screen. This Query removes all records from the Customers table where the last name starts with an "H." Notice that information for locating records is already in this query because the information was converted over from the original Select query that I used to list out these records.

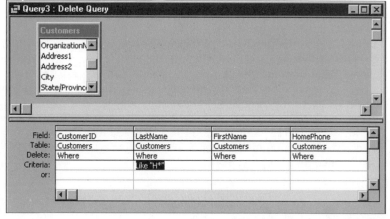

Figure 16-3:
The Delete Query window rubs out the data you don't want.

5. **Start the query.**

Access displays a message asking whether you're sure that you want to delete the records and reminding you that you won't be able to get the data back. Grit your teeth, remind yourself that you have a backup copy of the data in your tables (because you made one before starting this process) in case this doesn't work, and click on Yes. If you realize that this is all a bad dream and you really want to keep those records in your table, carefully click on No.

6. **The query runs and does its deed.**

If you clicked on Yes, Access goes out, finds the records that match the criteria, and removes those records from the table. That's all you need to do.

You cannot undo the changes made with the Delete query. After you delete these records, they are gone — period. Gone for good, never to be seen or heard from again. Are you sure you really mean to do this?

You can create Delete queries that use more than one table to locate their information. Be very careful when doing so, however, as the number of changes that you make can go up dramatically if things don't work quite right. Again, I suggest backing up your database and doing a Select query first to list out the records that you want to delete.

Making changes gets a bit more complicated when deleting from more than one table. Access can only figure these things out by itself when it needs to delete records that are linked one-to-one — in other words, each record is linked only to a single record in the other table. When you look at the relationship grid at the top of the Query screen, one-to-one links are shown with a point symbol. One-to-many relationships are indicated with a solid black arrow symbol "→", in which you need one query to delete all the matching records from the first table and a second query to delete the single record from the other end of the relationship.

Depending on the database settings, Access may not even *let* you delete the records. One-to-many deletions get into a very touchy and technical issue called *Referential Integrity*. Loosely translated, this means that records *must* exist in one table because *matching* records depend on them in some other table. Life gets very weird with referential integrity, but many corporate databases use it because it ensures that huge mistakes don't happen by accident. If you work in a big company and think that you need to delete data but keep running into a referential integrity error, contact your Information Systems folks. Once they stop hyperventilating, they can help you with the problem.

Making Big Changes

There comes a time in every database's life when it needs to change. Fortunately, you can make changes of the large variety automatically by using an Update query. An Update query enables you to use a query to select records and then use instructions to change the information.

As with other types of queries that modify your data, particularly the Delete query discussed previously in this chapter, making sure that your query works only with the records that you want to change is vitally important. Setting up and testing your criteria with a Select query before running the query for real is always a good idea.

 When you select the Update query, either by choosing Update Query from the Query menu or by choosing Update query from the Query Type list, your query grid changes to resemble the one shown in Figure 16-4.

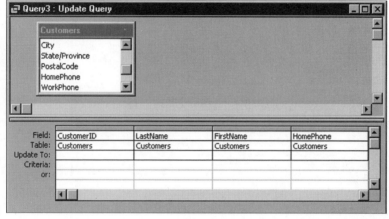

Figure 16-4:
The Update Query Design view gives you a field to update the entries of selected criteria.

Although the query looks pretty normal overall, this grid includes a new line labeled Update To. You can use any criteria to select your records, just as a normal Select query. For example, you may want to select all the records in your auction database that belong to the Allen-Brown family. To do so, set up your criteria with the LastName field and the entry "Allen-Brown" on the Criteria line. You may also want to include the ItemName and its MinimumBid to make sure that you find those records you want. When you run your Select query, your grid resembles the one shown in Figure 16-5.

Figure 16-5:
A Select Query window shows the items contributed by the Allen-Brown family.

Last Name	ItemName	MinimumBid
Allen-Brown	Asst hardback books (1 of 4)	$30.00
Allen-Brown	Asst hardback books (2 of 4)	$30.00
Allen-Brown	Asst hardback books (3 of 4)	$30.00
Allen-Brown	Asst hardback books (4 of 4)	$30.00

Record: 2 of 4

When you run this query, you see that, in fact, you are getting only the records for the items submitted by the Allen-Brown family — four boxes of assorted books.

The Allen-Brown family has decided to raise the price of the books that they have in the auction. You could simply go through and change each record by hand, but using an Update query is much easier. The Allen-Brown family has decided on a price of $35.00 as the MinimumBid. So, your Update query screen looks like the one shown in Figure 16-6. Notice that the new value is in the Update To row for the MinimumBid field.

Figure 16-6:
The Update query enables you to change the values of all the items in a field that correspond to your criteria.

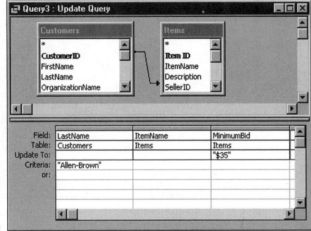

When you run the query, you get a warning message that you are about to update records. Click on Yes to go ahead and make your changes.

You can also make changes based upon the existing value in a field. To do that, you use a calculation like the ones described in Chapter 15.

Using the Expression Builder (also discussed in Chapter 15) to create your update calculation is easiest. Figure 16-7 shows an example from the auction database. In this case, the company decides to give a 10% discount on all items with a minimum bid over $100. The calculation changes the value in each MinimumBid field to .9 times the current MinimumBid value, thus leaving 90% of the current cost.

When you run this query, Access attempts to update 20 of the Auction records, discounting the MinimumBid price to 90 percent of its original price, but only on those records that have a MinimumBid of more than $100.00.

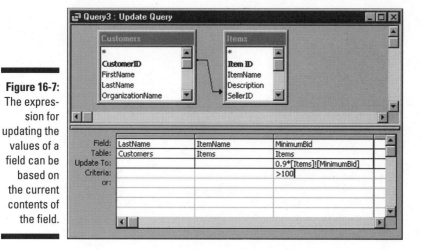

Figure 16-7:
The expression for updating the values of a field can be based on the current contents of the field.

To combine additional tables and criteria, you may want to update the MinimumBid of all the items that will be at one of the auction sites. To do that, you can use a grid like the one shown in Figure 16-8.

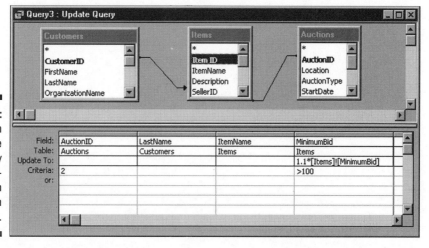

Figure 16-8:
You can update fields by using criteria from more than one table.

In Figure 16-8, the criteria being used is the AuctionID code for the auction, and MinimumBid are getting updated again — in this case, increasing the price of the items by 10 percent (multiply the old price by 1.1).

Part IV
Turning Your Table into a Book

The 5th Wave   By Rich Tennant

GRICHTENNANT

"WELL, SHOOT! THIS EGGPLANT CHART IS JUST AS CONFUSING AS THE BUTTERNUT SQUASH CHART AND THE GOURD CHART. CAN'T YOU JUST MAKE A PIE CHART LIKE EVERYONE ELSE?"

In this part . . .

Someone said that the computer revolution would do away with paper. Needless to say, that person was wrong. (Last I heard, that person is now compiling the annual psychic predictions page for one of the national tabloids.)

So far, this book's shown you how to put the data in and then mixed it up a little. Now it's time to pull the data out, clean it up a bit, and record it for posterity on the printed page. Access 2000 has some strong reporting tools to make your multi-thousand-page reports look truly cool. Better still, it offers some great summary tools to make those multi-thousand page reports a thing of the past. Stick your head in this part and see what you can see!

Chapter 17

AutoReport: Like the Model-T, It's Clunky but It Runs

In This Chapter

▶ Choosing between Columnar and Tabular AutoReports

▶ Creating an AutoReport

▶ Perusing your report with Print Preview

▶ Customizing your report with Page Layout

*W*hat do you do if someone (say, your boss) wants to see all the revelations you made using your datasheets, tables, and queries? And then, what if your boss wants to share the aforementioned revelations with the rest of the company? The odds are good that the whole management team doesn't want to crowd around your monitor and study thousands of records and dozens of queries (besides, your cubicle isn't *that* big).

Lucky for you, Access 2000 includes tools for creating and printing reports. In fact, Access sees report-making as just another part of the whole database experience. Reports take information from your database (specifically, reports can draw from either tables or queries) and organize that information according to your instructions. Access 2000 even includes report wizards to walk you through the steps of designing a report to meet your needs.

You probably found this chapter because the boss wants a report *right now*, so the following pages take you to the AutoReport factory, where a cadre of digital elves wait to create a quick report for you. If your boss gives you the time, the last section in this chapter (plus the other chapters in this part) helps you spruce up the finished report a bit, making it an thing of beauty in addition to an object of truth.

AutoReport Basics for High-Speed Information

Think of AutoReport as your very own information assembly line. The AutoReport tools excel at doing one thing very well. AutoReport builds a single-table report according to your specifications. Fire up the software, tell it what you want, and your report is as good as done.

Although AutoReport only works with one table at a time, it still offers some choices. AutoReport builds two kinds of reports: Columnar and Tabular. Both reports organize the same data, but in very different ways:

- *Tabular AutoReports* place all information for each record on one row, with a separate column for each field. The tabular format puts the field names above each column (often trimming the names until you can't make heads or tails of what they are) and squashes the columns themselves together in the name of fitting everything horizontally on a single page.

- *Columnar AutoReports* organize each record vertically on the page, in two columns — one for the names of the fields and one for the contents of the fields. Each record generally starts its own page.

I don't have a profound answer for when to use one AutoReport layout or the other. The choice is more a matter of personal taste and aesthetics than anything else. The only advice I can offer is that the Tabular format is generally more useful if your report has lots of records with small fields, whereas the Columnar format is often better for reports with large fields but fewer records.

Whether you choose the Tabular or Columnar format, feel free to change AutoReport's creation however you want. Use the report that is built as an easy starting point, and then add titles, headers, footers, cool formatting, and more. Because AutoReport builds a normal Access 2000 report, a quick trip into Design mode puts all of the report development and formatting tools at your command. For more about formatting, headers, and the other cool tricks available in the report system, flip ahead to Chapters 19 and 20.

Putting the Wheels of Informational Progress into Motion

Even though AutoReport includes separate tools for building Columnar and Tabular reports, the *good* news is that both systems work exactly the same way. The only difference between these two styles is in how they organize the data in the finished report. From a *how this works* standpoint, they're the same.

Follow these steps to create either a Columnar or Tabular AutoReport:

1. **Click the Reports button below the Objects bar of your main database window and then click on <u>N</u>ew.**

   The New Report dialog box appears, showing all the report types from which you can choose.

2. **Depending on your informational needs, click on AutoReport: Columnar or AutoReport: Tabular.**

   After you click on the AutoReport entry in the list, the graphic in the New Report window changes into a tiny image of the report layout (as Figure 17-1 shows). Isn't that cute? (Yes, sometimes it seems like the programmers really need to get out more.)

Figure 17-1:
Click on
your choice
of Columnar
or Tabular
and watch
the sample
change, too.

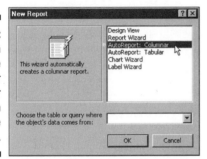

The query advantage

The fact that Access 2000 lets you base a report on a query is a truly wonderful thing. When you build a report on a table, you get a report containing each and every record in the table. But what if you only want a few of the records? Access makes it easy. Create a query and then base the report upon that query.

The advantages don't stop there. If you create a query based on multiple tables, Access neatly organizes your results into a single datasheet. If your query produces the information that you want in its datasheet, then a report, based on that query's results, organizes and presents the information in the way you want. (For more on creating queries using more than one table, see Chapter 12.)

3. Click on the drop-down list at the bottom of the dialog box to select which table or query you want to use.

Scroll through the options until you find the table or query on which you want to base your report. Remember that each AutoReport only covers one query or table.

4. Click on OK.

After a bit of clunking and thunking, Access displays your finished report on-screen in *Print Preview* mode (see Figure 17-2), which is pro-grammerese for "This is what the report looks like if you print it." Print Preview includes plenty of cool tools, so continue on to the next section for more about them.

Even though Access thinks quite a lot of the report already (it's having one of those proud parent moments), usually the report has a look that only a digital parent can love. Before sending the report out into the cold, cruel world, you probably should take it into Design view and dress it up a bit. Flip ahead a couple of pages for the basics of spiffing up a dull AutoReport.

Click here to leave Print Preview.

Click here to start printing.   Don't try this one yet.

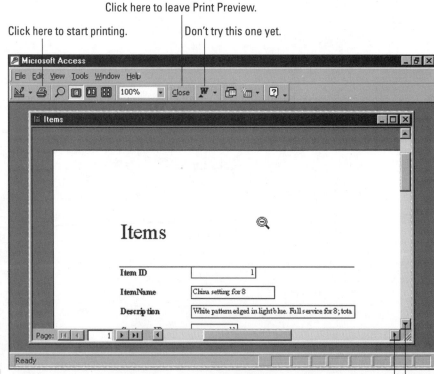

Figure 17-2:
In the Print Preview window, Access gives you an idea of what the report looks like on paper.

These let you see the rest of the page.

Previewing Your Informational Masterpiece

When you're in Print Preview, you can't do a whole lot with your report except print it. But Print Preview does give you the important ability to closely check out exactly what your document looks like. Table 17-1 shows the tools Print Preview provides to help with your inspection.

Table 17-1	Print Preview Tools
Tool	*What It Does*
	To flip between Print Preview and Design view, click here. The button art changes in Design view (the button looks like a page with a magnifying glass over it, which is supposed to remind you of Print Preview mode), but don't let that worry you.
	Click on the Print button and your printer begins spewing out your report. Pretty straightforward.
	Click the on the Zoom button to toggle between viewing the entire page on-screen and viewing the page at 100 percent magnification.
	View one page of your report on-screen.
	View two pages side-by-side.
	Select the number of pages to show (anything from one to six). Consult your optometrist before doing too much with this option.
Fit	Select a pre-set Zoom amount from the drop-down list or type your own custom setting.
Close	Close the Print Preview window and send your report back to its home in your database window.
	Send your report over to Microsoft Word or Excel (assuming, of course, that Word or Excel are installed on your computer).

Zooming around your report

In Figure 17-2, the entire page is not visible. The parts that show look pretty good, but you can't see the whole record, let alone the whole page. In this figure, Access displays the report full-size, just like it looks on the printed page. What if you need to see what the whole page will look like? Click on the Zoom button and change the setting to Fit. This displays the full-page view shown in Figure 17-3. Access calls the full-page view the Fit view because it *fits* the whole page on your screen. The Fit view is a good way to get an idea of the bigger picture. You can't read the text, but you can see what it looks like on the page. When you want to go back to the 100 percent view, click on the Zoom button again, and Access 2000 obligingly switches for you.

But what if you want to view a report that fits *more* into the Print Preview window than 100 percent view, but that is still legible (unlike Fit view)? Not a problem; just pick one of the percentage options in the Zoom Control. These percentages set the magnification of your page view. Click on a size and watch your view change. If you don't like any of the preset choices, type a percentage of your own directly into the Zoom Control and press Enter to see the results.

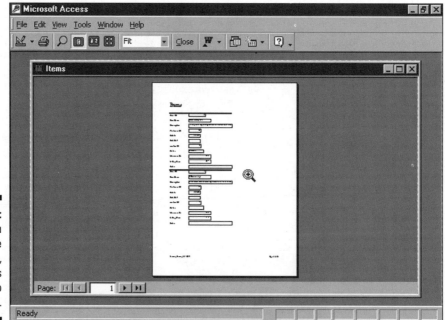

Figure 17-3:
When you view the whole page, the print is too tiny to read.

When you move your mouse pointer over the preview of your report, your pointer changes to look like a magnifying glass. Use this to zoom in closer to the report and check individual sections. Just click what you want to see and Access swoops down, enlarging that portion of the report so you can see it clearly. Click again, and your view changes back to the previous setting.

Note that clicking any of the page-number buttons (one page, two page, multiple pages) sets the Zoom view to the Fit view setting. When you have two pages showing, the odd-numbered page is always on the left unlike book publishing, which puts the odd-numbered page on the right — unless the production department is having a very, very bad day.

If you select View⇨Pages from the main menu, Access 2000 offers quite the selection of page view options, as you see in Figure 17-4. Set your system to show one page, two pages, or a mind-numbing (and eye-squinting) twelve pages on a single screen.

Clicking on one of the page view options changes your view to display a new, multipage arrangement. For example, Figure 17-5 shows the 12-page configuration.

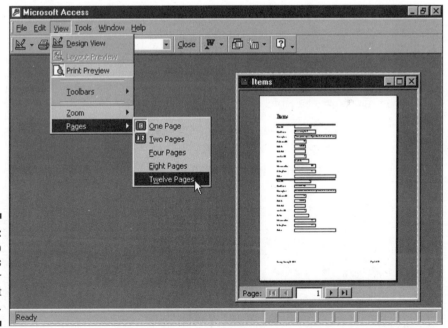

Figure 17-4: Preview up to 12 pages of your report at one time.

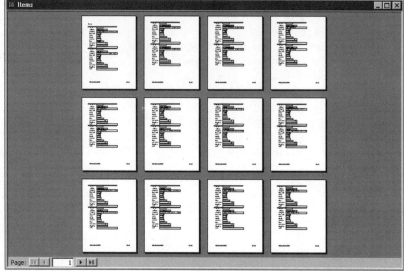

Figure 17-5:
You certainly can't read a lick of data, but multipage Print Previews still look cool.

Calling on the pop-up menu

You can right-click anywhere on the Print Preview screen to see a pop-up menu that gives you the choice of switching the Zoom or viewing a specific number of pages. When you select the Zoom command, a submenu appears with the same choices that appear on the Zoom Control. Two other commands are available when you right-click on the Print Preview screen:

- ✔ **Save As/Export:** Choose this command to save your Access 2000 report in a format used by another program.
- ✔ **Send:** Choose this command to take a copy of your Access 2000 report and send it as a mail message.

Truth Is Beauty, So Make Your Reports Look Great

After looking at your report in the Print Preview window, you have a decision to make. If you're happy with how your report looks, great! Go ahead and print the document. However, a few minutes of extra work does wonders for even the simplest reports.

Start with the basics in the Page Setup dialog box of Access 2000. To get there, select File⇨Page Setup from any Report view in Access 2000. This dialog box provides three tabs of options to insure that your report is as effective and attractive as it can be.

The Margins tab

No surprises here — the Margins tab of the Page Setup dialog box controls the width of the margins in your report. Figure 17-6 displays your options.

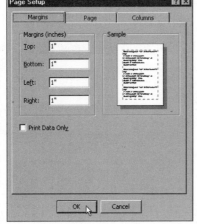

Figure 17-6: The Margins tab controls the space between the edge of the page and the start of your data.

Setting the Margins is really straightforward. The page has four margins, so the dialog box includes a setting for each one (Left, Right, Top, and Bottom). To change a margin, double-click in the appropriate box and type a new setting. Access automatically uses whatever Windows thinks is your local unit of measurement (inches, centimeters, or whatever else you measure with). On the right side of the dialog box, Access displays a sample image, which shows you how your current margin settings work on a page.

Make all of the changes you want to the layout of the report and then click on the OK button at the bottom of the dialog box. Take the report back into Print Preview to see first-hand how your adjustments worked. If you need to tweak a few more things, simply go back to Page Setup and play with the options until everything looks just right.

The last item on the Margins tab is the Print Data Only check box. I guess the programmers couldn't think of anywhere else to put this box, because it has *nothing* to do with margin settings. (Kinda like putting the controls for the toaster onto your refrigerator because it happened to be sitting nearby.) If you select this option (so that a check is showing), Access 2000 prints only the data in your records; field headings won't appear on the printed document. Use Print Data Only if you plan to use pre-printed forms. Otherwise, leave it alone, because your report looks pretty odd without any field labels.

The Page tab

The Page tab tells Access 2000 about the sheet of paper you actually print your report on, including its size, layout, and what printer you keep the paper in. You make some of the most fundamental decisions about how your report will look from the Page tab of the Page Setup dialog box (Figure 17-7).

Figure 17-7: The Page Setup dialog box lays the groundwork for a useful report.

The Orientation box sets the direction your report prints on the paper. The default choice is Portrait (the way that this book and most magazines appear). Your other choice is Landscape, which draws its name from the fact that when creating a picture of a landscape, the painter had to turn his canvas on its side to make everything fit. Likewise, Landscape report pages lay on their side, giving you more horizontal room, but less vertical space.

Deciding whether to go Portrait or Landscape is more important than you think. For Tabular reports, Landscape orientation displays more information for each field, thanks to the wider columns. Unfortunately, the columns get shorter in the process. (After all, that piece of paper is only so big.) Columnar reports don't do very well in Landscape, because they usually need more vertical space than horizontal space.

Your other choices for the Page tab are determined by your printing capabilities. The two drop-down lists in the Paper section of the tab enable you to pick the Size of the paper you want to use (refer to Figure 17-7). The Source drop-down list gives you the option to use your regular paper feed (the AutoSelect Tray choice), another automatic source, or to manually feed your paper into the printer.

The last part of the Page tab lets you choose a specific printer for this report. You can use either the Default Printer (Access uses whatever printer Windows says to use) or the Use Specific Printer option (where you pick the printer yourself). Most of the time, you can leave this setting alone; it's only useful if you want to force this report to always come out of one specific printer at your location. If you click on the Use Specific Printer radio button, the Printer button then comes to life. Click on this button to choose from among your available printers.

The Columns tab

After you finish with the Page tab, you're ready to click on the Columns tab (see Figure 17-8). Now, the real fun starts.

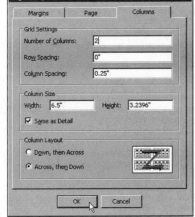

Figure 17-8: The Columns tab of the Page Setup dialog box lets you redesign your report.

The Columns tab of the Page Setup dialog box is divided into three sections:

- ✔ **Grid Settings:** Controls how many columns your report uses and how far apart the different elements are from each other

- ✔ **Column Size:** Adjusts the height and width of your columns

- ✔ **Column Layout:** Defines the way that Access 2000 places your data in columns (and uses a very easy-to-understand graphic to show you as well)

The default Grid Setting is one column to a page, but you can easily change the setting to suit your particular report. Just keep in mind that with more columns, your reports may show less information for each record. If you use so many columns that some of the information won't fit, you see a warning similar to the one displayed in Figure 17-9.

Figure 17-9:
You may not
be able to fit
more than
one column
on a page.

If the number of columns you select all fit (or if you're willing to lose your view of the information in some of your fields), click on OK to see a view of how your document will look with multiple columns.

The Grid Settings section of the Columns tab also adjusts row and column spacing:

- ✔ **Row Spacing:** To adjust the space (measured in your local unit of distance) between the horizontal rows, simply click on the Row Spacing box and enter the amount of space that you want to appear between each row. Again, this setting is a matter of personal preference.

- ✔ **Column Spacing:** Adjust the width of your columns. If you narrow this width, you make more room, but your entries are more difficult to read.

The bottom section of the Columns tab, called Column Layout, lets you control how your columns are organized on the page. You have two options here:

- ✔ **Down, then Across:** Access 2000 starts a new record in the same column (if the preceding record has not filled up the page). For example, Record 13 will start below Record 12 on the page (provided there's enough room), and then Records 14 and 15 will appear in the second column.

- ✔ **Across, then Down:** Access starts Record 13 across from 12, and then puts Record 14 below 12, and Record 15 below 13, and so on.

Chapter 18

Wizardly Help with Labels, Charts, and Multilevel Reports

. . . .

In This Chapter

▶ Printing labels with Label Wizard

▶ Adding charts with the Chart Wizard

▶ Organizing your report

▶ Using the Report Wizard

▶ Creating grouping levels

▶ Adding summaries

. . . .

AutoReports, covered in the preceding chapter, are just the tip of the Access report iceberg. If you have the inclination, you can use Access 2000 to generate much more complex reports. You can even create useful printouts that you probably never even thought of as reports — mailing labels and charts. Don't be daunted — Access provides kind, gentle wizards to help you along your report-creating journey.

Creating Labels

When the bulk-mailing urge strikes, there's nothing like a good stack of mailing labels to really make your day. At moments like this, Access 2000 rides to the rescue with the Label Wizard, one of the many report wizards in Access.

The Label Wizard formats your data for use with any size or type of label on the planet. Mailing labels, file labels, shipping labels, name tags — the list goes on forever. Best of all, the Label Wizard does all the hard stuff for you with the wave of a wand.

In the past, one of the hardest aspects about making labels was explaining the label layout to the software. At some point, Microsoft engineers obviously endured this hardship themselves because they built the specifications for hundreds of labels from popular manufacturers right into the Label Wizard. If you happen to use labels from Avery, Herma, Zweckform, or any other maker listed in the wizard's manufacturer list, just tell the wizard the manufacturer's product number. The wizard sets up the report dimensions for you according to the maker's specifications. Life just doesn't get much easier than this.

Before firing up the Label Wizard, figure out what information you want on the labels. Unless you want a label for everything in the table, you need to create a query that picks out the right pieces from your table, sorts them into order, and generally gets them ready for their trip to the sticky-backed paper. For more about that, flip back to the query sections of this book in Part III.

With your table or query in hand, you can make the labels. Follow these steps to create your Label report:

1. **Click on the Reports button under the Objects bar on your database window.**

   Access lists the reports that exist in your database. (Access may secretly hope that you create a new report to add to the list, but nobody knows the intimate thoughts and dreams of today's programs.)

2. **Click on <u>N</u>ew to create a new report.**

   The New Report dialog box appears, showing you all the available report types, including the all-important Label Wizard.

3. **Click on Label Wizard in the list of report types.**

   The little picture to the left of the list changes into a page of labels to prove that Access 2000 heard you correctly as shown in Figure 18-1.

Figure 18-1:
Access 2000 prepares to offer up some wizardly advice about labels.

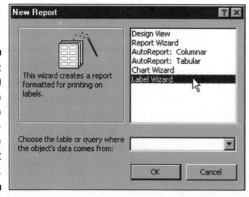

4. **Click on the down arrow near the bottom of the dialog box. In the drop-down list, click on the query or table to use with the labels.**

The wizard is ready, and the data awaits — it's time to make some labels!

5. **Take a deep breath and click on OK to start the Label Wizard.**

In a flurry of disk activity, the wizard performs his first trick by displaying the dialog box in Figure 18-2.

6. **Click on the down-arrow next to the Filter by manufacturer box and then look for the maker of your labels in the drop-down list.**

Access 2000 makes creating labels as painless as possible — provided, of course, that you use labels from a company that the Microsoft developers know about.

If your label manufacturer is on the Label Wizard's list, click the company name. In the top of the Label Wizard window, Access displays all that company's labels by product number. Scroll through the list until you find the number that matches the one on your label box. When you find it, skip merrily along to Step 8 (Lucky you!). If the number isn't on the list, proceed to the next step.

If your label manufacturer isn't on the Label Wizard's list, take another look at your box of labels. Because Avery controls so much of the label market, other manufacturers often put the equivalent Avery code number onto their product, usually with the notation *like Avery xxxx labels,* with the *xxxx* part replaced by an Avery code number. If you see that on your label box, select Avery as the label maker, then look for the right label number in the list. If you find it, skip ahead to Step 8. If you still don't find the number, go on to the next step.

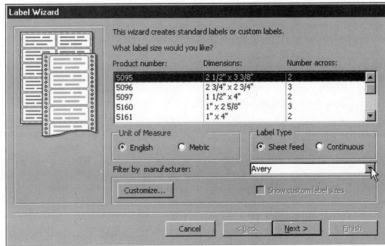

Figure 18-2: The first Label Wizard dialog box determines the size of your labels.

7. **If the Label Wizard doesn't know the details of your labels, click on Customize to add them to the Wizard's repertoire.**

   Building a customized label entry isn't hard, but it *does* take a few steps. For the details of this process, browse through the "It's a very *special* label" sidebar.

8. **When you find the label you want to use, click its entry on the label list, and then click on <u>N</u>ext.**

   With the Great Label Size Quandary solved, you can think about how your finished label can look. The Label Wizard offers you a slew of font choices in the next window as shown in Figure 18-3.

It's a very *special* label

Maybe they were on sale. Perhaps the Purchasing department landed a really *swell* deal on them. Whatever the reason, the labels lying in front of you draw their lineage from a family tree that the Label Wizard never heard of in its life. Don't despair, though, because the clever folks at Microsoft anticipated this very problem. That's why the Label Wizard includes a Customize button.

The Customize button leads to a whole series of screens dedicated to one purpose: adding the settings for the peculiar — er, *particular* — labels that your project demands.

To build a set of custom label settings, you need to know a bunch of measurement details about the labels in your possession. Often, the box of labels includes a sheet with all the measurements listed on it. If you don't have a measurement sheet, get out a ruler and prepare to wield it. Access makes customizing pretty easy by graphically showing all the measurements it needs. The Label Wizard steps you through the process pretty well, but you still need to keep your eyes open as you go. To make your new label, click on the Customize button in the Label Wizard. In the New Label Size dialog box, click on New. This brings up the New Label window, where all the fun starts.

Among other things, carefully check the label measurements as you enter them. Be sure that Label Type is set to Sheet Feed (unless you have a *roll* of labels and a dot matrix printer — in that case, use Continuous). Also check the Number Across setting, because the odds are good that your labels include two or three across on a page. Give your new label settings a memorable name, too (but be nice!). When you're done, click OK to finish the settings and then click Close to send away the New Label Size dialog box.

As you return to the Label Wizard, it proudly displays your new label on its main window. Take a moment to smile at a label-well-created, and then press onward with your labeling project. If you find that your new label settings don't work quite right, go back to the Customize button again, click on your label's name, and click on Edit. This takes you back to that wonderful label measurement window, so you can adjust whatever is out of whack with the settings. Good luck!

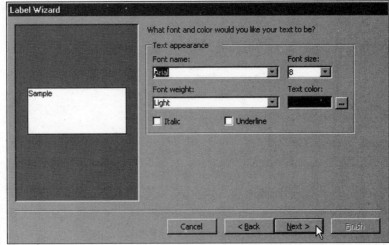

9. **Pick the font, size, weight, and color for the text on your label and then click on Next.**

   You can choose any font available in Windows: change the text size, change how bold it looks (what the techs call *font weight*), or even add italics, underline, and a new text color. (You need a color printer for this — otherwise, you get Henry Ford's *any color you want, as long as it's black* setting.) As you make changes, the sample text on the left side of the window shows your current settings.

   Unfortunately, the formatting you choose applies to *all* the text on *every* label. If you add italics, then the *whole label* — every label — comes out that way. Add special formatting sparingly because a little goes a long way.

10. **Select the data to appear on the label and type any other text that should print as well.**

   At this point, you tell the Wizard which data items from the table or query you want to put onto the label, and where you want them to go. You've done this drill before: Select the fields from the Available fields list on the left and click on the > button to transfer the field to the Prototype label box on the right. However, this procedure has one slight twist. The Label Wizard prints your fields *exactly* as you tell it to as shown in Figure 18-4.

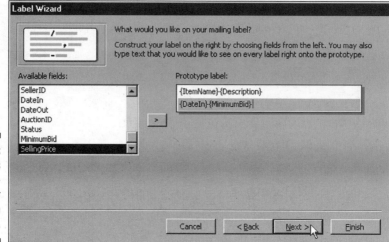

Figure 18-4:
At last, it's time to position your goodies on the label.

If you want fields on separate rows, press Enter or use an arrow key to move to the next row. When you double-click on a field (or click on the > button), that field always transfers to the highlighted line in the Prototype label box. Access 2000 figures out how many lines can print on your label, based upon the label's size and the font size you are using.

If you want to print a particular character, word, or other text message on every label, just click wherever you want it to appear and then type your text. For example, to insert a comma between the city, state, or province on your mailing labels, select the `City` field, type in a comma, press the spacebar, and then select the `StateOrProvince` field. When Access prints each label, it puts the city name, adds a comma, and then fills in the rest of the information.

11. **When the fields look simply marvelous (or at least passably cute), click on Next.**

    With the layout complete, the Label Wizard turns his attention to sorting the labels.

12. **Choose the field for Access to sort your labels (as in Figure 18-5) and click on Next.**

    Naming the report and saving it for posterity is the only step left!

13. **Type a name for the label report and then click on Finish to see your creation in action.**

    Hopefully, the labels look wonderful and work perfectly. If the labels are *almost* right but still need a few tweaks, click on the Design view button on the toolbar (the one that looks like a triangle and pencil) and modify the design as needed.

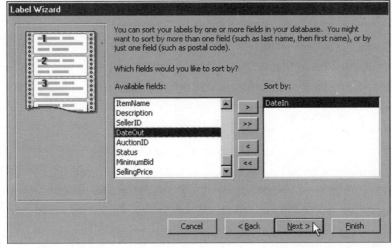

Figure 18-5:
Pick the field Access should use to sort your labels.

Using the Chart Wizard in Your Report

Generally, reports are just a collection of words and numbers, organized to allow you to make sense of the information. But sometimes, words and numbers don't paint enough of the story. At times like these, a graph makes the perfect antidote, filling in the heads, tails, and other sundry parts of your report's informational picture. As the saying goes, a picture is worth a thousand words (so add a few graphs and save a bunch of trees).

Access 2000 includes an artsy wizard for just such occasions. Say hello to the *Chart Wizard,* creator of penultimate pies, beautiful bars, and luscious lines — and all at the wave of a wand (plus a few mouse clicks for good measure).

The Chart Wizard in Access 2000 is one of those *install it when you ask for it* features. Don't be surprised if, immediately after Step 3 below, the Office 2000 installation program roars to life and demands your Office 2000 installation CD. If you work in a big company and don't have the CD at hand, contact your Information Systems folks for help. (If you work by yourself, look around the office — it *must* be there somewhere.)

To build a chart (or graph, since Access 2000 uses the terms interchangeably), you need *at least* two fields (but no more than six). One field contains the numbers making up the bars, lines, pie slices, or other graphical representations in your graph. The other field should hold labels identifying the various numbers (otherwise, your graph looks swell but says nothing). All the fields must come from a single-table or query.

Because the wizard is fluent in several types of charts, finding a layout that works perfectly for your data is easy. The Wizard offers five major types of charts:

✔ **Area charts:** A cross between a line chart and pie chart, these graphs show how the total of a *group* of figures changed over time. Perfect for showing how costs and profits add up to total revenue over several quarters.

✔ **Bar, Cone, and Column charts:** Variations of the line chart, these charts use vertical or horizontal bars to display your data. Good for comparing groups of data against each other (such as sales by quarter over a period of years).

✔ **Line charts:** The classic chart from Geometry class is reborn into the digital world and great for showing trends over time.

✔ **Pie and Donut charts:** These charts take a series of numbers and display them as percentages of a total. Perfect for showing how much each division contributed to total corporate profit, how many people from various countries buy a product, and anything else that requires a *slice of the pie* approach. (Of course, they also add a nice touch to breakfast meetings, particularly when accompanied by a steaming cappuccino or nice cup of hot chocolate.)

✔ **XY and Bubble charts:** These charts are the odd uncles and peculiar third cousins of the Access chart family. Technically speaking, they chart two data points as they relate to a third data point (such as *the number of women who visited the club each month, displayed by income group*). In the vernacular, that translates into *unless you have a darn good reason, don't even bother with these charts*. These charts are wonderful for engineers, economists, scientists, statisticians, and anyone else who probably needs more to do with their free time.

Building the chart-of-your-heart only takes a few minutes, thanks to the Wizard's helpful and competent assistance. Here's how it all works:

1. **Click the Reports button on the database screen and then click on New.**

   The New Report dialog box appears, proudly displaying your report options.

2. **Click on Chart Wizard in the list.**

   So far, so good — Access 2000 suspects that you want a chart. (You confirm its suspicions in the next step.)

3. **Click on the down-arrow next to the Choose the table or query text box and then choose the table or query for your chart. When you're all done, click on OK.**

   Access opens up the table or query you selected, takes a look inside, and then displays the fields available for the chart.

4. **Select the numeric and text fields for your chart, then click on Next.**

   Ever the one-trick pony, this field selection window looks a lot like every other one of its kind in the program. Use the > and < to add or remove fields in the list. The >> and << buttons do the same thing, but move *all* the available fields.

   When finished, click on Next to press onward through your graphical adventure.

5. **Access displays samples of every graph it knows how to make. Click on the picture of your chart type and then click on <u>N</u>ext.**

   As you click on each chart (as shown in Figure 18-6), the wizard briefly describes the chart and offers a few technical thoughts on how the chart works.

6. **The wizard explains how to display the data in your chart, but ultimately lets you make whatever changes you want. Click <u>N</u>ext when the chart meets your expectations, hopes, and desires (or when you simply tire of messing with the whole affair).**

   Although the wizard fills out almost everything in this window on its own, you can change anything you see. Drag and drop fields from the column on the left of the window into the various positions in the graph, double-click on the graph items to change their summary options, and do whatever else you wish. Click on the Preview Chart button (sitting quietly in the upper left corner of the window, as shown in Figure 18-7) to see how the chart look thus far.

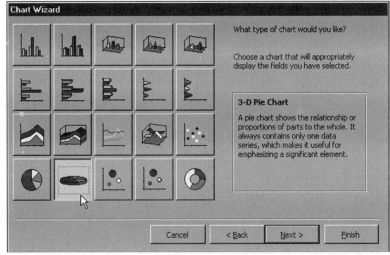

Figure 18-6: Like a mini-art gallery, Access displays and describes its available graphs.

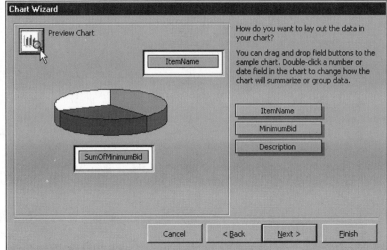

Figure 18-7:
Make a few
changes
and then
preview
your chart-
in-progress
with this
handy
button.

Each graph type offers slightly different options, so take a moment and explore the possibilities. After all, if something goes horribly wrong, just click on Cancel and start the graph again. (Aren't computers handy sometimes?)

7. **In this final screen, type a name for your new graph. Click on Finish to see the product of your labor.**

Use the radio buttons on this screen to add or remove the legend, and to either view the chart or take it straight into Design View for some detailed graph surgery.

Access adds the chart to the Reports page of your database. Why? Who knows — Access *is* merely software, you know.

For more information about charts and how to best use them, pick up a good book about public speaking or making technical presentations. These books usually include a section covering graphs of all kinds, including how to lay them out, what data you need to build each one, and which style best matches the information in your life.

Creating More Advanced Reports

The AutoReport Wizard (discussed back in Chapter 17) quickly creates simple reports from a single query or table. When you (or, more likely, your boss) need something *right now,* the AutoReport Wizard is a great tool.

Sometimes, your reporting needs call for more detail, more organization, or simply more data. For these more complex reports, seek help from the Report Wizard. This master of informational presentation lets you add fields from as many tables as you want, and organize those fields into as many levels as you choose. Each new level gets its own personalized section of the report, complete with a custom header and footer. After a spin with the Report Wizard, your data won't want to go anywhere else.

Creating complex reports involves more steps than the simple ones, but the results are _definitely_ worth the extra effort. Because complex reports include a lot more options, the steps to build the report are split into several sections according to topic. Each section includes some explanations of what the settings do and how to use them.

The first step: Starting the wizard and picking some fields

In the end, a multi-level report looks a lot different than a basic report, but they both start out the same way. Begin your report creation safari with these familiar steps:

1. **Click on the Reports button under the Objects bar on the left side of the main database screen.**

   As usual, Access displays the reports currently in your database.

2. **Click on <u>N</u>ew to create a new report.**

   The New Report dialog box appears, showing you all the report types you can choose from. (Bored yet? Don't worry — the cool stuff comes soon!)

3. **Click on the Report Wizard entry on the list and then click on OK.**

   After a moment, the dialog box shown in Figure 18-8 appears. The dialog box may look familiar because it's almost identical to the first dialog box of the Simple Query Wizard from Chapter 12. (At least you don't have to wrestle with new dialog box layouts all the time.)

   With the AutoReport Wizard, this is the point where you select a table or query to use in your report. With the _full_ Report Wizard, though, that step comes next.

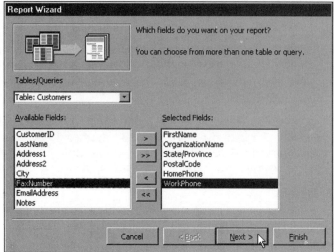

4. **In the Tables/Queries drop-down list, pick the first table or query that contains the fields you need for the report.**

   When you select the table or query, the Available Fields list updates to show everything that the selected item contains.

5. **Select the fields you want in the report by either double-clicking on the field names or clicking once by using the greater than (>, >>) or less than (<, <<) buttons.**

   The greater-than buttons move fields *into* the Selected Fields list, while the less-than buttons move fields *out of* the list.

   Although clicking on the buttons is fun, the easiest way to move a field from one side to another is by double-clicking on it. No matter which side the field starts on, double-clicking moves the field to the opposite list.

6. **After moving all the fields you want into the Selected Fields side of the dialog box, go back to Step 4 and repeat the process with the next table you need that contains fields for the report. When all the fields are listed in the Selected Fields side of the dialog box, click on Next. The window shown in Figure 18-9 appears.**

   If you *don't* see the window in Figure 18-9, that's okay. In that case, skip ahead to the next section. This screen only appears if the Report Wizard thinks that you need to see it. The screen lets you pick the field to use when organizing your report. The screen displays a sample page based on the Report Wizard's extensive analysis of your data (yes, that means the wizard *guessed*). Access 2000 may or may not correctly

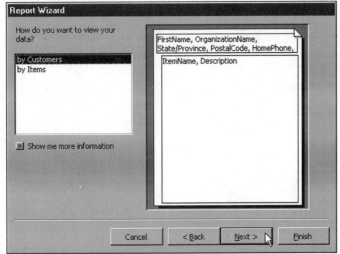

Figure 18-9:
This screen
lets you
choose how
you want
your infor-
mation
grouped.

discern how you want the data to appear (remember, it's only a program), so take a close look at each of the report-organization choices
and decide which one displays the information in the most effective
way. To see a different organization, click on one of the *by* choices on
the left side of the dialog box.

When you click on one of these choices, that field separates from the
other fields and appears at the top of the sample display (refer to Figure
18-9). All the information in the Details section (the main body) of your
report will be organized by the values in that field.

If you don't want the records sorted into groups, that's okay. Just click on the
very last entry in the *by* list (in this case, the *by Customers* entry). For reasons
beyond my comprehension (but that probably make sense to a demented
programmer somewhere), this action makes Access 2000 lump all the records
together, displaying the records without sorting them into groups.

More groups! More groups!

Up to this point, all the steps are the same whether you build a single-level or
a multilevel report. It's only with the next step that things start to get interesting. Click on Next to reveal the screen shown in Figure 18-10.

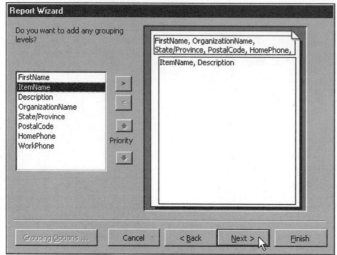

Figure 18-10:
The Report
Wizard
takes an
interesting
turn.

Access 2000 takes organization a step further by adding more grouping options — groups based on different fields than just the one you specified in the last section. The dialog box in Figure 18-10 lists the available fields on the left side of the window. Pick as many or as few as you want. To add a new group, based on a particular field, click on the field name and then click on the greater than > button. The wizard adjusts the sample page to show what your report looks like with the additional group, as shown in Figure 18-11.

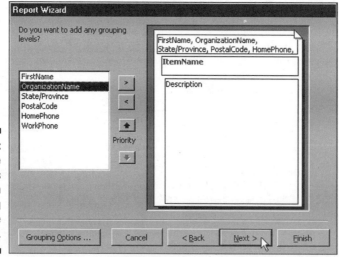

Figure 18-11:
Narrow the
report's
organization
by adding
more
groups.

What if you realize that you really want to organize the report by last name and *then,* within the LastName grouping, by site? All you have to do is rearrange the fields with the Priority buttons (as shown in Figure 18-11). If you highlight a field and click on the up-arrow Priority button, the field moves up a level in the organization. If you click on the down-arrow button, the highlighted field moves down a level.

If you highlight more than one field, the topmost one moves if you click on the up-arrow button; the lower field moves if you click on the down-arrow button. Then, if you repeat the click with the same button, the highlighted field next in line moves accordingly, and so on. You can play with this feature to your heart's content until the report is organized exactly as you want it.

Each of the fields you select to organize your report creates a new section. Each of these sections has its own header and footer area that can hold information from your database, or information that you add directly to the report through Design View after the wizard finishes its work.

Sorting out the details

After picking the fields for your report's groups, click on Next to go on with the sort order settings, shown in Figure 18-12.

Figure 18-12:
Set the report's sort order with a few swift clicks.

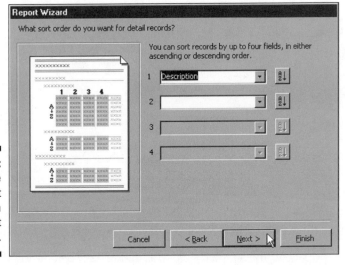

Access 2000 calls the fields that are not grouped as headers *Detail records*. The screen in Figure 18-12 lets you sort those records by the remaining fields, which you can organize in either ascending or descending order. To do that, simply select the field in the drop-down list and then click on the button at the right to change the sorting order from ascending (with the letters going from A at the top to Z at the bottom) to descending (with the letters going from Z at the top to A at the bottom). Don't ask me why the arrow doesn't just change directions. (Sorting on more than one field is discussed in more detail in Chapter 10.)

Notice that the lower middle of this dialog box contains a button labeled Summary Options. You can click on this button to see the dialog box shown in Figure 18-13. (If you don't see a Summary Options button on your screen, it's because your report doesn't include any number fields.) This dialog box lets you tell Access 2000 to summarize your data with a number of statistical tools, including totals (Sum), averages (Avg), minimums (Min), and maximums (Max). Check the boxes next to the operations that you want performed on the fields in your report.

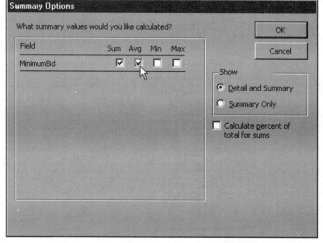

Figure 18-13:
Access 2000 can do statistical calculations on the data in your report. Better it than me.

In Figure 18-13, the auction company wants Access 2000 to add up all the minimum bids for each group (that's what the *Sum* checkmark does) and display the average minimum bid for each group (the purpose of the *Avg* entry).

On the right side of the Summary Options dialog box is an option labeled Show. If you want to see both the data *and* the summary, click on the Detail and Summary radio button. If you need to see only the summarized information, click on the Summary Only radio button. The last check box on this dialog box is Calculate the percent of total for sums. If you click on this button, Access 2000 calculates the total amount of the field and tells you the percentage of each record's contribution to that total.

The home stretch

After finishing the Summary Options and returning to the Report Wizard, click on Next to work on the report layout (shown in Figure 18-14).

The Report Wizard's Layout window offers a whole series of ready-to-use layouts to make your report both look great and read easily. Click on the styles in the Layout box, and then watch as Access shows you a sample of the layout on the left side of the screen. Your choices here vary depending on the data in your report.

The Orientation page lets you decide between having your report printed in Portrait (long edge along the side) or Landscape (long edge across the top and bottom) orientation. Again, this choice depends on your specific circumstances and preferences. Generally, if you have a lot of small fields or several large fields, Landscape orientation works best. For fewer fields of any shape or size, try Portrait.

The check box labeled, Adjust field width so all fields fit on a page, is important. If this box is checked (which it is by default), Access 2000 force-fits all of your fields onto one page, even if it has to squish some of them to do it. This is a dandy feature but it has a little, tiny drawback that you need to understand. During the highly scientific squishing process, the field may end up being too small to display the data it contains. For example, a field holding the name *Harriet Isa Finkelmeier* may only display *Harriet Isa Fink* after it gets squished. The rest of the name isn't lost — it just doesn't appear on the report. If you *don't* check the box, then Access 2000 packs as many fields onto the page as it can *without* changing any of the field widths. Fields that don't fit are left off the page, but the fields that *do* print appear in their normal, glorious size.

Figure 18-14: Access 2000 gives you several choices for report layout.

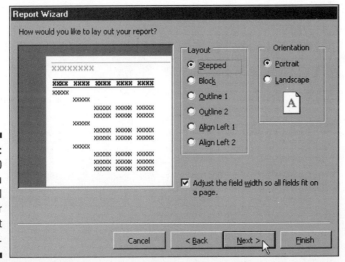

Click on Next one more time to see a dialog box that lets you choose from six predetermined styles for your report. The window at the left gives you a basic idea of what the style looks like. Again, this is a matter of taste, not what is "correct." Pick the one you like the most and move on.

Finally, you're ready to click on Next for the last time. In the final screen, you give your report a name. This action saves your report and provides it with its title. You also have the choice of previewing your report in Print Preview, modifying your report, or simply screaming for help. If you think that you are satisfied with what you've done, go ahead and preview your report. You should see something like the report shown in Figure 18-15.

If you want to make changes to the design of your report, you can click on the Modify report's design button before you click on Finish. If you do so, Access 2000 opens the Design view of your report, and you can tinker with the report to your heart's content. Chapter 19 explains how to modify and format your reports to create your own unique look.

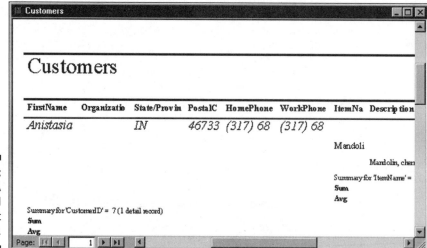

Figure 18-15:
Wow! A professional report at last.

Chapter 19

It's Amazing What a Little Formatting Can Do

In This Chapter

▶ Getting into Design view

▶ Working with report sections

▶ Marking text boxes and labels

▶ Previewing your stuff

▶ Putting AutoFormat to work for you

▶ Drawing lines and boxes

▶ Adding graphics to your reports

▶ Exporting reports to Microsoft Word and Excel

*T*he Access 2000 Report Wizard is a pretty swell fellow. After a brief round of 20 compu-questions, it sets up an informative, good-looking report for you automatically. Well, at least the report's *informative* — just between you and me, I think that the Report Wizard could use a little design training.

Although the Access 2000 Report Wizard does the best job it can, the results aren't always exactly what you need. Those clever engineers at Microsoft foresaw this problem and left a back door open for you. That door is called *Design view*. In Design view, you can change anything — and I mean *anything* — about your report's design. Reorganize the text boxes, add some text, emphasize certain text boxes with boxes and lines or do whatever else your heart desires.

This chapter guides you through some popular Design view tweaking and tuning techniques. With this information in hand, your reports are sure to be the envy of the office in no time. (And there's nothing like a well-envied report to start your day off just right.)

Taking Your Report to the Design View Tune-Up Shop

The first stop in your quest for a better-looking report is Design view itself. After all, you can't change *anything* in the report until the report is up on the jacks in the Design view. Thankfully, Access offers several easy ways to tow your report in for that much-needed tune-up. Precisely how you do it depends on where you are right now in Access 2000:

- ✔ After creating a report with the Report Wizard, the wizard asks if you want to preview your creation or modify its design (even the wizard knows that its design skills are lacking!). Click on the Modify the report's design radio button to send the wizard's creation straight into Design view.

- ✔ If the report is already on-screen in a preview, hop into Design view by clicking on the Design View button on the toolbar.

- ✔ To get into Design view from the Database window, click on the Reports button below the Objects bar and then click on the name of the report you want to work on. Click on the Design button (just above the report list in the Database window) to open the report in Design view.

No matter which method you use, Access 2000 sends you (and your report) to a Design view screen that looks a lot like Figure 19-1. Now you're ready to overhaul that report!

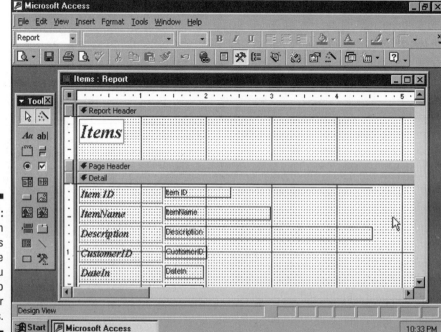

Figure 19-1: The Design view gives you all the tools you need to modify your reports.

Striking Up the Bands (And the Markers, Too)

When you look at a report in Design view, Access 2000 displays a slew of *markers* that are grouped into several bands (or *sections,* as they're called in Access 2000). The markers show where Access 2000 plans to put the text boxes and text that will appear on your final report. They also give you an idea of how the program plans to format everything.

Access 2000 uses two kinds of markers, depending on what kind of information the report includes:

- ✔ **Text boxes:** Boxes that display a particular field's data in the report. Every field you want to include in the final report has a text box in the Design view. If the report doesn't include a text box for one of the fields in your table, the data for that field won't end up in the report.

- ✔ **Labels:** Plain, simple text markers that display some kind of text message on the report. Sometimes, labels stand alone (such as "The information in this report is confidential. So there."); often, they accompany a text box to show people who read the report what kind of data they're looking at ("Customer ID" or "Right Shoe Size," for example).

Markers are organized into sections that represent the different parts of your report. The sections govern where and how often a particular field or text message is repeated in your report. The report design in Figure 19-2 displays the three most common sections: Report Header, Page Header, and Detail. Arrows to the left of the section names show you which markers each section contains.

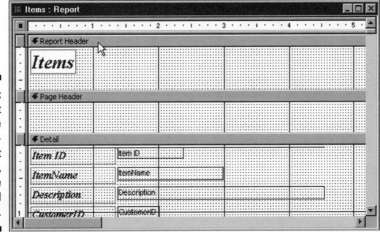

Figure 19-2:
Every report has three basic sections: Report Header, Page Header, and Detail.

The sections work in teams that straddle the Detail area. The teams are pretty easy to figure out (Report Header works with Report Footer, and Page Header works with Page Footer, for example). Figure 19-3 displays the mates to the sections shown in Figure 19-2.

Figure 19-3:
The Page Footer and Report Footer mirror their headers.

Here's how the most common sections work (including such important details as where and how often the sections appear in your printed report):

- ✔ **Report Header:** Anything that appears in the Report Header prints at the very start of the report. The information prints only once and appears at the top of the first page.

- ✔ **Page Header:** Information in the Page Header prints at the top of each and every page. The only exception is on the report's very first page, where Access 2000 prints the Report Header and *then* the Page Header.

- ✔ **Detail:** The meat of the report, the stuff in the Detail section fills the majority of each report page. The Detail section is repeated for every record included in the report.

- ✔ **Page Footer:** When each page is nearly full, Access finishes it off by printing the Page Footer at the bottom.

- ✔ **Report Footer:** At the bottom of the very last page, immediately following the Page Footer, the Report Footer wraps things up.

Being familiar with Glenn Miller, Claude Bolling, or John Philip Sousa won't help you when it comes to report bands in Access 2000. (Sorry, but I just couldn't let the term *band* go by without making some kind of musical note.) Because the how-to of bands (or, if you prefer, *sections*) is so important to your reports, Chapter 20 explores the topic in exhausting detail. Chapter 20 includes information on inserting and adjusting sections, and convincing them to perform all kinds of automated calculations.

Formatting This, That, These, and Those

You can artfully amend almost anything in a report's design with the help of the Formatting toolbar in Figure 19-4. Whether you want to change text color, font size, or the visual effect surrounding a text box, this toolbar has the goodies you need.

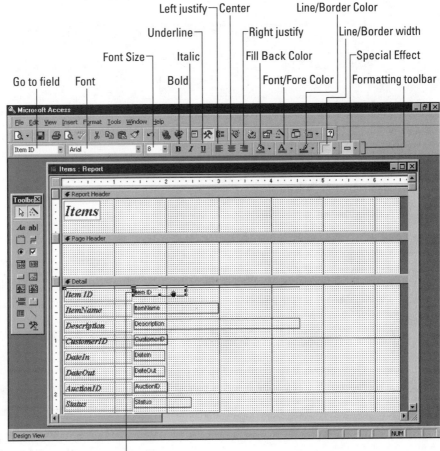

Figure 19-4: The tools to format the features of your report hop into action when you select a text box.

To adjust items in your report with the tools in the Formatting toolbar, follow these steps:

1. Click on the item you want to format.

Any text box, label, line, or box will do — Access 2000 is an equal-opportunity formatter. When you click on something, a bunch of little black boxes appear around it, much like Figure 19-5. (The little black boxes are a good sign.)

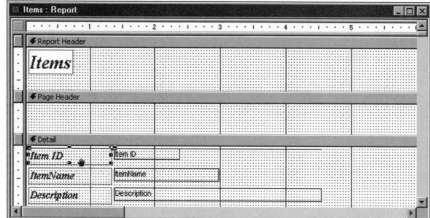

Figure 19-5:
The field marker for the label information is selected.

2. Click on the toolbar button for the formatting effect you want.

With most formatting tools, the new format immediately takes effect. Some tools (such as the ones for color, border, and 3D effect) also offer a pull-down list of choices. I cover these options in detail later in the chapter, so don't worry about them right now.

3. Repeat Steps 1 and 2 for all of the text boxes you want to modify.

If you make a mistake while formatting, just choose Edit⇨Undo Property Setting. Poof! Access removes the last formatting you applied.

The following sections step through some of the most common formatting tasks ahead of you. Just follow the instructions and soon your report will look like a cross between the Mona Lisa and a state tax form (I *think* that's a compliment, but I'll have to get back to you on that).

Taking control of your report

In addition to the normal goodies found on an everyday Access report (like labels and text boxes), you can also include all kinds of fascinating items called _controls._ You add controls to the report by using the Design view Toolbox (the floating island of buttons sitting somewhere around your screen).

Some controls work with specific types of fields. For example, a check box can graphically display the value of a Yes/No field. (Plus, controls look cool on the page.)

Anything this neat simply _must_ be a little complicated, and the controls certainly live up to these expectations. Access 2000 includes several control wizards to take the pain out of the process. These wizards, like their brethren elsewhere in the program, walk you through the steps for building your controls in a patient, step-by-step manner. The control wizards _usually_ come to life automatically after you place a control in the report.

If you create a new control but the control wizard doesn't show up to help, make sure that the Wizard button at the top of the Toolbox (the button emblazoned with a magic wand) is turned on. If it's on, the button looks as though it's pushed down a bit. If you aren't sure, click it a couple of times so you can see the difference.

Some of the controls (specifically the Line, Rectangle, Page Break, and image controls) are covered later in this chapter. The next chapter includes tips about using controls to create summaries in your report.

Colorizing your report

Nothing brightens up a drab report like a spot of color. Access 2000 makes adding color easy with the Font/Fore Color and the Fill/Back Color buttons. These buttons are located on your friendly Formatting toolbar (no surprises there).

Both buttons change the color of text markers in your report, but they differ a little in precisely how they do it:

- ✔ The Font/Fore Color button changes the color of text in a text box or label marker.

- ✔ The Fill/Back color button alters the marker's background color but leaves the text color alone.

To select a color to use, click on the arrow at the right of the Font/Fore Color or Fill/Back Color button. When the menu of colors appears, click on the color you want to use. Notice that your color choice also appears along the bottom of the toolbar button, too.

To change the color of a text box or label on your report, click on the marker that you want to work with. To change the font color, click on the Font/Fore Color button; to change the background, click on Fill/Back Color, instead. The new color settings appear right away on-screen, like the label in Figure 19-6 that proudly sports a new gray background.

Figure 19-6:
You can color the background of any item in your report.

You can also use the Font/Fore Color button to change the color of the text in a text box or any label. You can easily create special effects by choosing contrasting colors for the foreground and background, just like the white text floating on a black background in Figure 19-7.

Figure 19-7:
Combine and mix colors to create just the effect you want.

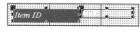

Be careful when choosing your colors — if you make the text and background colors the same, the text seems to disappear! If this happens, just choose Edit⇨Undo Property Setting to bring back the original color setting.

Moving things around

Feel like reorganizing things a little bit? You can easily move just about any element (text box, label, line, and such) in a report. In fact, moving things is *so* easy that you need to go slow and take extra care not to move things you shouldn't.

To move a line, box, label, or text box, follow these steps:

1. **Click on the item you want to move.**

   A bunch of black squares surround the item, letting you know that it's selected.

   If you have trouble selecting a line, try clicking near its ends. For some reason, Access 2000 has a tough time recognizing when you want to grab a line. Clicking right at the line's end seems to help the program figure out what you want to do.

2. **Move the mouse pointer to any edge of the selected item.**

   When you do this step, the mouse pointer turns into a little hand. Too cute, isn't it?

3. **Press and hold the left mouse button and then drag your item to a new position.**

   As you move the mouse, the little hand drags an outline of whatever object you selected. (Depending on your computer's video card, you *may* see the whole object move instead of just watching the outline box wander around the screen.)

4. **Release the mouse button when the item is hovering over its new home.**

   If something goes wrong, and you want to undo the movement, choose Edit⇨Undo Property Setting or just press Ctrl+Z (the universal Undo key). Access 2000 is *very* forgiving about such things.

In some Access 2000 reports (specifically the ones created by the Columnar Report Wizard), the text box and label for each field in the report are attached to each other. If you move one, the other automatically follows. In this case, you have to adjust the procedure a bit if you want to move one *without* moving the other. Follow the preceding steps, but instead of moving the cursor to the edge of the marker, move it to one of the big square handles shown in Figure 19-8.

Figure 19-8:
Use big handles to move a label or a text box separately.

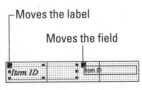

Moves the label

Moves the field

Item ID   Item ID

✔ The handle on the far left moves the label.

✔ The handle in the middle of the two markers moves the text box.

As the mouse pointer enters the handle, the cursor changes to a pointing finger. That's your sign that you can proceed with Step 3 — press and hold the mouse button and then start moving. Release the mouse button when you have the text box positioned where you want it. If the mouse pointer changes to a double-ended arrow instead of a pointing hand, try moving your mouse pointer onto the big handle again. That double-ended arrow tells Access to *resize* the item, not to move it.

Other types of reports, such as Tabular Reports or Labels, do not combine the label and the text box together the way Columnar reports do. In such reports, either no label appears, or the label appears only once in the Page Header section. When labels aren't linked to their respective text boxes, they each appear separately — without the special large handles shown in Figure 19-8.

Use the smaller handles around the edge of a text box to resize the text box. For example, if you discover that the information in one of your text boxes is getting cut off, you can click on the text box and use the small handles to make that text box somewhat longer. Or if a text box contains a lot of information, you can make the text box taller. Access wraps the information to more than one line.

The amount of space between the markers controls the space between items when you print the report. Increasing that spacing gives your report a less crowded look; decreasing the space enables you to fit more information on the page.

Bordering on beautiful

Organizationally speaking, lines and marker borders do wonderful things for your report. They draw your reader's eye to particular parts of the page, highlight certain sections of the report, and generally spruce up an otherwise drab page. The toolbar contains three buttons to put lines and borders through their paces: the Line/Border Color button, the Line/Border Width button, and the ever-popular Special Effects button.

Coloring your lines and borders

The Line/Border Color button changes the color of lines that mark a text box's border and lines drawn on your report with the Line tool. This button works just like the Back Color and the Font/Fore Color buttons did for text, so you probably know a lot about using it already. (Comforting feeling, isn't it?)

To change the color of a line or a marker's border, follow these steps:

1. **Click on the marker or line to select it.**

   Remember to click near the end of a line to select it; otherwise, you may end up clicking all around the line, but never highlighting it.

2. **Click on the arrow next to the Line/Border Color button.**

   A drop-down display of color choices appears on-screen (see Figure 19-9).

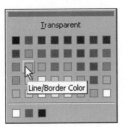

Figure 19-9:
Choose from an entire palette of colors.

3. **Click on your choice from the rainbow of options.**

Widening your lines and borders

In addition to colorizing lines and borders, you can also control their width:

1. **Click on the line or text marker you want to work with.**

2. **Click on the arrow next to the Line/Border Width button to display line- and border-width options.**

   Your choices for line and border width are represented in terms of *points* (a geeky publishing word that means ¹⁄₇₂ *inch*). The menu offers options for a hairline (half-point) line, 1 point, 2 points, 3 points, 4 points, 5 points, and finally the 6-point Monster Line that Devoured Toronto. (A 6-point line is ¹⁄₁₂ of an inch thick, but actually appears quite heavy on a report.)

3. **Click on the line- or border-width option you want.**

   That's all there is to it! As with everything else, choosing Edit⇨Undo Property Setting repairs any accidental damage, so feel free to experiment with the options.

Adding special effects to your lines and borders

You can change the style of a marker's border by using the Special Effects button. Six choices are available under this button, as shown in Figure 19-10.

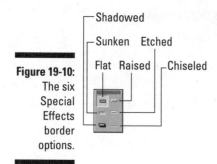

Figure 19-10:
The six
Special
Effects
border
options.

The Sunken and Raised options actually change the colors on two sides of the text box, but the effect makes the text box look three-dimensional. Selecting a sunken border makes the label or text box appear as though it is pushed into your text; a raised border makes it seem as though your text box is rising out of your text. Figure 19-11 shows an example of a raised border and a sunken border. Striking difference, isn't it? (Yes, I *am* kidding.)

Figure 19-11:
Can you
tell the
difference?

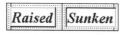

The Chiseled option gives a text box the appearance of having the bottom portion of its border raised upward, and the Etched option gives the effect of the border being etched into the background around the text box. The colors of your text box and of your report background affect how these borders look. Figure 19-12 shows examples of these two types of borders.

Figure 19-12:
You can't
miss the
difference
between
these
effects.

The Shadow option places a shadow around the lower-right of the text box. The Flat option simply puts a standard, single-line border around the entire text box.

To add special effects to a markers border, follow the same basic steps as you would for changing a border's color or width:

1. **Click on the marker whose border you want to change.**

2. **Click on the arrow next to the Special Effects button to display your six options.**

3. **Click on the special effect you want to add.**

If you have trouble reaching all the buttons on the drop-down Special Effects list, you can tear the list off the menu bar. Simply click on the down-arrow to display the list and then click on the bar at the top of the drop-down display area. When you drag the pointer down and to the left (outside the border of the list), a dotted rectangle the same size and shape as the list follows the pointer. When you can see all of the rectangle, release the mouse button. Ta da! A floating toolbar that displays the Special Effects options.

Tweaking your text

The tools on the left side of the Formatting toolbar change the style of the text within a selected text box. You can choose the font (the actual shape of the characters used to display text), the size of the font, and whether the font is **bold,** *italic,* or <u>underlined</u> — just use the formatting buttons shown in Figure 19-13.

Controls what letters look like

Controls letter size

Makes text bold

Figure 19-13:
These tools
change the
appearance
of your text.

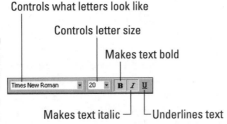

Makes text italic ⌐   └Underlines text

To change the font or the font size, simply click on the arrow to the right of the Font or Font Size list box and select from the drop-down list that appears. To turn on or off the bold, italic, or underline characteristics, select a block of text and click on the appropriate button. If the feature is off, clicking on the button turns it on. If the feature is on, clicking on the button turns it off. When one of these formatting features is turned on, the button appears to be pressed into the surface of the toolbar.

You can also control the alignment of the text within labels and text boxes. To change the alignment of the text for a label or text box, simply select the marker and then click on one of the three alignment buttons on the toolbar.

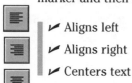

✔ Aligns left

✔ Aligns right

✔ Centers text

In Figure 19-14, the labels are both left-aligned, but the text boxes vary a bit. The top one is right-aligned, but the bottom one is left-aligned. As you can see, badly aligned text boxes are a little distracting. To make the best-looking report possible, pay attention to the little details like label and data alignment. Your effort may mean the difference between a hard-to-read report and an object of informational beauty.

Figure 19-14:
You can
change the
text alignment
for text boxes
and labels.

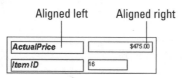

Taking a Peek

After fiddling around long enough in Design view, you inevitably reach a point where you want to view the *actual* report, rather than just looking at the technical magic being used to create it. No matter how good your imagination is, it's difficult to visualize how everything will actually look when it all comes together in the printed report. Access 2000 provides two distinct tools for previewing your report.

✔ **Layout Preview:** When you choose the Layout Preview, Access 2000 takes a portion of your data and arranges it to give you an idea of how your data will appear in the finished report. The preview shows only a sampling of your data (without performing any final calculations that you included). The idea is to see what the report *looks like,* not to review your calculations. To view Layout Preview, click on the down-arrow next to the Report View button and then select Layout Preview from the drop-down list, as shown in Figure 19-15.

✔ **Print Preview:** If you want to see a full preview of your report, complete with the calculations and all the data, select Print Preview by clicking on the Print Preview button. (Or you can go the long way around and click on the down-arrow next to the Report View button and then select Print Preview from the drop-down list shown in Figure 19-15.)

Regardless of which approach you use, you see a Print Preview screen similar to the one shown in Figure 19-16. The various items of your report appear as they will when you print the report. You can then use the controls at the top of the Print Preview window to change the appearance of the screen.

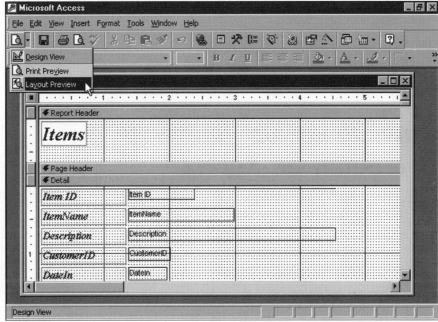

Figure 19-15: Choose Layout Preview to see how the report will look; choose Print Preview to see the report in full.

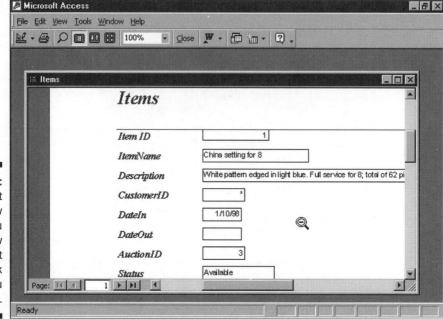

Figure 19-16:
Print
Preview
shows you
exactly how
your report
will look
when you
print it.

For more information about using Print Preview and Layout Preview, see
Chapter 17.

AutoFormatting Your Way to a Beautiful Report

When you want to change the look of the whole report in one (or two) easy
clicks, check out the AutoFormat button. When you click on this button,
Access 2000 offers several different format packages that reset everything
from the headline font to the color of lines that split up items in the report.

To use AutoFormat, follow these steps:

1. Click in the empty gray area below the Report Footer band.

This may sound like a strange first step, but there's reason behind my
peculiarity (or at least there is *this* time). Clicking in this area is the easiest way to tell Access 2000 that you don't want *any* report sections
selected. If any one section is selected when you do the AutoFormat
command, then AutoFormat *only* changes the contents of that one section. Although that kind of precision may be nice sometimes, most of the
time you want AutoFormat to redo your whole report.

2. **Click on the AutoFormat toolbar button.**

A dialog box appears, listing your various package-deal formatting choices.

3. **Click on the name of the format you want and then click on OK (see Figure 19-17).**

Access 2000 updates everything in your report with the newly selected look.

If just a few text boxes in one section change, but the majority of the report stays the same, go back to Step 1 and try that *click in the gray area* step again. The odds are good that you had one section selected when you clicked AutoFormat.

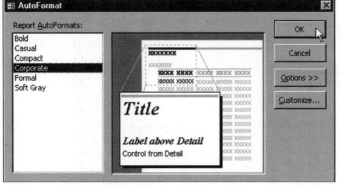

Figure 19-17:
Pick the look that you like and apply it to the whole report.

You can use the Customize button to create your own formats, which Access then stores on the AutoFormat page. Simply format your report using a consistent set of fonts, colors, and borders for everything on the report; then click on AutoFormat. In the AutoFormat dialog box, click on Customize. At this point, you have the option of adding your new format to the list or replacing one of the existing formats with your new definition. Don't redefine any of the default formats; instead, if you want to add your own format to the list, create a new AutoFormat for it. Give your new format a name and then click on Close to make the dialog box go away.

Lining Everything Up

When you start moving various items around on your report, you can easily wind up with a report that's out of alignment. For example, you may have put the column headings in the Page Header and the actual information farther down the page in a Detail line. Of course, you want the text boxes to line up with the headers, but simply moving the items around the page by hand and eyeballing the results may not do the trick.

The grid in the background of the screen can help you position screen elements by aligning them with the vertical lines or with the various dots on the Design screen. When you move an object on the report, you can choose Format➪Snap to Grid to control whether the object stays lined up with these dots that are "snapped to the grid," or whether you can move the object freely between the dots.

When you move an object with Snap to Grid turned on, the object's upper-left corner always aligns with one of the dots on the grid. Choose this command when you resize an object, and the side of the object that you move stays aligned with the dots on the grid.

Figure 19-18 shows several objects that I moved into position on-screen. I positioned the items in the left column with the help of the Snap to Grid command; I positioned the items in the right column freehand, without Snap to Grid steadying my hand. Notice how the label markers in the left column are lined up nicely, but the text boxes on the right are all over the page. So much for my dream of becoming a surgeon.

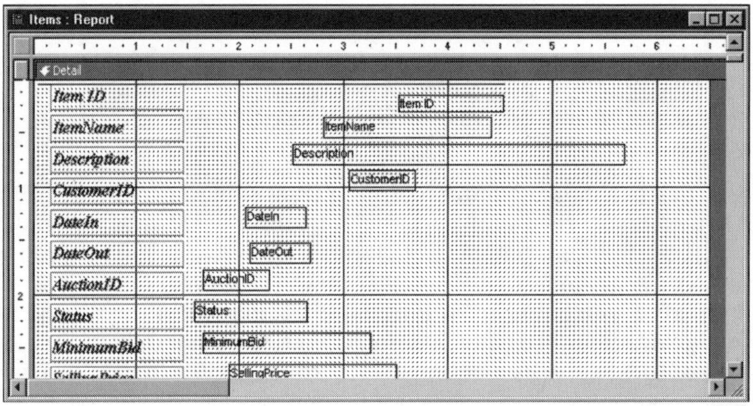

Figure 19-18:
The Snap to Grid feature helps you keep your reports neat and aligned, without driving yourself crazy.

Other commands on the Format menu that you may find useful for arranging objects on your reports include:

✔ **Align:** You can choose two or more objects and align them to each other or to the grid. Selecting Left, Right, Top, or Bottom causes the left, right, top, or bottom sides of the selected items to line up. For example, if you select three objects and then choose Format➪Align➪Left, the three objects move so that their left edges line up. By default, Access 2000 moves objects to line up with the object that is the farthest to the left.

✔ **Size:** You can change the size of a group of objects by selecting the objects and then selecting an option from the Size submenu. For example, you can choose Size⇨to Fit, which adjusts the size of the controls so that each one is just large enough to hold the information it contains. Choose Size⇨to Grid to adjust the controls so that all control corners are positioned on grid points.

Or adjust the controls relative to each other. If you choose Size⇨ to Tallest, Size⇨to Shortest, Size⇨to Widest, or Size⇨to Narrowest, each box in the selected group is adjusted to that characteristic. In other words, if you select a group of controls and then choose Size⇨to Tallest, each of the selected controls is resized to the same height as the tallest control in the selected group.

✔ **Horizontal Spacing, Vertical Spacing:** Use these commands to space a selected group of objects equally. This feature can be very useful if you're trying to spread out the title items for a report. Simply select the items in your group and then choose Format⇨Vertical Spacing⇨ Make Equal to have Access 2000 space the items equally.

Figure 19-19 shows four labels and text boxes in the top of the figure that are somewhat mushed together, and a duplicate set of four labels and text boxes lower down on the page that have been distributed with the Make Equal command.

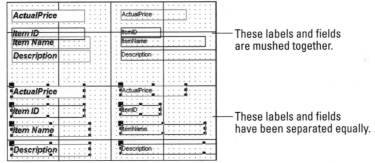

Figure 19-19:
Make Equal spreads the markers evenly on the page.

These labels and fields are mushed together.

These labels and fields have been separated equally.

Drawing Your Own Lines

An easy way to make your report a bit easier to read is to add lines that divide the various sections. To add lines to your report, follow these steps:

1. **Open the Toolbox by clicking on the Toolbox toolbar button.**

   Bet you can't say that five times fast!

2. **Click on the Line tool from the Toolbox.**

    When you select the Line tool, your cursor changes to a cross-hair with a line trailing off to the right.

3. **Click where you want to start the line, drag to the location where you want to end the line, and release the mouse button.**

    Access adds a line along the path you draw.

You can use the various toolbar buttons (discussed earlier in this chapter) to dress up your lines. For example, to change the line's color, thickness, and appearance, use the Line/Border Color, Line/Border Width, and Special Effects buttons.

You can use the Box tool to draw boxes around separate items on your report. Click on the point that you want to be the upper-left corner of your box, and drag the box shape down to the lower-right corner. When you release the mouse button, presto, you have a box.

Inserting Page Breaks

Most of the time, page breaks aren't high on the list of report priorities. Instead, you worry about things like making the summaries work, lining the data up into neat columns and rows, and selecting the proper shade of magenta (or was that more of a pinky russet?) for the lines and label borders.

Occasionally, though, you get the urge to tell Access 2000 precisely where a report page should end. Maybe you want to end each page with a special calculation, or just keep some information grouped on the same page. Regardless of the reason, inserting a page break into your report is as quick as a click.

To insert a page break into your Access 2000 report, follow these steps:

1. **Click on the Page Break button in the Toolbox.**

    The mouse pointer changes into a crosshair with a page next to it, signifying that you're about to do something that involves a page. (Someday, I want to be the person that gets paid to design mouse pointers for Windows programs. Can you imagine explaining that job to your kids' class on Parents Day?)

2. **Position the crosshair wherever you want the page break and then click on the left mouse button.**

    A couple of small black marks appear on the left side of the report. This little notation, believe it or not, is the page break marker. From now on, a new page will always begin here.

If you want to remove a page break that you so carefully added, click on the page break marker and then press Delete. That page break's outta there. If you want to move the page break, click on it, press and hold the mouse button, and then drag the page break marker to its new home. When the page break is hovering over the right spot, release the mouse button to place the page break.

Sprucing Up the Place with a Few Pictures

 A sure-fire way to spruce up a report is to add an image to it. You can use the Image button in the Toolbox to create a frame into which you can paste an image from your clip art collection.

 Images are great, but I strongly encourage you to add images only to the Report Header or Page Header. If you put an image in the Detail section, for example, the image would repeat so many times that the report would look as though you wanted a little information with your graphics, instead of a few graphics to perk up the information.

 If you don't have an image that you're ready to use, but rather have an image in progress, you may choose to use the Unbound Object Frame to add an OLE object. *OLE* (which stands for *object linking and embedding*) enables you to put an object onto your page, while maintaining the object's link to its original file. Any changes to that original file are reflected in the object you place into the report. You can link to an image or to *any* type of file that supports OLE.

When you click on either the Image or the Unbounded Object Frame tool, you get a plus-sign pointer, with the button's image to the lower right. You can then use this tool to draw a box onto your screen.

 ✔ **If you're using the Image tool:** Access opens the Insert Picture dialog box, which you can use to locate the image you want to insert.

 ✔ **If you're using the Unbound Object Frame tool:** Access opens the Insert Object dialog box so you can choose the type of object to insert. This option enables you to insert objects ranging from graphic images to digital sound files — you can even include a whole Microsoft Excel worksheet! (For more about the magic of OLE, see *OLE For Dummies,* by John Mueller and Wallace Wang.)

 You can also add an image to your report by cutting or copying the image from another program, storing it on the Clipboard, and then pasting it onto your design. This technique is the only easy way to include *part* of an image from a file.

Passing Your Reports around the (Microsoft) Office

You can do an awful lot with Access 2000, but sometimes a different program can get the job done better and make your life a little easier. The engineers at Microsoft gave Access 2000 the ability to send information directly to other Microsoft programs.

The key to this trick is the Tools⇨Office Links option on the main menu. This menu includes three options: two for sending your report to Microsoft Word and one for shipping it off to Excel.

From Access to Word

The Word option tells Access to convert the various items in your report into a form that Word understands and then builds the finished product as a new Word document. In fact, Access even opens the document for you in Word automatically. (If, of course, you own a copy of Word and your computer has enough memory to run both Word and Access at the same time.)

Of course, if you *do* own a copy of Word, you probably have *Word 2000 For Windows For Dummies,* by Dan Gookin (IDG Books Worldwide, Inc.). Right?

From Access to Excel

Analyze It with MS Excel takes your report (or whatever information you were working on in Access 2000), creates a datasheet, and then formats the data as an Excel worksheet. Each line of the report is placed in its own row, and the information that forms columns in your Access 2000 report becomes separate columns on your Excel worksheet. Your system then runs Excel and displays your newest creation. You can then use any of the Excel tools (including charting) to analyze, interpret, and generally abuse your data.

For more about making Excel 2000 do some rather impressive tricks, pick up a copy of Excel 2000 For Windows For Dummies, by Greg Harvey (IDG Books Worldwide, Inc.).

From Access to Mail Merge

The Merge It button is available only when you are working with a table or query. Unlike the other buttons, which just take your information and run with it, clicking on the Merge It button (or choosing the Merge It command) starts the Mail Merge Wizard. This wizard guides you through the steps of linking your database with a Word Mail Merge document.

Chapter 20

Headers and Footers for Groups, Pages, and Even (Egad) Whole Reports

• •

In This Chapter

▶ Getting into sections

▶ Grouping and sorting your records

▶ Adjusting the size of sections

▶ Fine-tuning the layout of your report

▶ Controlling your headers and footers

▶ Putting expressions into your footers

▶ Adding page numbers and dates

• •

*W*izards are great for creating reports, but they can only do so much for you. Even when you're working with a wizard, you still need to know a little something about how to group the fields of your report to get the optimum results. And someday after you've created your report, you may need to alter its organization or fine-tune its components to meet your changing needs. To tweak an existing report, you need to go into Design view and manually make the changes you want.

Don't despair! This chapter is designed to help you through these thorny issues. In this chapter, I explain the logic behind grouping your fields in a report, and I show you several options for your groups. I also walk you through the Design view thicket — a thorny place if ever there was one.

Everything in Its Place

The secret to successful report organization lies in the way you position the markers (known to programmers as *controls*) for the labels and fields within the report design. Each and every portion of the report design is separated into *sections* (called *bands* in other database programs) that identify different portions of the report. Which parts of the report land in which section depends on the report's layout:

- **Columnar:** In a standard Columnar report (see Figure 20-1), field descriptions print with every record's data. The layout behaves this way because both the field descriptions and data area are in the report's Detail section. Because the report title is in the Report Header section, it prints only once, at the very beginning of the report.

- **Tabular:** The setup is quite different in a standard Tabular report, such as the one in Figure 20-2. The title prints at the top of the report, just as in the Columnar report, but the similarity ends there. Instead of hanging out with the data, the field descriptions move to the Page Header section. Here, they print once per *page* instead of once per record. The data areas are by themselves in the Detail section.

Understanding the whole *section* concept is a prerequisite for performing any serious surgery on your report or for running off to build a report from scratch. Otherwise, your report groupings don't work right, fields are out of place, and life with Access 2000 is less fulfilling than it can be.

The most important point to understand about sections is that the contents of each section are printed *only* when certain events occur. For example, the information in the Page Header is repeated at the top of *each* page, but the Report Header only prints on the *first* page.

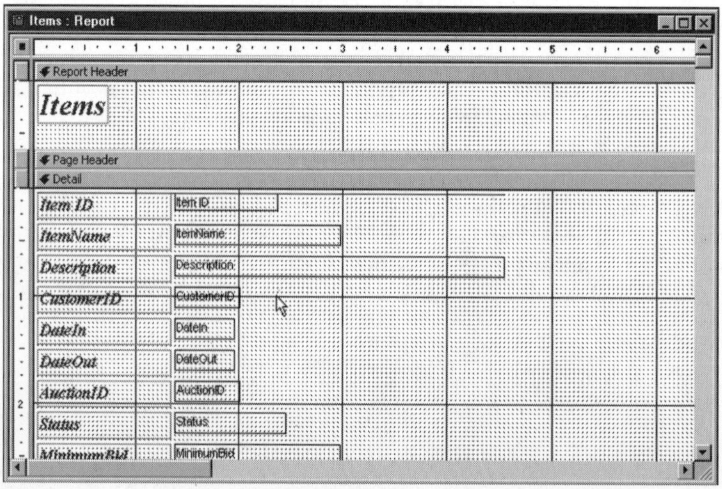

Figure 20-1:
The sections in Design view. In a Columnar report, the labels are to the left of the fields and repeat for each record.

Items : Report

Report Header

Items

Page Header
Detail

Item ID	Item ID
ItemName	ItemName
Description	Description
CustomerID	CustomerID
DateIn	DateIn
DateOut	DateOut
AuctionID	AuctionID
Status	Status
MinimumBid	MinimumBid

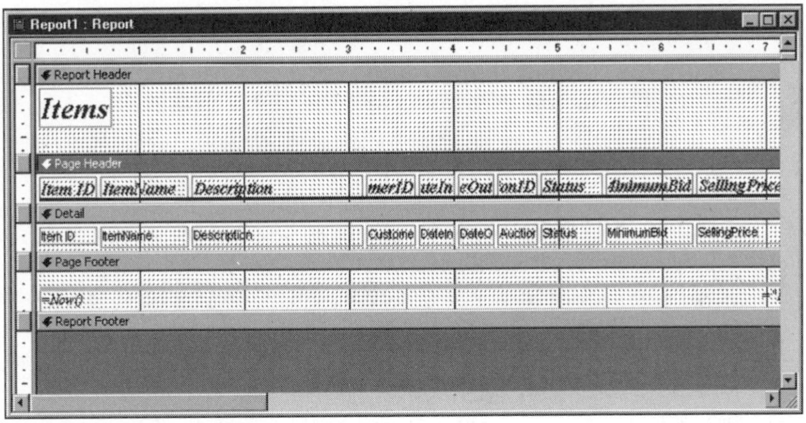

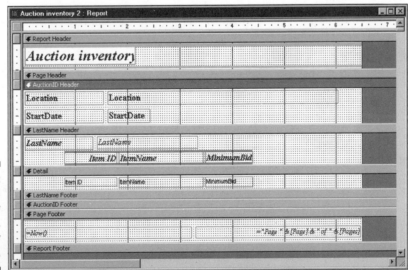

Figure 20-2:
In a Tabular report, labels are used as column headers for the fields and appear only once.

Getting a grip on sections is easy when you look at the innermost section of your report and work your way outward, like so:

✔ **Details:** At the center of every report is the Details section. Access prints items in this section each time it moves on to a new record. Your report includes a copy of the Details section for each and every record in the table.

✔ **Group headers and footers:** Moving outward from the Details section, you may have markers for one or more *group sections.* In Figure 20-3, information in the report is grouped by AuctionID, and then by LastName (you can tell by the section bars labeled `AuctionID Header` and `LastName Header` — the section bars identify which field is used for grouping).

Figure 20-3:
Grouping records by AuctionID, and then by LastName.

Group sections always come in pairs: the *group header* and the *group footer*. The header section is above the Details section in the report design; the footer is always below Details. Information in these sections is repeated for every unique value in the group's field. For example, the report in Figure 20-3 will reprint everything in the AuctionID Header for each unique auction number. Within the section for each auction, Access repeats the information in the LastName Header for each customer.

✔ **Page Header and Page Footer:** Above and below the group sections, you find the Page Header and Page Footer. These sections appear at the top and bottom of every page. They're among the few sections not controlled by the contents of your records. Use the information in the Page Header and Footer sections to identify the pages of your report.

✔ **Report Header and Footer:** The outermost sections are the Report Header, which appears at the start of your report, and the Report Footer, which appears at the end of your report. Both the Report Header and the Report Footer make only one appearance in your report — unlike the other sections, which pop up many times.

So when Access produces a report, what does it do with all these sections? The process goes a little something like this:

1. Access begins by printing the Report Header at the top of the first page.

2. Next, it prints the Page Header, if you choose to have the Page Header appear on the first page. (Otherwise, Access reprints this header at the top of every page except the first one.)

3. If your report has some groups, the Group Headers for the first set of records appear next.

4. When the headers are in place, Access finally prints the Detail lines for each record in the first group.

5. After it's done with all the Detail lines for the first group, Access prints that group's footer.

6. If you have more than one group, Access starts the process over again by printing the next group header, and then that group's Detail lines, and then that group's footer.

7. At the end of each page, Access prints the Page Footer.

8. When it finishes with the last group, Access prints the Report Footer — which, like the Report Header, only appears once in a given report.

Having all these headers and footers is great, but what do you *do* with them?

✔ The Report Header often provides general information about the report. This is a good place to add the report title, printing date, and version information.

✔ The Page Header contains any information you want to appear at the top of each page (such as the date, your company's logo, or whatever).

✔ The headers for each group usually identify the contents of that group and the field names.

✔ The footers for each group generally contain summary information, such as counts and calculations. The footer section of the Auction ID group, in this example, may hold a calculation that totals up the Minimum Bids.

✔ The Page Footer, which appears at the bottom of every page, traditionally holds the page number and report date fields. If the information is very important to your company, consider typing something like **Company Confidential** in the footer (won't your corporate lawyers be proud!).

✔ By the time the Report Footer prints, about the only information left is a master summary of what happened during the report. You may also include contact information (whom to call with questions about the report) if you plan to distribute the report widely throughout the company.

Grouping your records

If you're designing a report from scratch, you can use the Sorting and Grouping dialog box to create your groups and control how they behave. Perhaps more importantly, however, if you use a wizard to create a report for you, you can still use this dialog box to control how that report behaves and where information appears.

When the Report Wizard creates a report for you, it automatically includes a header and footer section for each group you want. If you tell the Report Wizard to group by the field AuctionID, it automatically creates both the AuctionID Header and the AuctionID Footer sections. You aren't limited to what the wizard does, though — if you're a little adventuresome, you can augment the wizard's work with your own grouping sections.

The key to creating your own grouping sections is the Sorting and Grouping dialog box in Figure 20-4. This dialog box controls how Access organizes the records in your report. Each grouping section in your report is automatically included in the sorting and grouping list (regardless of whether you created the section or the wizard did). You can also have additional entries that sort the records, although these entries don't generate their own section headers.

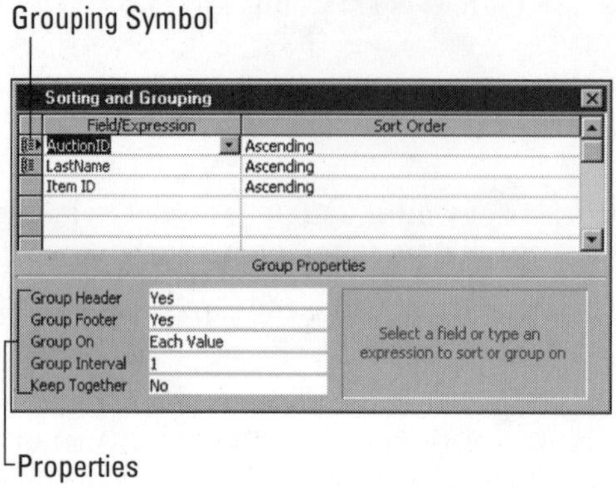

Grouping Symbol

Figure 20-4:
You can
adjust the
organization
of your
report with-
out going
back to see
the wizard.

Sorting and Grouping	
Field/Expression	Sort Order
AuctionID	Ascending
LastName	Ascending
Item ID	Ascending

Group Properties

Group Header	Yes
Group Footer	Yes
Group On	Each Value
Group Interval	1
Keep Together	No

Select a field or type an
expression to sort or group on

Properties

To build your own groupings, follow these steps:

1. **Choose View⇨Sorting and Grouping.**

   The Sorting and Grouping dialog box appears.

2. **Click on a blank line under Field/Expression.**

   The blinking toothpick cursor appears there, along with a down-arrow
   button.

3. **Click on the down-arrow to display a list of fields you can use for the
   group. Click on the field of your choice.**

   Access 2000 adds a new line for that field to the Sorting and Grouping
   list. By default, Access plans to do an ascending sort (smallest to
   largest) with the data in that field.

4. **To tell Access 2000 that you want the entry to be a full-fledged group,
   click in the Group Header area at the bottom of the dialog box. Click
   on the down-arrow that appears in the box and then select Yes from
   the drop-down menu.**

   Behind the scenes, Access 2000 adds a new group section to your report
   design. To include a footer for your new group as well, repeat this step
   in the Group Footer entry of the dialog box.

5. **When you're finished, close the dialog box.**

   That's it — your new group is in place.

To remove a group, click on the gray button next to the group's Field/Expression line and then press Delete. When Access frantically asks whether you really want to delete the group, click on Yes.

Notice that the first two entries in Figure 20-4 have a special symbol next to them. The symbol indicates that other groups are sorted or organized within *this* group. If you group records by more than one field (as this report does), the symbol is repeated in the list for each of the grouping fields.

If you want to change the order of the various groups, just dash back to the Sorting and Grouping dialog box (choose View➪Sorting and Grouping). Click on the gray button next to the group you want to move; then click and drag the group to its new location. Access automatically adjusts your report design accordingly.

Be *very* careful when changing the grouping order! It's easy to make an innocent-looking change and then discover that nothing in your report is organized correctly anymore. Before making any big adjustments to the report, take a minute to save the report (choose File➪Save). This way, if something goes wrong and the report becomes horribly disfigured, just close it (File➪Close) without saving your changes. Ahhh. Your original report is safe and sound.

The properties for the currently selected group appear at the bottom of the Sorting and Grouping dialog box.

- ✔ The first two properties — Group Header and Group Footer — specify whether you want this group to include a section for a Group Header, a section for a Group Footer, or both in your report.

- ✔ The Group On setting determines how Access 2000 creates the groups for that value. For more about this feature, check out the nearby "Group on, dude!" sidebar.

- ✔ The last property, Keep Together, controls whether all the information within that group must be printed on the same page, whether the first Detail line and the headings for that group must be printed on the same page, or whether Access can split the information any which way it wants, as long as it all gets printed on one page or another.

  You have three choices under the Keep Together property:

    - **No:** Tells Access to do whatever it pleases.

    - **Whole group:** Tells Access to print the entire group, from Header to Footer, on the same page.

    - **With first detail:** Tells Access to print all the information from the Header for the group through the Detail section for the first entry of the group in that group on the same page. Choose this option to ensure that each of your pages starts with a set of headings.

Group on, dude!

Groups are one of the too-cool-for-words features that make Access 2000 reports so flexible. But wait — groups have still *more* untapped power, thanks to the Group On setting in the Sorting and Grouping dialog box. This setting tells Access when to begin a new group of records on a report. The dialog box contains two settings for your grouping pleasure: *Each Value* and *Interval*.

The Each Value setting tells Access to group identical entries together. If any difference exists between values in the grouping field, Access puts them into different groups. Each Value is a great setting if you're grouping by customer numbers, vendor numbers, or government identification numbers. It's not such a great choice if you're working with names, because every little variation (Kaufield instead of Kaufeld, for example) ends up in its own group.

The Interval setting works a little differently. It tells Access that you're interested in organizing by a range of entries. Exactly how Access interprets the Interval setting depends on whether you're grouping with a number or text field.

If you're grouping a number field with the Interval setting, Access counts by the Interval setting when making the groups. For example, if your Interval is 10, then Access groups records that have values from 0 to 9, 10 to 19, 20 to 29, and so on.

To understand how the Interval setting works with a text field, think back to the way your grade-school teacher taught you to alphabetize words. You look at the first letter of the words, putting the As first, followed by the Bs. If two words start with A, you use the second letter in each word to break the tie. If those letters are identical, too, you try again with the third, and so on until the list is in perfect order or until recess time.

So what do blissful memories of childhood grammar lessons have to do with how the Interval setting works with a text field? In a nutshell, the Interval setting is the number of characters Access 2000 reads from each record when it's grouping them. An Interval of one makes Access 2000 group the entries by the first letter only; an Interval of two tells Access 2000 to consider the first and second letters of each entry.

For example, if you choose 1, 2, or 3 for your Interval setting, the words abandon and abalone would land in the same group because they start with the same three letters. You'd need an interval setting of 4 or more to split the words into separate groups.

Changing a section's size

One problem you may have with designing your own report is controlling how much space appears in a section. When you print a section — be it a Page Header, a Section Header, or a Detail line — it normally takes up the same amount of space as shown on the Design screen. You generally want to tighten the space within the group so that little space is wasted on your page, but your section needs to be large enough to contain all the markers and such that go into it. (To find out how to create sections that change size based on the information in them, flip ahead to the next section, "Fine-Tuning the Layout.")

Fortunately, changing the size of a section is quite easy. Figure 20-5 shows the Resizing cursor that appears when you position your pointer over the top portion of the bar representing the section. This resizing trick works a bit oddly, in that the bar you move increases or decreases the section *above* it, not the section for which it is labeled.

The Resizing cursor

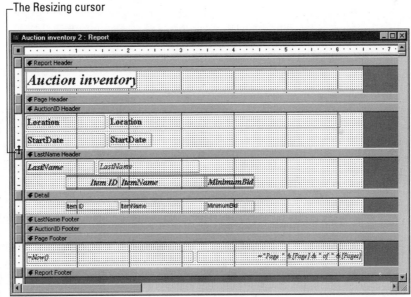

Figure 20-5:
The Resizing cursor enables you to change the size of header, footer, and detail sections.

Fine-Tuning the Layout

Most of the control you have over your report comes from setting the report's properties. Although *setting properties* is a formatting topic, it becomes useful only after you start dividing your report into sections.

Dressing up your report as a whole

To adjust the formatting of an entire report, double-click on the small box in the upper-left corner of the report window in Design view. Up pops the dialog box shown in Figure 20-6.

Playing with page headings

Of particular interest in the Report properties dialog box are controls on the Format Tab that affect when the Page Header and Page Footer will print. The default setting for the Page Header and Page Footer is All Pages, meaning that Access prints a header and footer on every page in the report. Choose Not with Rpt Hdr (or Not with Rprt Ftr for the footer) to tell Access to skip the first and last pages (where the Report Header and Report Footer are printed), but print the Page Header on all the others.

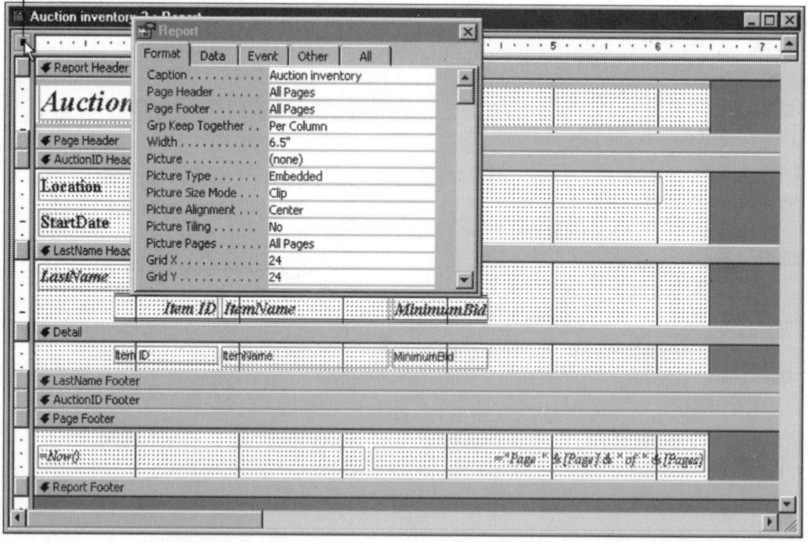

Properties button

Figure 20-6: In Design view, double-clicking on your report's Properties button opens the Report properties dialog box.

The Page Header itself comes with a bunch of options, too. Double-click on the Page Header to bring up the Page Header properties dialog box, which probably looks quite similar to the one shown in Figure 20-7.

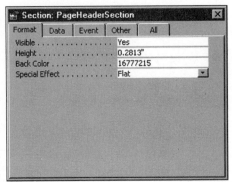

Figure 20-7: You can control how your page header looks with the Page Header properties dialog box.

- ✔ **Visible:** You can use this dialog box to control whether the Page Header appears at all.

- ✔ **Height:** Access automatically sets this property as you click and drag the section header up and down on the screen. To specify an exact size (for example, if you want the header area to be *precisely* 4 centimeters tall), type the size in this section. (Access automatically uses the units of measurement you chose for Windows itself.)

- ✔ **Back Color:** Although setting this property seems easy at first blush, Access 2000 couldn't let you get away with just typing **blue** as a color choice. No, it wants a big, technical number describing the color in gory, computerized detail. Luckily, generating that number is easy. If you want to adjust the section's color, click in this box and then click on the small gray button that appears to the right of the entry. This button brings up a color palette. Click on your choice and then let Access worry about the obnoxious color number that goes into the Back Color box.

Although you can control the color of your Page Header's background from the Report properties dialog box, an easier method is to click on the section in Design view and use the drop-down lists on the Formatting toolbar.

- ✔ **Special Effect:** This property adjusts the visual effect for the section heading, much as the Special Effect button does for the markers in the report itself. Your choices are somewhat limited here, though. Click in the Special Effect box and then click on the down-arrow to list what's available. Choose Flat (the default setting), Raised, or Sunken.

Keeping the right stuff together

The Grp Keep Together option on the Format tab of the Report properties dialog box affects the Keep Together entry, which you set in the Sorting and Grouping dialog box (see "Grouping your records," earlier in this chapter).

Choose Per Page to apply the Keep Together criteria to pages. Or, in a report with multiple columns, choose Per Column to apply the Keep Together criteria to columns.

Formatting individual sections of your report

What if you don't want to change the format of the whole report, but just of one section of the report — for example, the header for one group? Simple. In Design view, double-click on the Group Header to call upon the dialog box shown in Figure 20-8.

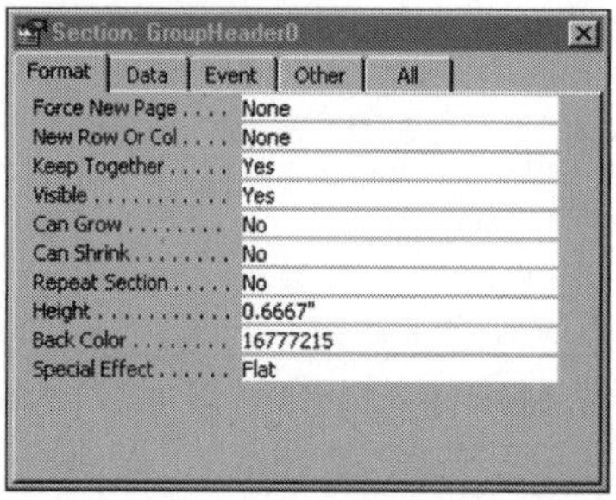

Figure 20-8:
This dialog box lets you fiddle with a single section of your report.

With the Force New Page option, you can control whether or not the change for that group automatically forces the information to start on a new page. When you set this option, you can determine whether this page break occurs only before the header, only after the footer, or in both places. Similarly, you can control the way in which section starts and endings are handled for multiple column reports (such as having the group always start in a separate column). As with the previous dialog boxes, you can control whether or not the group is kept together and whether or not the section is visible.

Perhaps the most important settings in this dialog box are Can Grow, Can Shrink, and Repeat Section.

✔ When the Can Grow option is turned on, the section expands as necessary, based upon the data within it.

Can Grow is particularly useful when you're printing a report that contains a Memo field. You set the width of the field so that it is as wide as you want. Then you can use the Can Grow property to enable Access 2000 to adjust the height available for the information.

✔ With Can Shrink turned on, the section can become smaller if, for example, some of the fields are empty. In order to use the Can Grow and Can Shrink properties, you need to set them for both the section and the items within the section that are able to grow or shrink.

✔ You can use the Repeat Section option to control whether or not, when a group is split across pages or columns, Access 2000 repeats the heading on the new page (or pages, if the section is so big that it covers more than two pages).

Taking it one item at a time

Double-clicking doesn't just work for sections. When you want to adjust the formatting of any item of your report — a field, a label, or something you've drawn on your report — just double-click on that item in Design view. Access 2000 leads you to a marvelous dialog box from which you can perform all manner of technical nit-picking.

Filling in Those Sections

Although Access includes several default settings for headers and footers, those settings aren't very personalized or imaginative. You can do much more with headers and footers than simply display labels for your data. You can build expressions in these sections or insert text that introduces or summarizes your data. Now that's the kind of header and footer that impresses your friends, influences your coworkers, and wins over your boss.

At the head of the class

How you place the labels within the report's Header sections controls how the final report both looks and works, so you really oughta put some thought into those Headers. You want to make sure that all your headings are easy to understand and that they actually add some useful information to the report.

When you're setting up a report, feel free to play around with the header layouts. Experiment with your options and see what you can come up with — the way that information repeats through the report may surprise you.

For example, Figure 20-9 shows a common header configuration in Design view. Figure 20-10 shows the same report in action. In this case, the column headings are printed above the site name. The descriptions for the column headings appear at the top of each and every page because they're in the Page Header section. This example is certainly not a bad layout, but you can accomplish the same goal in other ways.

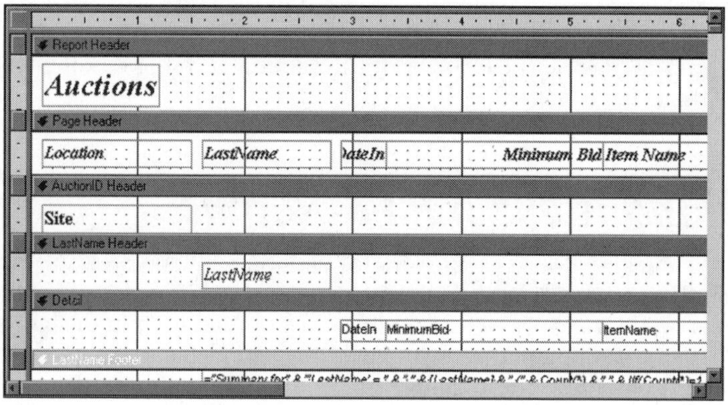

Figure 20-9:
The Design View of the Auctions report.

Figures 20-11 and 20-12 show an alternate arrangement. In this case, the DateIn, Minimum Bid, and Item Name headings repeat every time the LastName Header is printed. This is a little easier to read than the version in Figure 20-10 because the column descriptions are right above their matching columns.

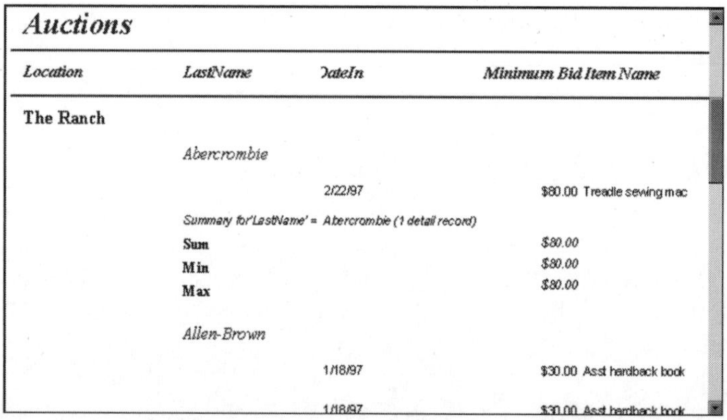

Figure 20-10:
What the Auctions Report actually looks like.

Figure 20-11:
Another arrange-ment for the Auctions report. Notice the new posi-tions for the headers.

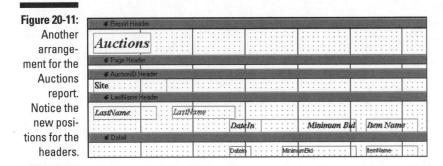

Figure 20-12:
How the new arrangement looks in Print Preview. Compare this report to Figure 20-10.

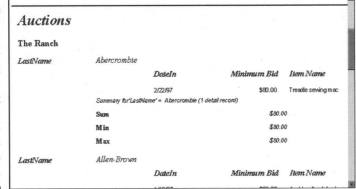

In comparing the figures, you may notice that some of the labels (such as LastName) were also moved, and the various sections were resized. In addition, the pair of lines used to mark the top and bottom of the Page Header were removed in order to close that space.

Expressing yourself in footers

Footers are most often used to produce summary statistics and general infor-mation. Figure 20-13 shows some of the markers that commonly appear in a simple Access 2000 report.

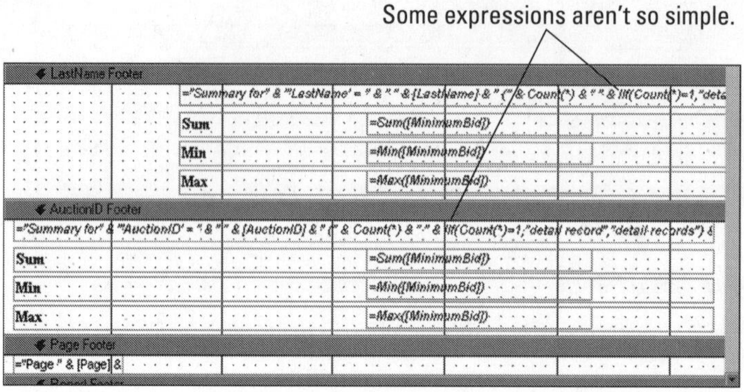

Some expressions aren't so simple.

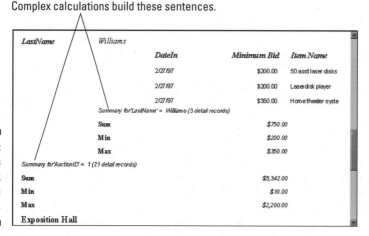

Figure 20-13: You can select from a plethora of footers to include in your reports.

Most of the time, the markers in the footer simply print the page number or some other kind of text. That doesn't mean that you *can't* put something more complex in there, however. Notice the first field in each of the footer sections in Figure 20-13. These fields involve a somewhat complex-looking formula. This formula mixes some text with the current value of a field in the report to produce an informative note for the report. Figure 20-14 shows the results of this complicated bit of computer wizardry.

Complex calculations build these sentences.

Figure 20-14: The results of the work shown in Figure 20-13.

In the example, the actual last name is inserted along with some standard text ("Summary for"), and a function is used to count the number of records being reported in the group. The expression at the end is just used to determine whether the sentence ends with "record" or "records." In order to help you better understand the formula used for this last bit of magic, Figure 20-15 shows the expression in the Expression Builder.

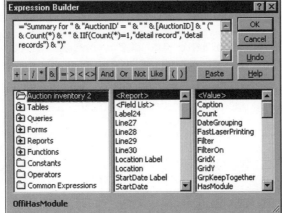

Figure 20-15: Some expressions you don't want to develop yourself.

REMEMBER

Remember that the names enclosed in square brackets represent fields from the database. The last portion of the expression, starting with the *If,* controls whether the sentence ends with the singular *detail record* or the plural *detail records,* and it does this by determining whether the count of records is equal to one or to some other number (that is, more than one). If there were no records, the section wouldn't have been printed at all, so no summary for it would appear.

These feet were made for summing

Access 2000 contains many functions, but the ones listed in Table 20-1 win the award for Most Likely to Be Used in a Normal Human's Report. These functions create different summaries of the fields in your report.

Table 20-1	**Summary Functions**	
Function	**Description**	**Example**
Sum	Adds up all of the values in the field	Sum([MinimumBid])
Maximum	Finds the largest value in the values listed in this section for this field	Max([MinimumBid])
Minimum	Finds the smallest value in the values listed in this section for this field	Min([MinimumBid])
Average	Finds the average value of all of the values listed within this section for this field	Avg([MinimumBid])
Count	Counts up how many values are listed in this section for this field	Count([MinimumBid])

By double-clicking on a calculated field in a report, you open the Properties dialog box, like the one shown in Figure 20-16. You can use the first line of the Format tab to select a format for displaying the information in the field. This control is the most useful for setting the look of your report. You also have options for whether duplicates within the field are shown or whether the fields after the first instance of the same entry are left blank. These options are most useful in the Detail section, where you may want to show only the first record of several records with the same entry in a field.

Figure 20-16:
The Properties dialog box lets you control more settings than you ever thought possible.

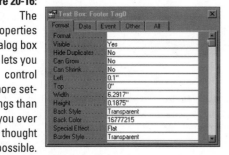

The Data tab contains four entries, one of which is the Control Source that provides the calculation's information. The easiest way to get to this page is to double-click on the field itself, which brings up the Properties dialog box, and then click on the Data tab.

At the bottom of the Data tab is an option for whether or not the entry is a Running Sum. This tells Access whether to reset the total at zero each time the corresponding Header appears, or if it should simply keep on summing and build a massive total. If this is set to No, then every time the Header for the group is printed (every time the entries in the grouping field change), the total is reset to zero.

If Running Sum is set to Over Group or Over All, then the value from the previous group is carried forward across all the groups. This setting can be useful for giving a grand total or a grand average of a group of records. Use it to obtain such calculations as the average across regions in a report summarizing information about regions.

With the Over Group option, the calculation is continued across all the groups contained within that section (any sections that fall between the header for the group and the footer for the group). With Over All, the calculation continues no matter how the group changes.

Page numbers and dates

Access can insert certain types of information for you in either the headers or the footers. Most notably, Access can insert page numbers or dates, using the Page Number command and the Date and Time command under the Insert menu.

Hey, what page is this?

Choosing Insert⇨Page Number displays the dialog box shown in Figure 20-17.

Figure 20-17: From this dialog box, you can fiddle with how your reports generate their page numbers.

From this dialog box, you have several options for your page-numbering pleasure:

- ✔ **Format:** Choose Page N to tell Access to print the word "Page" followed by the appropriate page number. Or choose Page N of M to have Access count the total number of pages in the report and print that number in addition to the current page (as in "Page 2 of 15").

- ✔ **Position:** Tell Access whether to print the page number in the Page Header or the Page Footer.

- ✔ **Alignment:** Set the position of the page number on the page. Click on the arrow at the right edge of the list box to scroll through your options.

- ✔ **Show Number on First Page:** Select this check box to include a page number on the first page of your report. Deselect it to keep your first page unnumbered and pristine.

If you want to change the way that the page numbers work on your report, first manually delete the existing page number field by clicking on it and pressing the Delete key. Once the number is gone, choose Insert⇨ Page Numbers to build the new page numbers.

When did you print this report, anyway?

Choosing Insert⇨Date and Time displays the dialog box shown in Figure 20-18. The most important options to consider here are Include Date and Include Time.

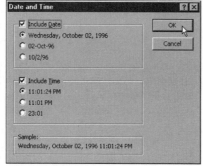

Figure 20-18:
You can even tell Access how you want the date displayed on your report.

You then can select the format for both the date and the time from a somewhat limited set of choices.

You don't have a choice of where the date and time go — Access always puts them in the Page Header. But, if you're feeling a bit sneaky, here's a tip: Use the Cut and Paste commands to move the date and time markers to the section where you want to place them.

Part V
Wizards, Forms, and Other Mystical Stuff

The 5th Wave   By Rich Tennant

"MY GIRLFRIEND RAN A SPREADSHEET OF MY LIFE, AND GENERATED THIS CHART. MY BEST HOPE IS THAT SHE'LL CHANGE HER MAJOR FROM 'COMPUTER SCIENCES' TO 'REHABILITATIVE SERVICES.'"

In this part . . .

Part V defies rational explanation. (How's *that* for a compelling tag line?) Its four chapters introduce a wide range of stuff that's all individually useful, but collectively unrelated. When you get down to it, the only thing tying these topics together is the fact that they're not related to anything else.

Chapter 21 (appropriately enough) takes you and your databases into the 21st century with Internet integration — one of the much-heralded features of Access 2000.

Also, be sure to check out Chapter 22 to find out all about forms in Access 2000. (Uh oh — my *inner nerd* is starting to get excited. . . .) Forms are really powerful and flexible . . . and they're fun to make — that's right, I said *fun*.

Chapter 23 delves into the wonderful world of importing and exporting data. Chapter 24 shows you how to analyze the heck out of your tables. (Perhaps you should just go ahead and read the part while I try to get the nerd back under control before it's too late.)

Chapter 21

Spinning Your Data into (And onto) the Web

. . . .

In This Chapter

▶ What Access 2000 knows about the Internet

▶ Entering and using hyperlinks

▶ Publishing stuff on the Web

▶ Advanced topics to challenge your hair retention

. . . .

*Y*es, it's true — I couldn't make something like this up by myself. Yesterday, Access was merely a database, just another tool for pushing data around your hard drive or local area network. Today, Access 2000 is a powerhouse of Internet and intranet information. If you're itching to join the online revolution, or if you yearn for fun and profit on the electronic super-highway, then Access 2000 (and the rest of the Office 2000 suite, for that matter) is ready to get you started.

This chapter takes a quick look at the technology behind newfound online capabilities of Access 2000 and then discusses some of the details of hyper-links and online database publishing. The chapter closes with some advanced topics for your further research pleasure. (Trust me, these topics are just too high on the old technonerd scale for this book.)

Right from outset, this chapter dives headlong into things like the Internet, corporate intranets, and the World Wide Web. If these terms make you think of a technology-based conspiracy theory, you need to relax a little (after all, they're not *all* out to get just you). When you're nice and rested, pick up a copy of *The Internet For Dummies,* 6th Edition, by John Levine, Carol Baroudi, and Margaret Levine Young (published by IDG Books Worldwide, Inc.). To try out the Internet in an easy, low-stress environment, get *America Online For Dummies,* 5th Edition, by Yours Truly, and get ready to join the fun. Either way, invest some time to discover more about the online world — it's vital informa-tion for the coming years of your career. (Yes, it really *is* that important.)

Access 2000 and the Internet: A Match Made in Redmond

These days, it seems that all software makers are touting their products' cozy linkage with the Internet. Whether it's a natural fit or the marketing equivalent of a shotgun wedding, everyone's joining the rush to cyberspace.

Thankfully, Internet integration with Access 2000 is on the *natural fit* end of the scale. Databases are a perfect complement to the Net's popular World Wide Web information system. The Web always offers lots of interactivity and a flexible presentation medium. But until now, publishing a database on the Web was a complex process requiring time, effort, and a willingness to cheerfully rip your hair out by the roots.

To make the data-publishing process much easier and less hair-intensive, Microsoft came up with a way to bring the Net right into Access 2000. The key to the behind-the-scenes magic is a new Microsoft technology called ActiveX.

ActiveX is the Microsoft answer to another popular Internet innovation: Java. Don't stress out yet about the technology — I have some good news. You don't need to know *anything* technical about either ActiveX or Java to make Access 2000 sing duets with either the Internet or your company's intranet. Just make a mental note that ActiveX is like a super-duper version of *Object Linking and Embedding* (OLE), the technology that lets you store an Access database inside a Microsoft Word document and perform other equally amazing feats of technological magic. ActiveX has capabilities that go beyond OLE, because ActiveX knows how to do its thing over networks instead of being limited to just your hard drive.

If anyone asks for your opinion of ActiveX or Java, just say something about how "ActiveX and Java are both very robust and promising technologies." Be sure to use the term *robust* in your answer — it's one of those amazing buzzwords that nobody really understands, but everybody agrees with.

The Internet power of Access 2000 comes directly from the Microsoft Web browser, Internet Explorer, through a cool ActiveX pipeline. When you work with hyperlinks, browse the Net from a form, or search your company's intranet, Internet Explorer does all of the work behind the scenes. Even when it looks as though Access 2000 is in the thick of things, the Internet information is coming directly from Internet Explorer. The ActiveX technology makes everything appear so seamless.

To make Access 2000 do its Internet tricks, you must install Internet Explorer 5.0. (Newer versions can work as well — goodness only knows how many updates Microsoft may create by the time you read this.) In addition, you need a connection to the Internet (or to your company's intranet) that uses the built-in Windows 32-bit Winsock file. (Internet Explorer 5.0 doesn't work with a 16-bit Winsock — sorry, but it's a fact of life.) Winsock is yet another special piece of Windows code that helps Windows applications talk to the Internet.

If you don't know the technical details of your computer's Internet connection, that's okay — you're allowed to ask questions. In that case, I suggest consulting your company's computer gurus before going any further. If you're on your own and don't have a corporate techweenie department handy, try calling your Internet Service Provider for help, because you pay them to know stuff like this.

Can't Hyperlinks Take Something to Calm Down?

Sitting right in the center of the whole Internet discussion is the term *hyperlink*. Although "hyperlink" sounds vaguely like a frenzied game show host, hyperlinks are actually the special storage compartments for whatever you want to link with. Hyperlinks can connect to a variety of Internet or intranet locations, as Table 21-1 shows.

Table 21-1	Hyperlinks in Access 2000
Link	*Description*
file://	Opens a local or network-based file
ftp://	File Transfer Protocol; links to an FTP server
gopher://	Links to a Gopher server on the network or Internet
http://	Hypertext Transfer Protocol; links to a World Wide Web page
mailto	Sends e-mail to a network or Internet address
news	Opens an Internet newsgroup

Table 21-1 contains the most popular and commonly used tags. For a complete list of the hyperlink tags that Access 2000 understands, press F1 to open the Access 2000 Help system and then search for the term *hyperlink*.

If you regularly surf the World Wide Web, many of these tags should look familiar. Although most of them are geared toward Internet/intranet applications, Access 2000 can also use hyperlinks to identify locally stored Microsoft Office documents. This technology is so flexible, the sky's the limit.

Adding a hyperlink field to your table

You can't let hyperlinks just stand around without a permanent home, so Access 2000 sports a new field type specifically for this special data. As you probably guessed, this type is called the hyperlink field. Figure 21-1 shows a table design containing a hyperlink field. Notice that the hyperlink field is no different from the other mundane fields surrounding it.

There aren't any special steps for adding a hyperlink field to a table. Just use the same steps you would for adding *any* new field to a table:

1. **Open your table in Design view.**

   A window that shows the table's structure appears on-screen.

2. **Click on the spot where you want the new field and then choose Insert⇨Rows from the main menu.**

   A blank row appears in your table design, as shown in Figure 21-2.

3. **Type a name for the field and then press Tab to place the cursor in the Data Type column.**

   Hyperlink fields have names just like all the other fields. Goodness knows you don't want them to feel left out.

4. **Click on the down arrow in the Data Type column, choose Hyperlink from the pull-down menu, and press Tab after you're finished.**

   So much for the mystique — you use the same steps for any new field. (Even though they're special, hyperlink fields behave just like all the other fields in Design view.)

5. **Type a field description if you want one.**

6. **Choose File⇨Save from the main menu to save your design changes.**

   The new hyperlink field proudly takes its place in your table, just as in Figure 21-3.

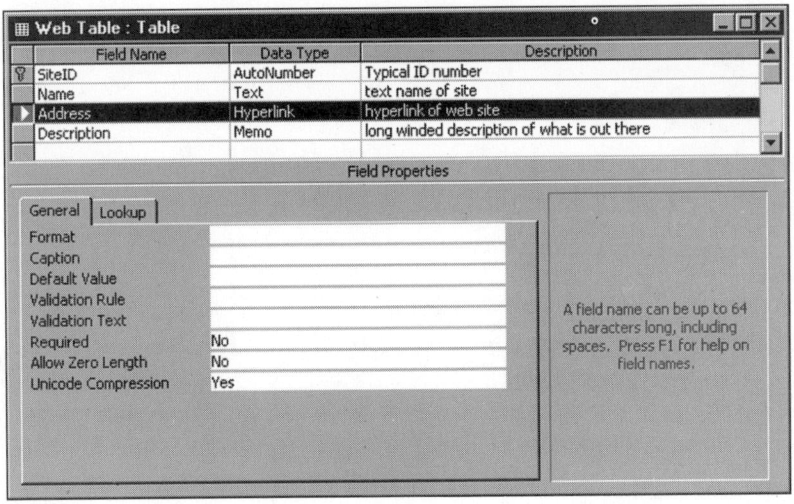

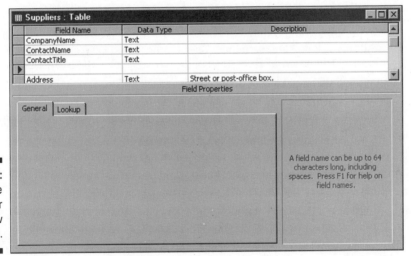

Figure 21-1: This table contains a hyperlink field.

Figure 21-2: A space opens for the new field.

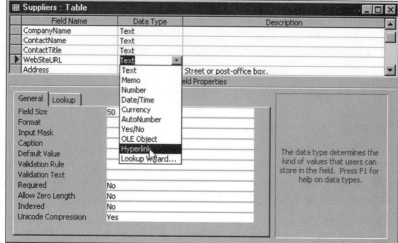

Figure 21-3:
Adding a
hyperlink is
just like
adding any
other field.

Typing hyperlinks (and using them, too)

Hyperlinks are just data, so you don't have to do anything special to coax them into your tables. In fact, all you have to do is type! Granted, hyperlinks look a little different than normal data (see Figure 21-4), but that's okay. They're just like plain fields most of the time — they need to have some fun.

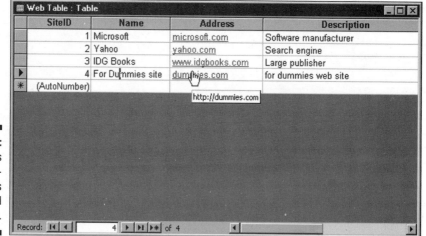

Figure 21-4:
Hyperlinks
automati-
cally dress
up in special
formatting.

Although most hyperlinks store World Wide Web or other Internet addresses, they can point to just about anything in the known world. Thanks to their flexible tags, hyperlinks understand Web pages, intranet servers, database objects (reports, forms, and such), and even plain Microsoft Office documents on your computer or another networked PC.

Using the hyperlink is easy, too. Here are the steps:

1. **Either log onto your network or start your Internet connection.**

   Internet Explorer needs to see that everything is up and running before it consents to making an appearance. (Silly prima donna software.)

2. **Open the Access 2000 database you want to use and then open the table containing those wonderful hyperlinks.**

   The fun is about to begin!

3. **Click on the hyperlink of your choice.**

   After a few moments of thought, Internet Explorer leaps on-screen, displaying the Web site from the link, just as in Figure 21-5. If the link leads to something other than a Web site, Windows automatically fires up the right program to handle whatever the link has to offer. (Isn't technology amazing when it works?)

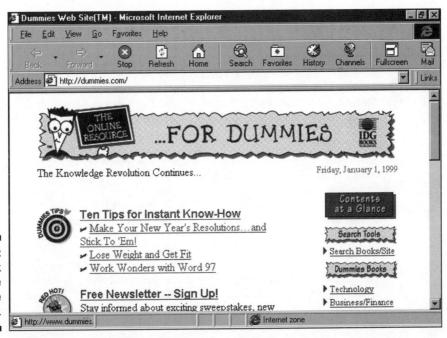

Figure 21-5: One click later, the Web site appears.

A few words about the World Wide Web (and why you care)

Although this whole hyperlink thing may seem like just so much technohype, it really *is* important. More and more businesses are moving information to the World Wide Web. Companies are also creating in-house *intranets* (custom Web servers offering information to networked employees).

The new abilities of Access 2000 put it in the middle of the Web and intranet excitement — and that presents a cool opportunity for you.

Everything about the Web and intranet technology is so new that it cuts across all kinds of organizational boundaries. Duties that used to belong exclusively to *those computer people* are landing in graphic arts, marketing, and almost everywhere else. New jobs are born overnight as companies wrestle with the Web's powerful communication features. It may sound a little chaotic, and that's okay — it is.

If you're looking for a new career path in your corporate life, knowledge of the Web may just be the ticket. Whether you move into Web site development, information management, or even your own Web-oriented consulting business, this is an exciting time full of new possibilities. Dive in and discover what's waiting for you!

Pushing Your Data onto the Web

Now that Access 2000 contains all of your coolest information, why not share your stuff with others in your company — or even publish it for the world? Whether you're building a commercial site geared toward fame and online fortune, or a cross-department intranet to supercharge your company, Access 2000 contains all the tools you need to whip your data into Web-ready shape in no time at all.

Although you don't need to know anything about HTML to build Web pages with Access 2000, you probably *will* need to know some HTML before your project is done. For a painless introduction to HTML, check out *HTML 4 For Dummies,* by Ed Tittel and Steve James. Or pick up a copy of *Creating Cool HTML 4 Web Pages,* by Dave Taylor (both published by IDG Books Worldwide, Inc.).

Access 2000 helps you publish data in two ways: static and dynamic. The one to choose for your project depends on the equipment, goals and expertise available in your immediate surroundings. Here's a quick comparison of the options:

✔ **Static:** This option is a straight conversion from Access 2000 into HTML. Its name reflects the fact that the stuff you convert doesn't change over time — it's a lot like taking a picture of your data. If you add more records to your table and want to include them in your Web-based stuff, you need to re-create the Web pages. Static conversion is a great option for address lists and catalogs that don't change very often. It's also a good place to start when you're exploring the possibilities of the Web. You can convert almost any Access 2000 object — including tables, queries, forms, and reports — into a static Web page with the File➪Export option. (See the next section for more about exporting files.)

✔ **Dynamic:** Instead of creating a simple HTML page that contains all of your data, the Dynamic option builds a special goodie that Access 2000 calls a *data access page.* This is an HTML page that gives people *access* to your data, so they can see (and even change) your information through the corporate network or the Web. Data access pages work only with Access tables and queries.

Thanks to the Data Access Page Wizard, building a data access page isn't tough at all. But because all this technical magic requires some serious cooperation between the Web server, Access 2000, and your database, *implementing* the finished data access page isn't necessarily a task for beginners. For more about this, see the sidebar "What about this data access page thing?" later in this chapter.

Even though the details of making a data access page work may require some help from a trained (and, like me, often balding) computer professional, literally anyone can create a data access page with the wizard. The process works a lot like the Form or Report Wizard. Here are the step-by-step details:

1. **Open the database containing data destined for your intranet or the Web.**

   The database window hops to the screen.

2. **Click on the Pages Objects bar button on the left side of the window.**

   The database window changes, displaying three options dealing with data access pages.

3. **Double-click on the Create data access page by using wizard option (as shown in Figure 21-6).**

   After a gratuitous amount of hard drive activity, the Data Access Page Wizard ambles forth.

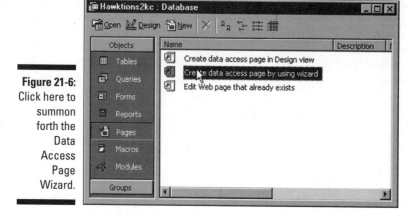

Figure 21-6:
Click here to
summon
forth the
Data
Access
Page
Wizard.

4. **Click on the down arrow in the Tables/Queries box to display a list of tables and queries in the current database. Click on the one you want on the data access page.**

   The Available Fields window lists all of the fields in the selected table or query. The fields themselves wait in anxious anticipation of Step 5.

5. **For each field you want in the data access page, click on the field name, then click on the > button (greater than symbol).**

   The highlighted field hops into the Selected Fields list.

   To copy all of the possible fields into the Selected Fields list, click on the >> button (double greater than symbol). To remove a field, click on its entry in the Selected Fields list, then click on the < button (less than symbol). To clear the whole list out and start over, click on the << button (double less than symbol).

6. **Repeat Steps 4 and 5 for each table or query you want to include. After all of the fields are ready, click on Next.**

   Data access pages understand how related tables work together so that you can include fields from several tables in one data access page. For more about data relationships, flip back to Chapter 5. For tips about other relationships, consult a good counselor.

7. **To show your data in groups on your new data access page, click on the fields you want to subtotal your records with and click on the > button (greater than symbol) to add the new groups. After you finish, click on Next.**

With grouping complete, Access moves along to sorting and summary information.

TIP

Groups in a data access page work just like groups in a report. For more grouping details, flip back to Chapter 18.

8. **To sort the detail records even further, select a field on the Sort order and summary information page. Click on Next after you're finished.**

   Most of the time, you won't need yet *another* layer of organization for your data. By this time, the data is already sliced and diced a couple of times, thanks to the grouping options. If you *do* need more layers though, feel free to add up to four more levels of sorting and summarizing.

9. **Finally, Access 2000 wants a title for your page. Type the title you want and then click on Finish.**

   The Wizard clunks, shimmies, and generally ambles around for a bit. After making you wait just long enough to prove that the whole process is woefully complex, the Wizard delivers your finished data access page, as shown in Figure 21-7.

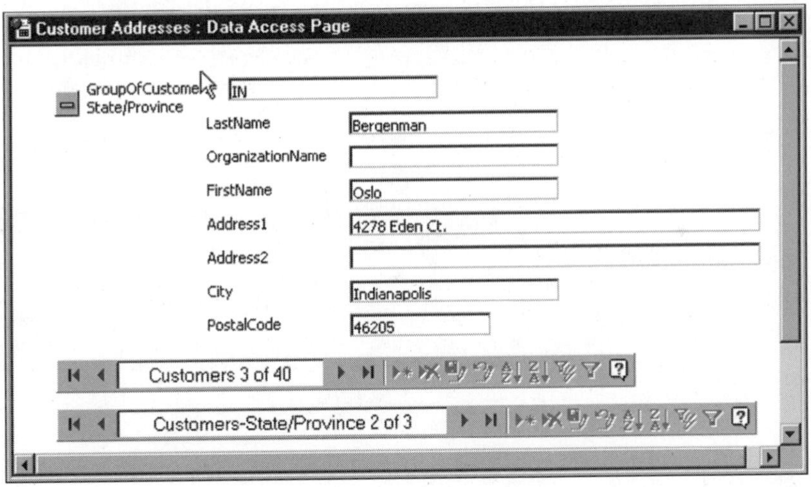

Figure 21-7:
The finished data access page, looking very cool and useful.

Customer Addresses : Data Access Page	
GroupOfCustomers State/Province	IN
LastName	Bergenman
OrganizationName	
FirstName	Oslo
Address1	4278 Eden Ct.
Address2	
City	Indianapolis
PostalCode	46205

Customers 3 of 40

Customers-State/Province 2 of 3

10. **Test your new page by running your Web browser and loading the page up for a quick look (as shown in Figure 21-8).**

    If this page is destined to be part of a big commercial Web site, check the page in a variety of Web browsers. The file may need some adjusting before it looks right (or at least looks passable) when viewed from the many different Web browsers out there.

What about this data access page thing?

Data access pages are pretty cool. They offer totally current, up-to-the-second data through the Internet's most popular information system. What else could you ask? Well, frankly, you *could* ask for the implementation process to be a little less complex.

It takes a bevy of Microsoft products working together behind the scenes in sweet harmony to make dynamic Web pages work. Even though you already have the first piece, Access 2000, that's only about one third of the story.

Next on the shopping list is your Web server itself. A high-volume system — a Web server connected directly to the Internet, for example — requires Microsoft Windows NT Server running the Microsoft Internet Information Server product. (If you think that sounds vaguely expensive and unavoidably technical,

you're right.) The odds are good that you'll also need some help assembling, tweaking, and generally beating the system into submission.

If your sights are set a little lower, though, you just may be able to do this yourself. For a small Web server running on a local area network, try using the Microsoft Personal Web Server product. It uses a networked Windows computer as the base for a fully functional Web server. Don't expect to attach a Personal Web Server to the Internet, though — it's strictly a low volume, local network type of product. The good news is, if you bought Microsoft Office 2000 on a CD-ROM, you may already have the software.

For more details about either of these options, press F1 or click on the Office Assistant; then type web server and press Enter.

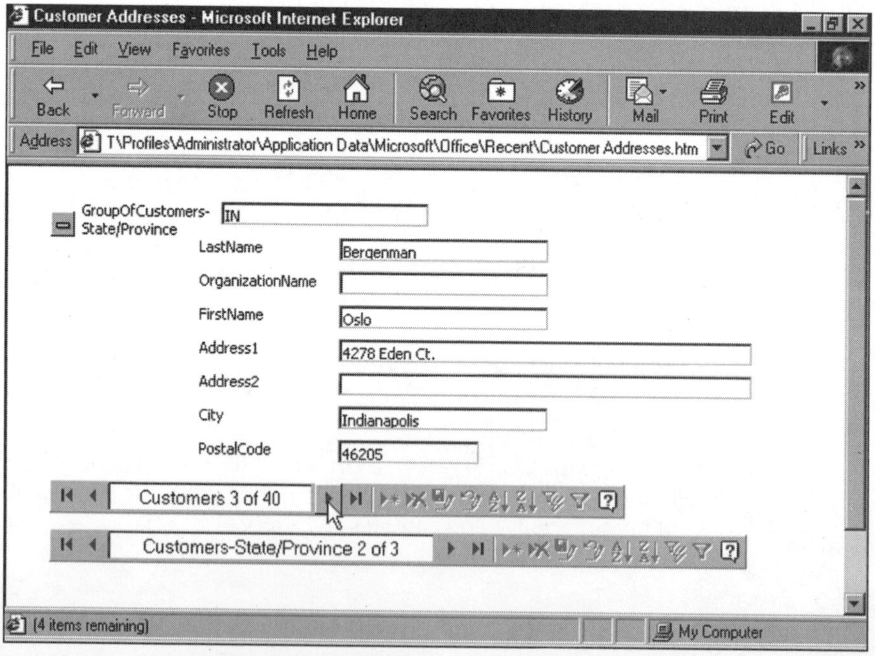

Figure 21-8: Not a bad job, considering it came from a mere piece of software.

Advanced Topics for Your Copious Nerd Time

If all the stuff in this chapter doesn't quell your technological impulses, don't worry — there's plenty more where this came from. Here are a few ideas to keep your mind active, your Web pages sharp, and your Access 2000 forms looking truly cool.

Each item includes a brief summary, plus a term to give to the Office Assistant if you want all of the details.

- ✔ Export datasheets, reports, and forms directly as static HTML pages with the File➪Export menu selection. One or two quick clicks is all it takes to convert your data into a simple, unchanging Web page. This option is great when you're fluent in HTML and want to quickly generate a few pages of information that are ready for manual tweaking. Search for: **export to HTML**.

- ✔ Put hyperlinks right into your reports and forms. Access 2000 lets you attach hyperlinks directly to command buttons, labels, or images. Search for: **add hyperlink to form**.

- ✔ Build HTML template files to make your exported tables look, act, and dress the same. If you're building the mother of all database Web sites, template files are a big time-saver. Plus, they give your site a consistent, professional feel. Search for: **HTML template files**.

- ✔ Add a Web browser to any Access 2000 form. Navigate through Web documents directly from a form — no need to switch between Access 2000 and your Web browser! This feature has incredible possibilities for corporate intranets, plus a lot of promise on the Internet, too. Search for: **Web page on a form**.

These features just scratch the surface of all the special capabilities of Access 2000. In addition to working with the Net, Access 2000 also works very closely with the other members of the Microsoft Office 2000 suite. There's so much to know about how the programs interact that Microsoft created a huge informational file on the subject. Amazingly, the file is available for free through the Internet. To get all the details, ask the Office Assistant for information about the Office 2000 resource kit.

Chapter 22

Making Forms That Look Cool and Work Great

In This Chapter

▶ Taking a look at forms in Access 2000

▶ Building a form with the Form Wizard

▶ Making simple forms with the AutoForm Wizard

▶ Improving on the Form Wizard's creation

*P*aper forms are the lifeblood of almost every enterprise. If they weren't, life would probably be simpler and we might have more trees, but that's beside the point. Because real life is the mirror that software engineers peer into (and frequently faint while looking at) when they design programs, Access 2000 includes the ever-cherished capability to view and work with forms.

Fear not, though, because electronic forms are infinitely friendlier than their old-fashioned counterparts, the dreaded PBFs *(paper-based forms)*. In fact, you may even discover that you *like* messing around with forms in Access 2000. (If that happens to you, don't tell anyone.) This chapter looks at what forms can do for you, explores a couple different ways to make forms, and tosses out some tips for customizing forms so that they're exactly what you need.

Tax Forms and Data Forms Are Very Different Animals

All forms are *not* created equal. Paper forms make cool airplanes, take up physical space, are hard to update, and (depending on the number of forms involved) may constitute a safety hazard when stacked. Access 2000 forms, on the other hand, are simple to update, easy to store, and are rarely a safety risk (although designing a form *can* be hazardous to your productivity, because it's kinda fun).

Forms in Access 2000 are something like digital versions of their paper cousins, but the similarity ends with the name. Access 2000 forms have all kinds of advantages over old-fashioned paper forms — and they'll spoil you if you're used to wandering through your data in Datasheet view. Here's just a sampling of how forms in Access 2000 make viewing your data easier:

✔ **Escape the clutches of Datasheet view:** Instead of scrolling back and forth through a datasheet, you focus on one record at a time, with all the data pleasantly laid out on a single screen.

✔ **Modify at will:** When your needs change, take the form into Design view and update it. And, unlike with its paper cousins, you don't have to worry about recycling 10,000 leftover copies of the old form.

✔ **See your data any way you want:** Access 2000 lets you take one set of data and present it in as many different forms as you want — all without re-entering a bit of data for the new form. Create a special form for the data-entry folks, another for your analysts, and a third for yourself. Well-designed forms give the right information to the right people *without* revealing data they don't need to.

✔ **View the entries in a table or the results of a query:** Forms pull information from tables or queries with equal ease. Forms based on queries are especially flexible because they always display the latest information.

✔ **Combine data from linked tables:** One form can display data from several related tables. Forms automatically use the relationships built into your database.

Like reports and queries, forms are stored in the database file under their own button, as Figure 22-1 shows. Forms are full-fledged Access 2000 objects, so you can do all kinds of cool tricks with them.

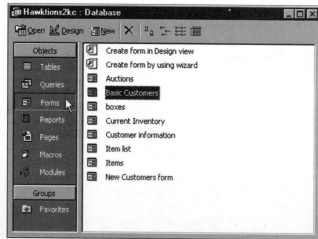

Figure 22-1: Knowing that the forms are just where I left them is comforting.

Depending on your needs, you can use any of three ways to make forms. The *Form Wizard* offers a take-you-by-the-hand approach, walking you through a series of questions and then proudly producing a rather bland-looking form. The three *AutoForm* tools make the same forms as the Form Wizard but don't ask any questions. Finally, in the *by-hand* approach, Access 2000 sets up a blank form, drops off a toolbox full of form-related goodies, shakes your hand, and then wanders off to do something fun while you make a form from scratch.

I believe in keeping things as simple as possible, so this chapter explains how to enlist the Form Wizard and the AutoForm tools to build basic forms *for* you. The chapter closes with tips and tricks for manually tweaking these Masterpieces of Vanilla into Truly Cool Forms.

Creating a Form at the Wave of a Wand

The easiest path to the best in computer-designed forms (notice that I didn't say *stunning forms* or *incredibly useful forms*) is through the Form Wizard. As with all the other Access 2000 wizards, the Form Wizard steps you through the creation process, bombarding you with questions to the point that you sometimes want to tell it to just grow up and start making its own decisions.

To get the Form Wizard up and running, follow these steps:

1. **Open your database file and click on the Forms button on the Objects bar on the left side of the window.**

   Access 2000 displays a list of the forms currently in your database. Don't fret if the list is currently empty — you're about to change that.

2. **Click on <u>N</u>ew.**

   The New Form dialog box appears.

   The next time you want to create a form, you also can double-click on the Create form by using the wizard option instead of using New. Think of this option as a shortcut to the wizard's lair.

3. **Double-click on Form Wizard in the dialog box (see Figure 22-2).**

   At this point, the computer's hard disk usually sounds like it's having a massive fight with itself. When the noise dies down, the Form Wizard poofs into action.

4. **Click on the down arrow in the Tables/Queries box to list the tables and queries in your database and then select the one that contains the fields you want to view with this form.**

   The Form Wizard lists the available fields. Now tell the wizard what you want to display in the form.

5. **Double-click on a field name in the Available Fields list to include the field in your form.**

If you want to see *all* the fields, click the >> button in the middle of the screen. To remove a field that you accidentally picked, double-click on its name in the Selected Fields list. The field jumps back to the Available Fields side of the dialog box.

Figure 22-2:
Ringing the
Form
Wizard's
bell.

6. **Repeat the process on each field destined for the form. After you're done with all the fields, click on Next (see Figure 22-3).**

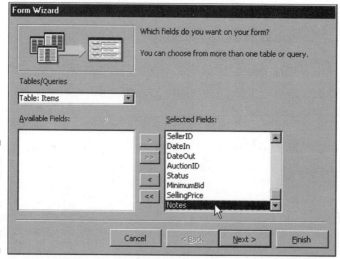

Figure 22-3:
The fields
are ready,
so it's time
to move
along.

7. **If you select fields from more than one table, the Form Wizard takes a moment to ask how you want to organize the data in your form. Click on your choice in the by (fieldname) list on the left side of the dialog box and then click on Next.**

   If the Form Wizard asks about form layout at this point, go on to the next step.

8. **Next, the Form Wizard wants to know how you want to display the data on the form. Leave the option set to Columnar (or Datasheet, if that's the default option on your screen) and then click on Next.**

   This is another one of those points where Access 2000 has too many options for its own good. If you saw the dialog box that I mention in Step 7, your screen probably shows only two options: Tabular and Datasheet. On the other hand, if you skipped Step 7 and came directly to Step 8, you should have four options on-screen: Columnar, Tabular, Datasheet, and Justified. The Report Wizard offers only the options that it thinks are most appropriate for your data. (Of course, this kind of *help* often leads to confusion, which is why I get to write these cool books. Keep up the good work, Microsoft!)

   The other formats (Tabular and Justified) are interesting, but they create really complicated forms that aren't very easy to work with or customize. Sometime in the future, when you're all caught up on work and want to spend some intimate moments with Access 2000, give one of the other formats a try.

9. **In the name of sprucing up a bland form, the wizard offers to use some interesting color and background styles to display your data. For now, click on the Standard option (shown in Figure 22-4) and click on Next to continue.**

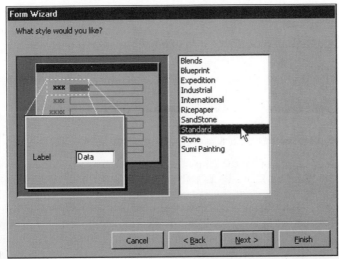

Figure 22-4:
Even though the options are tempting, stick with simplicity at first.

Most of the color and background combinations *really* slow down the performance of your forms. If you absolutely *must* have some color in your forms, try the Colorful or Stone settings. They provide some lively highlights without affecting your form's performance.

10. **Type a descriptive title for your form in the What title do you want for your form? box at the top of the Form Wizard screen.**

By default, the Form Wizard offers you the name of the table that you used to feed the form, but *please* use something more descriptive than just that.

11. **Click on Finish after you're done.**

After a few moments (or a few *minutes,* if you have a slow computer), your new form appears on-screen, ready for action (see Figure 22-5).

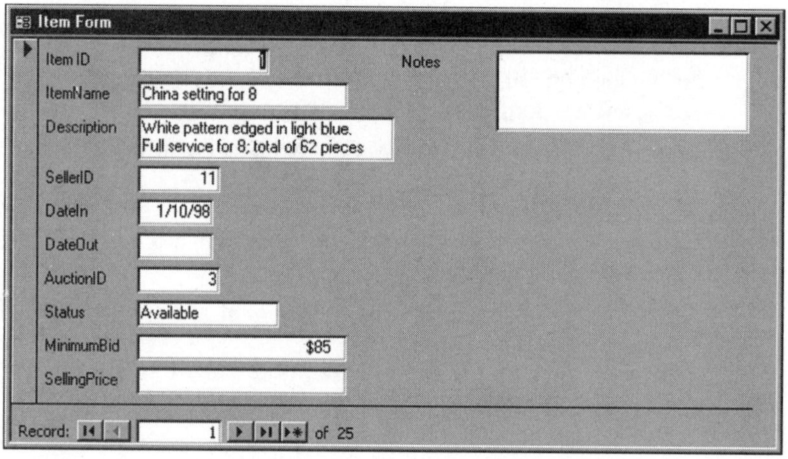

Figure 22-5:
The new form's no Mona Lisa, but it's not a finger painting, either.

Item Form	
Item ID	1
ItemName	China setting for 8
Description	White pattern edged in light blue. Full service for 8; total of 62 pieces
SellerID	11
DateIn	1/10/98
DateOut	
AuctionID	3
Status	Available
MinimumBid	$85
SellingPrice	
Notes	

Record: 1 of 25

The Form Wizard automatically saves the form as part of the creation process, so you don't need to manually save and name it.

Mass Production at Its Best: Forms from the Auto Factory

When I was a kid, I became fascinated with business and how it worked. The move from hand-built products to Henry Ford's automated assembly line particularly amazed me. (Yes, I *was* a little different. Why do you ask?) The assembly line had its good and bad points, but the quote that always defined the Ford assembly line for me was, "You can have any color you want, as long as it's black."

With that thought in mind, let me welcome you to the AutoForm Factory. Our motto: "You can have any form you want, as long as it's one of the three we make." Ah, the joys of flexible production management. . . .

Access 2000 claims that the AutoForms are wizards, but because they're so limited — er, I mean *focused* — I don't think of them as full-fledged purveyors of the magical arts. Semantics aside, each of the three AutoForms builds a different kind of form:

- ✔ *Columnar* assembles a classic, one-record-per-page form.

- ✔ Tabular makes a rather cool, multiple-record-per-page form, but be ready for some cosmetic surgery to grind away the rough edges and make the form truly useful (see Figure 22-6).

- ✔ *Datasheet* creates (hold on tight for this one) a *form* that looks, acts, smells, and feels just like a classic *datasheet.* Check out Figure 22-7 to see for yourself. Does the world *need* a form that pretends to be a datasheet? (I don't think so, but nobody at Microsoft ever asks me these things.)

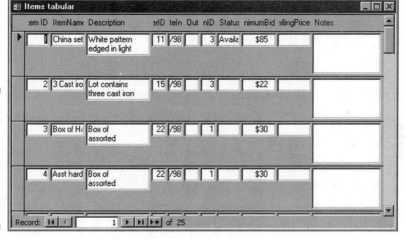

Figure 22-6: Tabular forms are more avant-garde, but those headings are a mess.

Using the AutoForms is a quick process. Despite their alleged *wizard* status, AutoForms are more like office temps: Just point them at data, stand back, and before you know it, the form is done. Here are the details of the process:

1. **With your database open, click on the Form button on the Objects bar on the left side of the database window and then click on New.**

   The New Form dialog box hops onto the screen, ready to help.

Figure 22-7:
Is it a datasheet or a form pretending to be a datasheet? Only its properties know for sure.

	Item ID	ItemName	Description	SellerID	D
	1	China setting for 8	White pattern edged in light blue.	11	1.
	2	3 Cast iron toys	Lot contains three cast iron toys,	15	1.
	3	Box of Ham Radio Magaz	Box of assorted hardback books.	22	1.
	4	Asst hardback books (2 o	Box of assorted hardback books.	22	1.
	5	Asst hardback books (3 o	Box of assorted hardback books.	22	1.
	6	Asst hardback books (4 o	Box of assorted hardback books.	22	1.
	7	Painting -- boat on lake	16x20 original oil painting	37	1.
	8	Painting -- Children	16x20 original oil painting	37	1.
	9	Painting -- Convertible	16x20 original oil painting	37	1.
	10	Painting -- Old man	16x20 original oil painting	37	1.
	11	Painting -- Round Barn	16x20 original oil painting	37	1.
	12	Mandolin	Mandolin, cherry front. Good cond	7	1.
	13	HF Radio	Ham radio transceiver. Covers 20	24	1.
	14	2m Handi-talkie	Ham radio hand-held transceiver. I	24	1.
	15	20m Yagi antenna	Single-band Yagi antenna. Include	24	1.

Items tabular

Record: 1 of 25

2. **Depending on which look you're after, click on AutoForm: Columnar, AutoForm: Tabular, or AutoForm: Datasheet.**

   Access 2000 highlights the appropriate mini-wizard name.

3. **Click on the down arrow next to the Choose the table text box below the Wizard list.**

   A drop-down list of tables and queries in the current database appears.

4. **In the drop-down list, click on the table or query that you want to provide information for this form. After you're done, click on OK.**

   The appropriate mini-wizard begins its focused little job, and your new form appears on-screen in a few moments.

5. **If you like the form, preserve it for posterity by choosing File⇨Save or by clicking on the Save button on the toolbar. When the Save As dialog box appears, type a name for the form and then click on OK.**

   Unlike the Form Wizard, AutoForms *don't* automatically save the form they create, so you have to save the form manually. The form is added to your database on the Forms button.

Ultimate Beauty through Cosmetic Surgery

I have a question for you. Tell me the brutal truth, okay? Don't hold back. I want your honest opinion on this. Ready? Would you rather slavishly toil away in the data-entry sweatshop of Figure 22-8 or casually pop a few records into Figure 22-9 between tennis sets? Take your time to answer.

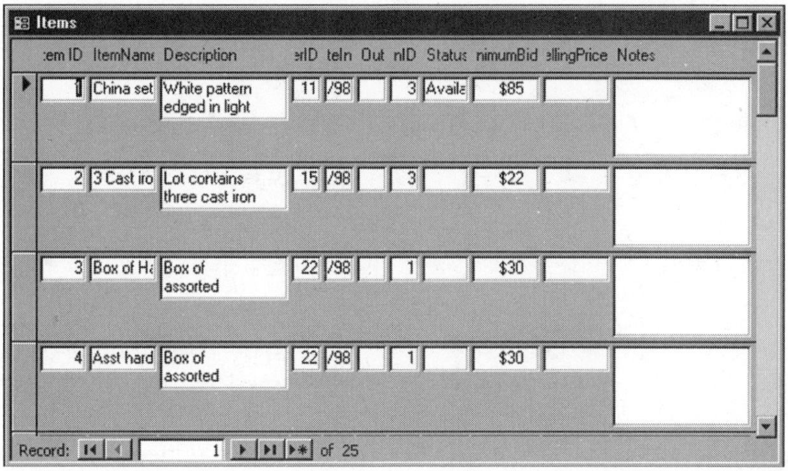

Figure 22-8:
Before: An unimaginative form created by a mindless software automation.

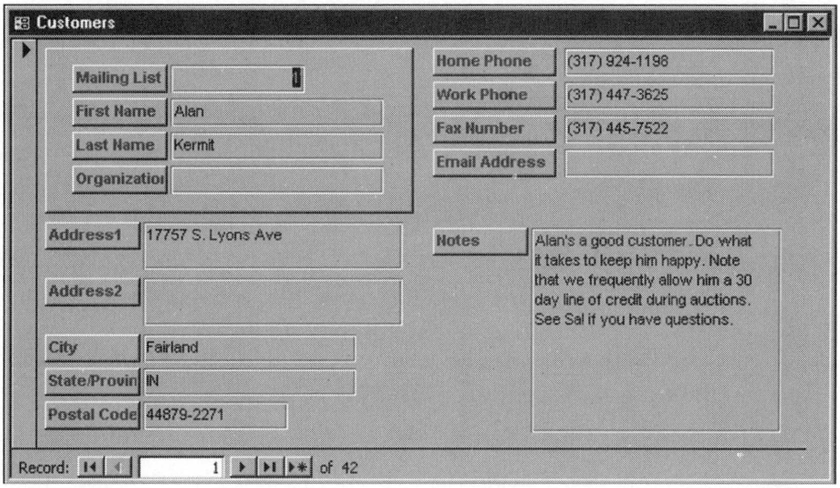

Figure 22-9:
After: The same form rescued from the depths of digital despair, thanks to cosmetic surgery.

Believe it or not, those images are the *same kind of form.* Yup, it's true. The *Before* image in Figure 22-8 is a standard columnar form straight from the AutoForm Factory of the previous section. The *After* image, also a standard columnar form, in Figure 22-9 emerges poised, beautiful, and easy to use after just one visit to Dr. John's School for Operationally Inept Forms. To bring about the transformation, I moved the fields around, added some graphics to segment the form, and changed the tab order to make data entry more intuitive.

Because the school is a small, private institution, it doesn't have enough space for the thousands upon thousands of forms that desperately require this treatment. So instead of sending your forms to my school, I'm sending the school to you. This section outfits you with the basic tool kit used by top form surgeons around the country. In no time at all, your frumpy forms will be sleek data-entry machines, both functionally useful and visually appealing.

Taking a form into Design view

Before you can make *any* of these changes, the form has to be in Design view. Access provides two easy ways to get there, depending on where you happen to be right now:

✔ **From the database window:** Click on the Forms button on the Objects bar to list the available forms. Click on the form you want to change and then click on Design.

✔ **From a form window:** Click on the Design button on the toolbar or choose View➪Form Design from the menu.

Don't let Design view stress you out. It *looks* more complicated than normal life, but that's okay. If something goes wrong and you accidentally mess up your form, just choose File➪Close from the menu. When Access 2000 asks about saving your changes, politely click on No. This step throws out all the horrible changes you just made to the form. Take a few deep breaths to calm your nerves and then start the design process over again.

Moving fields

To move a field around in Design view, follow these steps:

1. **Put the mouse pointer anywhere on the field that you want to move.**

   You can point to the field name or the box where the field value goes. Either place is equally fine for what you're doing.

   If the field is already selected (the name has a box around it that's decorated with small, filled-in squares), click on any blank spot of your form to deselect the field; then start with Step 1. Otherwise, Access gets confused and thinks you want to do something *other* than just move the field.

2. **Press and hold down the left mouse button.**

   The mouse pointer turns into a hand, which is how Access 2000 tells you that it's ready to move something. Strange response, isn't it?

3. **Drag the field to its new location.**

   As you move the field, a pair of white boxes moves along with the cursor to show you precisely where the field will land.

4. **When the field is in position, release the mouse button.**

The field drops smoothly into place.

If you don't like where the field landed, either move it again or press Ctrl+Z to undo the move and start over from scratch.

Adding lines and boxes

Two buttons near the bottom of Design view enable you to do the following:

- ✔ Create lines on your form.
- ✔ Create boxes (or borders) on your form.

Here's how to use these tools:

1. **Click on the tool of your choice.**

   To show you that it's selected, the tool visually *pushes in,* just like a toggle button.

2. **Put the mouse pointer where you want to start the line or place the corner of a box; then press and hold down the left mouse button.**

   Aim is important, but you can always undo or move the graphic if the project doesn't work out quite right.

3. **Move the cursor to the spot where the line ends or to the opposite corner of your box and then release the mouse button.**

   The line or box appears on-screen.

When adding line or box graphics, remember that several special effects are available to you, depending on what you're adding:

- ✔ Lines can be *flat* or *raised.* Even though the other options seem to be available, they don't look any different from *raised* when you're working with a line.

- ✔ Boxes respond to *all* the special effects options, as you can see in Figure 22-10.

To use these special effects, draw your line or box and then right-click on it (if it's a line, right-click on one end). Choose Special Effects from the pop-up menu and then click on the particular effect you like best.

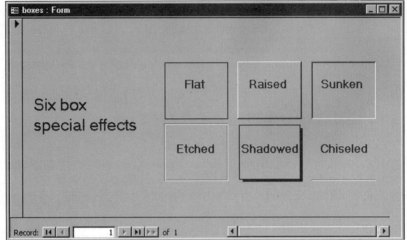

Figure 22-10:
Boxes are by far the more stylish graphic element.

If you want to customize your line or box a little further, give the Border settings a try. Begin by opening the Special Effects dialog box as I previously describe and then click on the Format button.

- ✔ *Border Style* adjusts how the line looks, with options ranging from solid to dotted.
- ✔ *Border Color* changes the line's color.
- ✔ *Border Width* makes the line anything from a wispy hairline to a bold 6-point behemoth.

Experiment with the settings to come up with the best combination for you. As with the special effects settings, click on the X button to close the Properties box after you're done.

Changing the field tab order

Changing the field tab order isn't quite as simple and fun-loving as the other options in this section, but changing the order is extremely rewarding. If you move the fields around on the form and then try to use the form, you quickly discover that the fields remember their *old* order when you move from one field to the next with the Tab key. To fix this problem, you need to change the Tab Index property of the fields.

Changing the field tab order is a slightly more technical undertaking than drawing boxes, but it doesn't hold a candle to flying a Boeing 747 aircraft. Now that the issue is in perspective, here's how to change the tab order:

1. **With the form open in Design view, choose View➪Tab Order.**

   The Tab Order dialog box opens, listing the fields in their current tab order.

2. **Click on the small button to the left of the field you want to work with (as shown in Figure 22-11).**

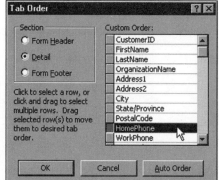

Figure 22-11: The HomePhone field is ready to go.

The field highlights in response to your click. (Isn't that special?)

To have Access 2000 automatically set the tab order for all the fields in the form, click on the Auto Order button at the bottom of the Tab Order dialog box. Access 2000 sets the order according to where the field is in the form. It starts from the upper-left side of the form and goes across, and then moves down one line and repeats the process. Fields end up in order horizontally (fields on line one, fields on line two, and so on).

3. **Click and drag the field to its new position in the tab order.**

   As you drag the field, a dark gray bar moves with it, showing where the field will fit into the tab order. When the bar is in the right place, release the button. Access moves the field into its new position in the tab order.

4. **Repeat Steps 2 and 3 for any other fields you want to change.**

   Access doesn't care how much you work with the tab order, so play to your heart's content.

5. **After you're done adjusting the tab order, click on OK.**

   The Tab Order dialog box runs off to wherever dialog boxes hang out when they're not on-screen.

6. **Click on the Form View button on the toolbar and test your work.**

   If any fields are still out of order, note which ones they are and then work back through these steps to fix the order.

Chapter 23

If Love Is Universal, Why Can't I Export to It?

• •

In This Chapter
▶ Pulling data into Access 2000
▶ Deciding when to import and when to link data
▶ Speaking in foreign data tongues
▶ Pushing your comfortable data into the cold, cruel outside world

• •

*T*o achieve true success these days, speaking only the tongue of the country that bore you isn't enough. You need to be comfortable with several languages before the pinnacle of achievement is within your grasp. I, for example, am fluent in *American English,* a language that the British view as a poor substitute for grunting and knocking rocks together. For work, I also studied several variants of the vernacular *Nerd,* including *Windows, DOS,* the pictorial troubleshooting tongue *$%@&#!,* and the esoteric dialect *Macintosh* (which is particularly challenging because all the words in it look and act alike).

Access 2000 is multilingual as well, because its electronic world is filled with more disagreeing tongues than the United Nations in general session. To simplify your life, Access 2000 understands a couple of spreadsheets, several competing databases, and even plain old text files. Because of this capability, you can exchange data with almost any source out there. Access 2000 is one of the most flexible programs I've ever seen (and I've seen a *bunch* of programs).

This chapter looks at the import and export capabilities of Access 2000, how they work, and what you can do with them. If you work with Access 2000 and almost *any* other program, you need this chapter, because sometime soon, some data will be in the wrong place — and guess whose job it is to move it. . . .

Importing Only the Best Information for Your Databases

Access 2000 includes two ways of sucking data into its greedy clutches. *Importing* involves translating the data from a foreign format into the Access 2000 database file format (which, according to Microsoft, all the world's data should be stored in). The other method is *linking*, where you build a temporary bridge between the external data and Access 2000.

If you worked with older versions of Access, *linking* used to be called *attaching*. The concept is the same; only the name has been changed to confuse the innocent.

Translating file formats

Regardless of whether you import or link the data, Access 2000 understands only certain data formats. Table 23-1 lists the most common file types that Access interacts with. Believe it or not, the entries in this table cover the majority of data stored on PCs around the world.

Table 23-1	The Access 2000 List of Language Fluencies		
Program	**File extension**	**Versions**	**Notes**
Access	.MDB	2.0, 7.0, 97	Even though they share the same name, these versions use slightly different file formats than Access 2000.
dBASE	.DBF	III, III+, IV, V	One of the most popular formats out there; many programs use the dBASE format.
FoxPro	.DBF	2.0, 2.5, 2.6, 3.0	The other database program of Microsoft; not directly compatible with dBASE in some cases.
Paradox	.DB	3.x, 4.x, 5.x	A competing database from Borland.
Excel	.XLS	2.0, 3.0, 4.0, 5.0, 7.0, 8.0	Although it's a spreadsheet, many people use Excel as a simple flat-file database manager.
Lotus 1-2-3	.WKS, .WK1, .WK3	1.x, 2.x, 3.x, 4.x	At one time, the most popular spreadsheet around.

Program	File extension	Versions	Notes
Text	.TXT	N/A	The "if all else fails" format; Access 2000 understands both delimited and fixed-width text files.
Rich Text Format	.RTF	N/A	This is a format good for many word processors because more formatting is maintained then you get in text.
Active Server Pages	.ASP	N/A	This is a special scripting language for Microsoft's Internet Information Server which tells it how to generate HTML.
HTML	.HTM, .HTML	More than you can imagine	The web page codes that make a web page a web page.

Although Access 2000 is pretty intelligent about the translation process, you need to watch out for some quirks. Here are some specific tips to keep in mind as you play The Great Data Liberator and set imperiled information free to enjoy a new life in Access 2000:

✔ When working with dBASE and FoxPro files, keep careful track of the index files that go along with the database files. Access 2000 needs the index to work with the table. If Access can't find the index or if it is corrupt, try canceling the prompt that requests the index file and see if the import worked.

✔ Access 2000 has problems linking to Paradox tables that don't have a primary key. Specifically, Access 2000 can't write changes to the unkeyed Paradox table. To fix the problem, use Paradox to create a primary key in the table and *then* link the table to Access 2000.

✔ Remember that data in Paradox tables *isn't* stored in a single file. Having a .PX (the primary index) and a .MB (memo data — I don't know what the *B* is supposed to stand for) file lurking around the .DB file is common. If you copy a Paradox table from one computer to another, take care to copy *all* the associated files!

✔ Double-check information coming from any spreadsheet program to be sure that it's *consistent* and *complete*. Above all, make sure that all of the entries in each column (field) are the same type (all numbers, text, or whatever). Otherwise, the import won't work right (and you know how forgiving software is of such "little" problems).

✔ If you have difficulty importing a given format then you may try using the old database product to open the respective file, and export the database tables as text files (the data techies use its formal name, *ASCII*). Text may be cumbersome to manage but it is the most widely recognized form of data known to man (or computer).

Always back up your data before importing, exporting, or even leaving the office for a short vacation. The computer person's advice always begins "Well, nothing should go wrong," but wise folks prepare for the worst. Make copies of your databases *before* trying the techniques in this chapter.

Importing or linking your files

The precise details of importing and linking depend greatly on the type of file you're importing, but here are the general steps to get you started in the right direction. Although the instructions are written mainly for importing, they include supporting notes about linking as well.

Ready to take a spin at the *Data Import Polka?* Here goes:

1. **Open the Access 2000 database you're pulling data into.**

   If you're not familiar with this step, *stop* — don't go any further. Flip to Chapter 1 and spend some time getting comfy with Access 2000 before attempting an import.

2. **Choose File➪Get External Data➪Import.**

   The dialog box in Figure 23-1 appears.

3. **Click on the down arrow in the Files of type box (at the bottom of the window) and click on the kind of data you're importing. If necessary, use the Look in list box to navigate your way to the files.**

   The dialog box displays the matching files for your selection pleasure. Make sure that you choose the correct file type. Otherwise, Access doesn't list the file you're looking for in the dialog box!

   If your database file has a strange, nonstandard extension on the end of the filename (like .FOO, .DTA, or .XXX), Access 2000 may not be able to make heads or tails of the file. In that case, seek help from your technical support people or local computer jockey.

Figure 23-1:
Make sure
that you
pick the cor-
rect data
type.

4. **Double-click on the file that you want to import.**

   Here's where the process takes off in wildly different directions depending on the file format you're importing and whether you're doing a link or an import. The only sage advice I can give is to cross your fingers, follow the on-screen instructions carefully, refer to the preceding tips, hope for the best, and take comfort in the knowledge that you made backup copies of your databases before starting this sordid process. (You *did* make those backups, right?)

One final thought: If you're importing and the process is taking *forever,* Access is probably struggling with errors in the inbound data. Press Ctrl+Break to stop the import process and check the data that's being imported for obvious errors (bad or corrupt data, badly organized spreadsheet data, invalid index, and so on).

Sending Your Data on a Long, One-Way Trip

In the interest of keeping you awake, I'll keep this explanation short: Exporting is just like importing, except where it's different.

Hmm . . . perhaps that explanation was a little *too* short.

Exporting a table involves reorganizing the data it contains into a different format. Like importing, Access 2000 can translate the data into a variety of "languages," depending on your needs. The master list of export formats is the same one governing imports, given earlier in the chapter.

The main problem to keep an eye out for when exporting is *data loss.* Not all storage formats are created equal (after all, Microsoft didn't come up with them *all,* which is arguably a good situation). Just because the data looked glorious in your Access 2000 table doesn't mean a suitable home is waiting when you ship the information off to, say, Paradox or FoxPro. Special Access 2000 data types such as *AutoNumber, Yes/No, Memo,* and *OLE* are almost sure to cause problems. Be ready for some creative problem solving to make the data work just the way you want it to.

Likewise, field names can be trouble. Access 2000 is very generous about what you can put into a field name. dBASE, on the other hand, is downright totalitarian about field names. This attitude can lead to multiple fields with the same name — a frustrating (if slightly humorous) problem. If you export an Access 2000 table with fields called Projected2000Sales, Projected2000Net, and Projected2000Overhead, ending up with three fields named *Projected1* is distinctly possible — *not* a pleasant thought. Be ready to spend some time tuning the export so that it works just the way you thought it would.

To import or to link — the answer is, *It depends*

Because Access 2000 offers two different ways to get data in, a logical question comes up: *Which method should I use?* Because this question involves a computer, the simple answer is *It depends.*

The answer mainly depends on the other program and its fate within your organization. Are you still using the other program to update the data? Do other people use the program to access the data? If so, use a link with Access 2000. This option lets you play with the data while keeping it in the original format so that everyone else can use it as well.

On the other hand, if the other application was mothballed and you're doing data rescue duty, import the data permanently and give it a comfortable new home. Preserving a data format that nobody cares about anymore makes no sense.

The steps to exporting a table are much simpler than they are for importing. Here goes:

1. **With the database open, click on the table you want to export.**

    As you may expect, the table name is highlighted for the world to see.

2. **Choose File⇨ Export from the main menu.**

    The Export Table dialog box bounds merrily onto the screen.

3. **Click on the down arrow in the Save as type box to list the available exporting formats; then click on the one you want (see Figure 23-2).**

Figure 23-2:
I think that an Excel 2000 spreadsheet would be great for my less sophisticated friends who did not learn about Access 2000.

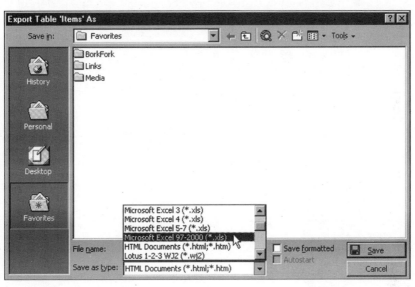

If the format you're looking for is in Table 23-1 but is *not* in your list on-screen, run the Access 2000 setup program again (oh joy, oh rapture!) and install that format on your system. This procedure may require the help of your Information Systems folks, depending on where your copy of Access 2000 is stored and who has custody of the installation disks.

What if you try these steps and Access 2000 *still* doesn't understand your data file? Here's one last trick you can try, but be forewarned: This is *truly* a last resort. Go back to your old program (where you created these data files in the first place) and see if that program has an *export* option. If the old program does, try exporting your data to one of the formats that Access 2000 understands (see Table 23-1 earlier in this chapter for a complete list).

There's danger here, though — every time you export and import data, you risk messing up part of it. The export/import process isn't perfect, so tread carefully (and make a couple backup copies of the original data file before you begin!).

4. **To use a different name for the table, click on the File name list box, highlight the existing table name, and then type a new name.**

If the table is headed back to an old DOS or Windows 3.*x* world, remember to limit yourself to eight letters, numbers, or combination thereof. Don't worry about the extension (the three character part after period in an old filename), because Access 2000 handles that automatically.

5. **If you want to stow the newly exported file in a different folder from the current one, use the Save in list box at the top of the window to explain the destination to Access 2000.**

To leave the file in the folder you're in, just skip this step and forge ahead.

6. **Brace yourself and click on Export (see Figure 23-3).**

Figure 23-3:
Crossing your fingers helps, too.

In true computer style, if the process is a success you get absolutely *no* feedback from Access 2000. You only hear about it if something dreadful goes wrong. Luckily, few things ever go wrong with exports, so your computer is probably sitting there looking smug even as you read this.

Chapter 24

The Analyzer: Your Data's Dr. Freud, Dr. Watson, and Dr. Jekyll

In This Chapter

▶ Becoming relational with the Table Analyzer
▶ Making the database document itself
▶ Steering clear of the Performance Analyzer

*I*f I didn't know better, I'd file this chapter under the heading *Oh Sure, That's What It Does* (said with heavy sarcasm). After all, the Analyzer promises to do the three tasks that are nearest to a database person's heart: automatically convert flat files into relational databases; document the database and all its sundry parts (including tables, queries, forms, reports, and more); and analyze the structure of your tables to make sure that everything is set up in the best possible way. If the Analyzer does all that and cooks, too (or at least orders pizza), a nearsighted technoweenie may accidentally fall in love!

Even though technology has come a *long* way in recent years, it's not as advanced as you expect. That caveat is true of the Analyzer, too — it promises more than it delivers. On the bright side, it does deliver a great deal, so the Analyzer gets a chapter of its very own, a place to extol its two virtues and reveal its shortcoming. (I guess one out of three isn't bad.)

It Slices, It Dices, It Builds Relational Databases!

Arguably, the Analyzer's biggest promise is hiding under Tools⇨Analyze⇨ Table. This piece of software claims it can turn a flat file table into a relational database with minimal human intervention *and* check for spelling errors in the data at the same time.

Truth be told, the Analyzer *tries* awfully hard to convert the flat file into a relational database. But like most software, sometimes it gets confused and vaults off in the wrong direction. I still recommend giving the Analyzer a try, simply because it *may* work on your table, and if it does, you just saved a ton of time and effort.

The Analyzer works best with a flat file table that contains plenty of duplicate information. For example, imagine a flat file table that stores video rental information. Each record contains customer and video data. If the same customer rents six tapes, the table has six separate records with the customer's name, address, and other information duplicated in each one. Multiply that by 100 customers and you have precisely the kind of flat file mess that the Analyzer is designed to solve.

With that thought in mind, here's how to inflict — er, invoke — the Table Analyzer Wizard:

1. **With your database open, choose <u>T</u>ools⇨<u>A</u>nalyze⇨<u>T</u>able from the main menu.**

   After a period of thought punctuated with hard disk activity, the Table Analyzer Wizard dialog box appears on-screen (see Figure 24-1).

2. **The first two screens are interesting, but strictly educational. Read them if you want and then click on <u>N</u>ext.**

   Stop clicking on Next when you get to the screen in Figure 24-2 (which should be precisely two Next clicks from Step 1).

3. **Click on the name of the flat file you want to do the relational magic on and then click on <u>N</u>ext.**

   Although some call it superstition, I firmly believe in crossing my fingers at moments such as this.

4. **The wizard wants to know whether it can analyze the table and offer suggestions on how the table ought to work. Click on the <u>Y</u>es radio button (if it's not already selected) and then click on <u>N</u>ext.**

   This step is the pivotal one in the whole process. The wizard leaps into the task, displaying a couple of horizontal bar charts to show how the project's progressing. When the Analysis Stages bar gets all the way to the end, the wizard's done. With the analysis complete, the results look like those shown in Figure 24-3.

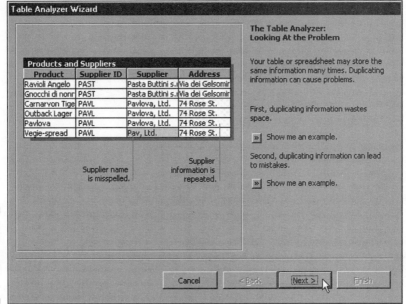

Figure 24-1:
So far, so good — the wizard shows up.

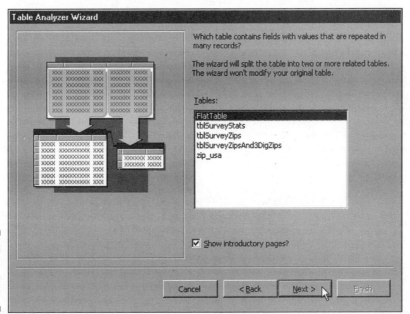

Figure 24-2:
Getting ready to do the deed.

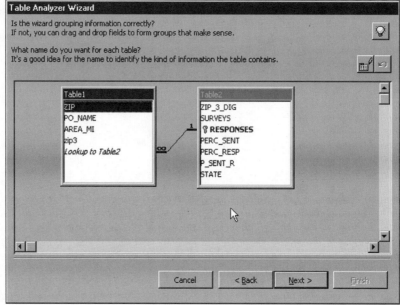

Figure 24-3:
The results
are a little
odd, but not
bad for a
piece of
hardware.

5. **If you like what the wizard came up with, name the tables by clicking on each table and then clicking on the Name Table button (the one that looks like a pencil doodling on a table). When you're done, click on Next.**

   If you're not sure about what the wizard wants to do or if the plan just makes no sense (and believe it or not, that *does* happen sometimes), click on Cancel and seek human help. (See the sidebar "When in doubt, ask a human" for more about that option.)

   If the wizard recommends that you don't split your table, carefully click on the Cancel button and pat yourself on the head for a job well done. That's the wizard's way of saying that it thinks your table is fine just as it is.

6. **The wizard wants your input about key fields for the tables. To designate a key field, click on a field in the table and then click on the Key button.**

   This step lets you replace many of the Generated Unique ID entries that the wizard put in the tables.

   Make sure that each table has a key field before continuing!

7. **The structure is basically complete, so the wizard turns its attention to typographical errors within the database. If it finds records that *seem* to be the same except for minor changes, it asks for your help to fix them (see Figure 24-4). Follow the on-screen instructions to make the repairs.**

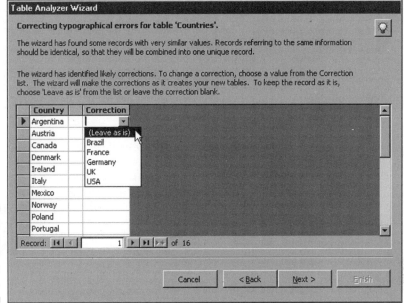

Figure 24-4:
What seems
to be a little
trouble is
easily fixed.

Depending on the condition of your data, you may have *many* records to correct. Be patient — the wizard really *is* helping!

8. **After the correction process is done, the wizard offers to create a query that looks and acts like your original table. If you have reports and forms that work with the flat file, let the wizard create the query for you (the default action). Otherwise, click on the N̲o radio button. Click on F̲inish when you're through.**

When in doubt, ask a human

The Table Analyzer may not be able to make heads or tails of your table. The Analyzer always tries, but it may fail rather spectacularly. If it does, the project falls back into your lap.

If you're trying to split a flat file database into a relational database and you don't know where to start, a good place to begin is the snack food aisle at the local food store. Get some goodies

(preferably chocolate) and use them to bribe your local database nerd into helping you.

If this database is important to your business or life (and it must be, or you wouldn't be haggling with it so much), the database is important enough to get some live, human help to put it together correctly.

Documentation: What to Give the Nerd in Your Life

Pardon me while I put on my technoweenie hat and taped-together glasses for a moment. One thing the world needs more of (can't ever have enough of, in fact) is *documentation*. If life were a little better documented, things would be different.

(I'm taking off the technoweenie outfit now. Thanks for your patience.)

In truth, documentation is probably the furthest task from your mind right now, but it's still important, especially if you're creating something for your business. I know that you barely have time to get the database running and tested, but you *absolutely* need to document what you're doing.

Like many problems, documenting your work is a trade-off between a dire need and a lack of time. What's a person to do? Call the Documentor!

This second piece of the Analyzer puzzle browses through everything in your database (and I do mean *everything*) and documents the living daylights out of it all. This thing collects information so obscure that I'm not even sure the programmers know what some of it means.

The neat part of the Documentor is that it works *by itself.* Really. You start it, sic it on a database, and nip off for a spot of lunch. When you come back, the Documentor's report is done and waiting. {Poof!} Instant documentation.

Here's how to put the Documentor to work on your database:

1. **With the database file open, choose Tools➪Analyze➪Documentor from the main menu.**

   The Database Documentor rises from the hard drive like a digital Phoenix and appears on-screen. (Okay, so I'm in a poetic mood — I'm still giddy about the prospect of the program doing my documentation for me.)

2. **In the Documentor dialog box, click the All Object Types tab and then click on the Select All button to document your entire database (see Figure 24-5). When you're ready, click on OK to start the process.**

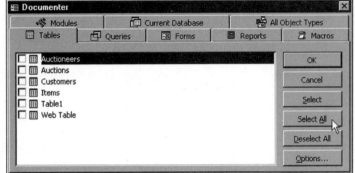

Figure 24-5:
One click
ensures that
everything
gets
included.

The Documentor begins by examining all the objects in your database, starting with the tables, and moving on to the queries, forms, reports, and so on. During the process, your forms appear on-screen for a moment — that's normal.

The process often takes a while, so this is a good time for lunch or a little coffee break.

When the Documentor finishes, it leaves a report packed with information about your database (see Figure 24-6).

4. **Click on the Print button on the toolbar or choose File⇨Print to get a paper copy.**

   If you want to store the report for posterity, choose File⇨Save as Table and then give the table a name.

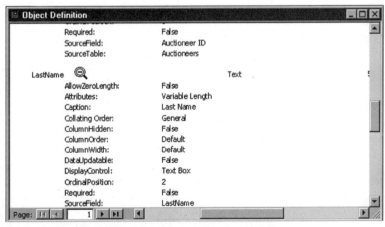

Figure 24-6:
The info's all
here in
black and
white —
you barely
lifted a
finger.

Let the Performance Analyzer Work on Someone Else's Tables

I don't usually come right out and drop a great big *hands off* notice in your lap, but I'm afraid that the Performance Analyzer deserves to be the exception to the rule.

Don't get me wrong — this feature shows great promise. After all, who wouldn't like something that claims to dig around in your tables, ferret out the technoid tweaks that are the key to better performance, and then implement them for you? But at least for now, forgo the temptation to tinker and instead let someone *else* (preferably someone you don't like) use the Performance Analyzer on his or her data first.

In my tests, the analyzer came up with some pretty lame ideas, such as an ever-present suggestion that I change the postal code field from text to a long integer type. For as smart as the software is supposed to be, it certainly *ought* to find some more impressive suggestions than that. I tried several combinations, including some with obvious problems in field type. The Performance Analyzer never came up with anything really useful to say.

Keep this feature in the back of your mind and try it out when Access 3000 comes out on the market in the next millennium.

Part VI
The Part of Tens

5th Wave Power Tip: To increase application speed, punch the Command Key over and over and over as rapidly as possible. The computer will sense your impatience and move your data along quicker than if you just sat and waited. Hint: This also works on elevator buttons and cross walk signals.

In this part . . .

All hail the traditional Part of Tens, purveyor of numerically organized information, keeper of the sacred decimal count, and upholder of the proud ...*For Dummies* tradition.

Every ...*For Dummies* book closes with a Part of Tens. I guess it's the *Dummies* version of denouement. Anyway, this book's final part includes stuff you can use today, stuff you may need tomorrow, and stuff for *way* on down the road. I tried to include a little something for everyone, so read every chapter *very* closely and see if you can find the stuff that I put in just for you.

By the way, no animals were harmed, exploited, or even consulted in the quest to bring you this information (although I did remember to feed my dog periodically throughout the project). One technoweenie was slightly miffed, but I'm sure he'll get over it.

Chapter 25

Ten Timesaving Keyboard Shortcuts

In This Chapter

▶ Keystrokes to save you time, energy, and hair

*J*ust because Windows 95/98 is supposed to be the ultimate graphical user environment doesn't mean that you won't need the keyboard anymore. In fact, Access 2000 has some cool shortcuts up its sleeve that are available only through this special, keyboard-based offer.

This chapter highlights ten cool shortcuts designed to make your life a little easier. Some keystroke combinations enter data automatically, some make editing quicker, and others are for fun.

Select an Entire Field — F2

This shortcut is particularly handy when you're replacing a lengthy address or description field. Instead of wrestling with the mouse to make sure that you have *everything* in the field highlighted, simply press F2 and you *know* that it's done. The keystroke works in both Datasheet view and Form view.

Insert the Current Date — Ctrl+; (Semicolon)

This keystroke combination and the one following not only save time, but also increase accuracy. Ever mistyped a date because you were in a hurry (or because the keyboard couldn't spell)? Ctrl+; resolves the issue completely by doing the work for you. To properly execute this command, press the Ctrl button first and while holding the Ctrl button down, press the semicolon button at the same time. The keystroke works in Datasheet view and Form view.

Insert the Current Time — Ctrl+: (Colon)

This shortcut is another nod to accuracy. To insert the current time, you actually press the Ctrl button and Shift button first, and while holding the two buttons down, press the semicolon button at the same time. Although Ctrl+: is the actual keystroke to get a colon, you have to do the Shift+; (semicolon) routine. The keystroke works in Datasheet view and Form view.

Insert the Same Field Value as the Last Record Ctrl+' (Apostrophe)

While entering data, you often come across a whole bunch of records containing similar information — for instance, people from the same city and state. Instead of manually typing the duplicate information in every record, the Ctrl+' (apostrophe) keystroke quickly enters it for you in both the Datasheet view and Form view.

Ctrl+' (apostrophe) isn't psychic, though. Instead, it merely says, "Well, I see that you're in the City field. In the last record, the city was *Tucumcari,* so I bet that's what you want in this record, too." And then it promptly copies the value from the previous record into the current one. (Of course, this works for any field, not just address information.)

Insert a Line Break — Ctrl+Enter

When a long entry in a memo or large text field feels like it's never going to quit, end the monotony with a line break. Well-placed line breaks make your data more legible, too. The keystroke is available in Datasheet view and Form view.

Add a New Record — Ctrl++ (Plus Sign)

Although Ctrl++ looks funny (just how _do_ you write _plus_ + without spelling it out?), this keyboard shortcut keeps you on the go when you're in a hot-and-heavy edit mode. Because you don't have to keep switching between the keyboard and the mouse to insert new records, your speed increases, as does your accuracy. This keystroke may seem strange but this one works with Ctrl+= (equal) also. I guess the Access gurus figured that because the + sign and = sign are on the same button on many keyboards, it's easier to remember that + means adding something such as a record, then the = sign. No doubt to your surprise, this shortcut works in Datasheet view and Form view.

Delete the Current Record — Ctrl+– (Minus Sign)

Do you suffer from pesky, unsightly, or unneeded records in your tables? Ctrl+– painlessly excises the records that you want to delete. And just like this shortcut's cousin, Ctrl++, this shortcut works in both Datasheet view and Form view.

Save the Record — Shift+Enter

After a long, hard edit, make sure that the record is saved with a quick Shift+Enter. That signals Access 2000 that you're truly done working on this one and are ready to store it for posterity. The software takes the cue and saves your changes immediately. Use this key combo in Datasheet view or Form view. It's a real time-saver!

Undo Your Last Changes — Ctrl+Z

Everyone should have this one memorized. The Undo keystroke is a golden oldie. With the propensity of Access 2000 to automatically save things every time you turn around, it can really save your bacon. When something goes wrong, don't panic — try Ctrl+Z instead. This keystroke combination works almost everywhere in Access 2000 and even beyond in many Windows applications.

Open the Selected Object in Design View — Ctrl+Enter

Hey, what's this? Ctrl+Enter does *two* things in Access 2000? You're right. When you're editing a table in Datasheet view or Form view, Ctrl+Enter inserts a line break. When you're in *Database* view, use Ctrl+Enter to whip open something in Design view. Let the *ordinary folks* use the mouse — be different and do it from the keyboard!

Chapter 26

Ten Common Crises and How to Survive Them

. . . .

In This Chapter

▶ Common hair-raising problems solved (or at least explained)

▶ Misplacing tables

▶ Mysteriously changing numbers

▶ Vanishing files and records

▶ Unasked questions

. . . .

*W*here there are computers, so also is there software, because a computer is nothing without its software. Where there is software, so also are there problems, because software without problems is obviously outdated and in need of replacement.

Problems are a part of life. When the problems strike in or around your precious data, they seem all the more fearsome. This chapter touches on only ten problems you may encounter while using Access 2000. If your problem is covered here, try the solution I outline. If your particular trouble isn't on the list, refer to Chapter 3 for some other spots to seek help.

And good luck. (I mean it!)

You Built Several Tables, but Put Them in Different Databases

Misplacing your tables is an easy mistake to make at first, especially if you have experience with one of those *other* database programs such as Paradox or FoxPro. Those systems store each table in a separate file. Working from that experience, it's only natural to start creating databases right and left, each one containing a single table.

Of course, separate tables make a great deal of extra work for you in Access 2000 because the confused program can't figure out what you're trying to accomplish. Rather than setting up all kinds of links among a slew of different database files, pull your tables together into a single database, the way Access 2000 is designed to work with them.

To pull all your tables together, open an Access database file, right-click on the table you want to move, and select Copy from the pop-up menu. Now open the database you're moving the table to. Click on the Tables Objects bar button, right-click in the Table list, and select Paste on the pop-up menu. The table hops into the database. Repeat the process for all the orphan tables rattling around in their own Access database files.

If you're feeling really rambunctious and adventuresome, try feeding your new database to the mighty Access 2000 Analyzer. For more about the Analyzer, flip back to Chapter 24.

You Type 73.725, but It Changes to 74 by Itself

Automatic rounding can frustrate the living daylights out of you, but fixing it is easy. By default, Access 2000 sets all number fields to accept *long integers* — numbers without decimal places. You need to change the setting to *single,* which is short for *single precision number,* not *hey you swinging text field, let's go party with the forms.*

To fix the problem, open the table in Design view and then click on the field that's giving you fits. On the General tab of the Properties area at the bottom of the screen, click in the Field Size box. Click on the down arrow that appears on the end of the box; then select single from the drop-down menu. Save the table and (voilà!) your automatic rounding problem is over.

You're Almost Completely Sure That's Not the Question You Asked

Remember the old saying, "Kids say the darnedest things?" Well, this problem falls under the heading, "Queries return the darnedest results." Every now and then, one of your queries returns the most *fascinating* answers. In fact, they're *so* fascinating that you begin to wonder precisely what color the sky is in the query's world, because the query's world is obviously different from the one you're in.

Because the actual cause can be any number of things, this problem doesn't have a tried-and-true solution, but I can offer some steps to send you in the right direction:

1. **Make sure that no stray characters are in the query.**

   A single misplaced keystroke can send Access 2000 on a wild data chase. Tidy things up and then try the query again. If you still get flaky results, go on to the next step.

2. **Double-check the query logic itself.**

   Are you asking the question that you *think* you're asking? Access 2000 always tries hard to get the query right, but if it misunderstands the question, all its work is for naught. If you're doing one incredibly complex query, try to split it into a few simple queries that build on each other instead.

3. **Try closing the query and rebuilding it from scratch.**

   Every now and then, queries simply freak out (after all, it's *just* a computer). If nothing seems to help, make a backup of your data and call your friendly neighborhood computer guru.

If the query *still* doesn't work right, enlist your local database nerd for a quick consultation. Something very subtle may be wrong with either your query or (horrors!) your tables.

And When You Looked Again, the Record Was Gone

"The record was there — right there!" The key word in that sentence is the verb, because it indicates that the record *isn't* there now. Precisely *where* the record went is a moot point because only the computer knows, and machines have a code of silence about these details. (It's a subset of the rules that make all the copiers break at the same time.)

First, *don't panic.* Panicky people do strange things, and you need your wits about you for the next few minutes. You can panic later after the dust settles.

Before doing anything technical with Access 2000 (or hitting the computer with a baseball bat), press Ctrl+Z. That's the Undo key. If the record comes back, you're done. In that case, close the table and go have a panic attack in the break room.

If the Undo key didn't accomplish anything, you're in slightly more trouble. The next best solution is to copy the record from a backup of the database file. This solution works only if you backed up your database at some point. If you have a paper copy of the data, you can always manually re-enter it into the database. If that record was your only copy of the information, then raise your hand, look at the computer, and wave good-bye, because it's gone now (you have my deepest sympathy).

Please, oh *please,* keep current backups of your information. You never know when bad things will happen (insert eerie organ music here).

The Validation That Never Was

Validations are one of my favorite features of Access 2000. But like anything, validations can cause problems if they're not used properly.

The biggest concern is a validation rule that *can't* be valid. For example, suppose that someone (certainly not you or I, but *someone*) wants to limit a particular field so that it only accepts entries between 0 and 100. To accomplish that, the person creates a validation that says `<0 And >100`. Unfortunately, that rule won't work — ever! The person mixed up the symbols and created a rule that only accepts a number that's less than 0 *and* greater than 100. According to my college math professor, not too many numbers like that are running loose in the world.

Don't let this problem happen to your validations. To avoid such crises, write your rule on paper and then test it with some sample data. Be sure to include examples of both good and bad entries to make sure that the rule works just like it's supposed to.

The Sometimes-There, Sometimes-Gone Menus

Thanks to someone in the *Conceptually Cool, But Functionally Frustrating New Feature Division* of Microsoft, the menus in Access 2000 (and all of its brethren in Office 2000) don't automatically show all of the possible menu items available. Instead, they show only the most commonly used menu items, plus a little down-pointing chevron at the bottom of the menu. (Yes, this is *supposed* to make your life easier. Isn't that nice to know?)

That little chevron is your key to the full menu. When you click on the chevron, the menu magically expands to its full size, proudly displaying all of the options available on it. At this point, click on whichever menu item you want.

After you click the chevron and select an item from the full menu, Access 2000 automatically adds that item to the *short* version of the menu.

You Can't Link to a FoxPro or dBASE Table

In this bet on the cause of the failed link, the odds-on favorite is a bad index file. Access 2000 has a specific problem linking to FoxPro and dBASE tables that have bad indexes. Before getting frustrated — even before panicking — go back to the original program, rebuild the table's index, and then try the link again. Most of the time, that procedure solves the problem.

If this snag happens to be the one time in 10,000 where the index file *isn't* at fault, pick up a bag of nacho chips at the convenience store and invite the guru over for a snack and some troubleshooting.

Be *really* careful when updating a FoxPro or dBASE file through Access 2000. Make sure that you attach the index — otherwise, you're crawling around on your knees, begging for trouble.

You Get a Key Violation While Importing a Table

When you get a key violation while importing a table, Access 2000 is trying as hard as it can, but the data you're importing contains a duplicate key value. Because Access 2000 can't arbitrarily change the data in question, you need to do the repair. Go back to the master program, find the offending record, and build a good key to replace the duplicated one. After you're sure that the key values are all unique, then try, try again.

Try as You Might, the Program Won't Start

After picking Access 2000 from the Start menu, the oh-so-cool Access 2000 splash screen (the pretty picture that keeps you entertained while the program takes too long to load) flows smoothly onto the screen. Suddenly, the serene moment shatters as a small warning box bursts in, shouting that Windows `Can't find ODD_ESOTERIC_FILE.MDB`. The Access 2000 splash screen fades and you're left facing the Windows 95/98 desktop once more.

This sequence really does happen from time to time. Honestly, such events are just part of life with computers. I teach my troubleshooting classes a simple mantra to cover precisely this problem: *It's a file. Files go bad.*

Because the error message was kind enough to give you a filename (not all errors are so generous), use the Explorer to look for the file. If it's there, odds are that the file is corrupt. If the file isn't there, well, at least you know why Access 2000 didn't find it.

Either way, you need to replace the file with a healthy version from your original Access 2000 program disks. If you have a CD-ROM copy of Access 2000, this process is easy. Just point the Explorer at the installation CD-ROM, find the file, and copy it to the Access 2000 subdirectory.

If Access 2000 lives on your company's network, contact your friendly Information Systems support folks for guidance. In that case, the problem is very likely out of your hands. Wish the computer gurus luck, and then take a coffee break while they work on the problem.

The Wizard Won't Come Out of His Castle

This one is a more focused version of the preceding problem where Access 2000 won't start. Now the problem is localized to a particular wizard. The solution is the same: Look for the missing file, replace it from the master disks, and then see whether that solves the problem. If all else fails (which may happen), pick up a bag of nacho chips and call in your favorite nerd for some assistance.

By default, the Access 2000 menus and other dialog boxes show *all* of the *possible* options — not just the options currently installed on your computer. This means that as you use Access 2000, it may periodically say that a menu option you select doesn't exist on your computer. In that case, whip out the Access 2000 CD-ROM and install it. If your computer is part of a network in a business, contact your computer support folks, because they probably need (or want) to handle the installation themselves.

Chapter 27

Ten Tips from the Database Nerds

∙∙∙

In This Chapter

▶ Cool ideas from that most uncool of all populations

∙∙∙

*L*ike 'em or loathe 'em, the technical experts are always with you. Everywhere you turn, you see someone who may know more about technology than you do. Granted, these folks sometimes look funny, frequently act strange, and often seem amazingly disconnected from reality. (I know this because I'm one of them and my friends often catalog my behaviors for me. Isn't it great to be loved?)

In their more lucid moments, though, the technical experts possess incredible nuggets of wisdom. This chapter is a distillation of good advice that I picked up over the years. Some of it is very focused, while other parts are downright philosophical. Such is life with the technical experts (but you knew that already).

Document As If Your Life Depends on It

Yes, it's a pain. Yes, it's a bother. Yes, *I* do it myself (kinda scary when a guy actually listens to his own advice). If you build a database, make sure that you document every little detail about it. Here's a list of items to start with:

✔ **General information about the database:** Include file locations, an explanation of what the database does, and information on how it works.

✔ **Table layouts, including field names, sizes, contents, and sample contents:** If some of the data comes from esoteric or temporary sources (like the shipping report that you shred right after data entry), note that fact in the documentation so that people know.

- ✔ **Report names, an explanation of the information on the report, and lists of who gets a copy of the report when it's printed:** If you need to run some queries before doing a report, document the process (or better yet, get a nerd to help you automate the whole thing). Documenting who receives the report is *particularly* important. Jot down the job title in the documentation as well as the current person in the position.

- ✔ **Queries and logic:** For every query, provide a detailed explanation of how the query works, especially if it involves multiple tables or data sources outside of Access (like SQL tables or other big-time information storage areas).

- ✔ **Answer the question "Why?":** As you document your database, focus on *why* things work they way that they do. Why do the queries use those particular tables? Why do the reports go to those people? Granted, if you work in a corporate environment, you may not *know* why some things happen the way they do, but it never hurts to inquire.

- ✔ **Miscellaneous details:** Provide information such as the backup process and schedule, where back-up tapes are located (you *are* doing backups, right?), and what to do if the computer isn't working. If your database runs a particularly important business function, such as accounting, inventory, point-of-sale, or order entry, make sure that some kind of manual process is in place to keep the business going if the computer breaks down — and remember to document the process!

One final thought: Keep the documentation up to date. Every six to 12 months, review your documentation to see whether some updates are needed. Documentation is only useful if it's up to date and if someone other than yourself can understand it. Likewise, make sure you (or your counterparts in the department) know where the documentation is located. If you have an electronic version, keep it backed up and have a printout handy.

Don't Make Your Fields Way Too Big

When you're building a table, take a moment to make your text fields the appropriate size for the data you're keeping in those fields. By default, Access 2000 sets up text fields to hold 50 characters — a pretty generous setting, particularly if the field happens to be holding two-letter state abbreviations. Granted, 48 characters of space aren't anything to write home about, but multiply that space across a table with 100,000 customer addresses in it and you get 4.8MB of storage space that's very busy holding absolutely *nothing*.

Adjust the field size with the Field Size setting on the General tab in Design view.

Real Numbers Use Number Fields

Use number fields for *numbers,* not for text *pretending* to be a number. Computers perceive a difference between the postal code *47201* and the number *47,201.* The postal code is stored as a series of five characters that all happen to be digits, but the number is stored as an actual number that you can use for math (just try that on a postal code field, sometime) and all kinds of other fun numeric stuff.

When choosing the type for a new field with numbers in it, ask yourself a simple question: Are you *ever* going to make a calculation or do anything math-related with the field? If so, use a number type. If not, store the field as text and go on with your life.

Better Validations Make Better Data

Validations work hand in hand with masks to prevent bad data from getting close to your tables. Validations are easy to make, quick to set up, and ever vigilant (even when you're so tired you can't see straight). If you aren't using validations to protect the integrity of your database, you really should start. Flip to Chapter 7 and have a look at the topic.

Use Understandable Names

When building a table or creating a database, think about the names you use. Will you remember what they mean three months from now? Six months from now? Are they intuitive enough for someone else to look at the table and figure out what it does, long after your knowledge of Access 2000 puts your career on the fast track?

Now that Windows 95/98 *finally* offers long filenames, please use them. You don't need to get carried away, but now you have no excuse for files called *99Q1bdg5.* Using *Q1 1999 Budget Rev 5* makes *much* more sense to everyone involved.

Take Great Care When Deleting

Whenever you're deleting field values from a table, make sure that you're killing the values in the *right* record, check again, and — only when you're sure — delete the original. Even then, you can still do a quick Ctrl+Z and recover the little bugger.

Why all the checking and double-checking? Because after you delete a field value *and do anything else in the table,* Access 2000 completely forgets about your old value. It's gone, just as if it never existed. If you delete a record from a table, then the record is really gone because there is no Undo available for an entire record. If that record happened to be important and you don't have a current back-up file, you're out of luck. Sorry!

Keep Backups

There's no substitute for a current backup of your data, particularly if the data is vital to your company. Effective strategies often include maintaining back up copies at another location just in case a disaster destroys your work facility. Don't believe me? Let the phrase *no receivables* float through your mind for a while. How do you feel about backups now? I thought you'd see it my way.

Think First and Then Think Again

Apply this rule to any Access 2000 step that contains the word *delete* or *redesign.* Think about what you're doing. Then think again. Software makes handling large amounts of data easier than ever before, but it also offers the tools to screw up your data on a scale not seen since the time of P.T. Barnum.

Thomas Watson, Sr., the president of IBM for years and years, said it best: "Think."

Get Organized and Keep It Simple

Although they may seem different at first blush, these two tips work together to promote classic nerd values like *a place for every gadget* and *my query ran faster than yours, so there.* By keeping your computer orderly and organizing your entire workspace, you have everything you need at hand. Get yourself a Barcalounger and a remote control, and you never need to leave the office again.

Yes, you can get *too* organized. In fact, doing so is altogether too easy. Temper your desire to organize with a passion for doing work with as few steps as possible. On your computer, limit the number of folders and subfolders you use — a maximum of five levels of folders is *more* than enough for just about anybody. If you go much beyond five levels, your organization starts bumping into your productivity (and nobody likes a productivity loss, least of all the people who come up with those silly little slogans for the corporate feel-good posters).

Know When to Ask for Help

If you're having trouble with something, swallow your ego and ask for help. Saying *I don't know* and then trying to find out holds no shame. This rule is *especially* important when you're riding herd on thousands of records in a database. Small missteps quickly magnify and multiply a small problem into a huge crisis. Ask for help *before* the situation becomes dire.

Index

• *Numbers & Symbols* •

+ (plus signs) as related table indicator, 30

& (ampersand)
  for blanks, 102
  joining fields in expressions or formulas, 204

@ (at sign) for padding data with spaces, 102

\ (backslash) for integer division, 206

^ (caret) for exponentiation, 206

! (exclamation point)
  for adding fields in Expression Builder, 206
  for mask-filling from left, 111

> (greater-than symbol)
  as comparison operator, 158
  in expressions, 207
  for uppercase, 102

< (less-than symbol)
  as comparison operator, 158
  in expressions, 207
  for lowercase, 102

(pound sign) around dates, 178
  (sigma) (mathematical symbol for "Sum"), 186

16-bit Winsock, 297

[] (square brackets) around field names for calculations, 196–197

32-bit Winsock, 297

• *A* •

Access file imports, 324

Access 2000 for Windows
  Analyzer, 331–338
  customizing toolbar icon size, 34
  main window, 26–27
  starting, 10
  troubleshooting problems with starting, 349–350
  users' mailing list, 46

Active Server Page imports, 325

ActiveX, 296

address field type, 57

Advanced Filter/Sort, 155–159

aligning
  report items to grids, 267
  text on reports, 264

alignment buttons, 264

Alt+key combinations. *See* keyboard shortcuts

America Online (AOL), online help, 45

America Online For Dummies, 45, 295

ampersand (&)
  for blanks, 102
  joining fields in expressions or formulas, 204

Analyzer
  converting flat files to relational databases, 331–335
  documenting database structures, 336–337
  invoking, 332
  pros and cons, 331
  suggesting performance enhancements, 338

AND Boolean operator, 178–180, 182–184

Answer Wizard, 42
Append queries, 212
Apply Filter button, 159
area charts, 240
arithmetic operators. *See also*
   calculations
  described, 206
  summary functions, 289
arrow keys for next/previous field/
   record, 116, 117
ASCII (text file) imports, 325, 326
.asp file imports, 325
at sign (@) for padding data with
   spaces, 102
attaching. *See* linking
AutoFormat button, 267
AutoFormatting reports, 266–267
AutoForms, 314–316
automated editing queries, 210–217
Autonumber fields
  caution on exports, 328
  described, 56
AutoReports
  column adjustments, 231–232
  columnar, 222
  creating, 223–224
  described, 221
  margin adjustments, 229–230
  paper size and orientation specifica-
    tions, 230–231
  previewing, 224–228
  saving as exports, 228
  sending as e-mail, 228
  tabular, 222
  zooming, 226–228
Avery label stock, 234, 235
Avg function, 194, 289

• *B* •

Back Color option of Page Header
  properties dialog box, 283

backslash (\) for integer division, 206
backups
  caution on Access's automatic save
   feature, 21
  caution on non-undoable deletions,
   353–354
  documenting system and schedule
   for, 352
  importance of, 22, 97, 209–210, 326,
   348, 354
bands on reports. *See* sections (bands)
   on reports
bar charts, 240
blanks. *See* spaces
Bold button, 255, 263
Boolean operators
  AND, 178–179
  AND and/or OR, 182–184
  described, 177–178
  multiple ANDs, 179–180
  OR, 180–182
borders. *See* lines, borders, or boxes
Box tool, 270
boxes. *See* lines, borders, or boxes
bubble charts, 240

• *C* •

calculations
  with Expression Builder, 204–207
  in queries, 185–194
  for updating records, 216–217
  upon fields, 195–207
  upon fields in multiple tables, 198
Can Grow/Shrink options of Group
   Header properties dialog box,
   284–285
caret (^) for exponentiation, 206
case
  formatting for lowercase, 102
  formatting for uppercase, 102
  matching in searches, 144

catalogs (in dBASE and FoxPro), 54
Cell Effects: Raised/Sunken, 127
cellular phone number data, 57
changing records. *See* editing
charts
  creating with Chart Wizard, 239–242
  types available, 240
chiseled text on reports, 262
city data, 57
Clear Grid button, 151
clicking (and dragging) the mouse
    (highlighting), 4
Clippit, 39
colors
  for lines or borders on reports, 260–261
  on datasheets, 126
  on reports, 257–258
column charts, 240
columnar AutoReports, 222, 274
columns in tables
  adjusting width, 118–119
  deleting, 124
  as fields, 131
  freezing on-screen, 124–125
  hiding, 122–123
  inserting, 124
  rearranging, 120–122
  renaming, 124, 353
columns on reports, formatting, 231–232
command buttons, adding hyperlinks
    to, 307
Common Expressions, 207
company data in database fields, 57
comparison operators for queries, 158
CompuServe For Dummies, 45
CompuServe online help, 45
cone charts, 240
constants, 206
Contacts (sample table in Table
    Wizard), 72

context-sensitive menus, 34
Control Menu button, 27
controls on reports, 257, 274
correcting records. *See* editing
Count function, 188–189, 194, 289
counting tools, 185
country data in database fields, 57
Creating Cool HTML 4 Web Pages, 302
crosstab queries (tabulations), 189–190
Crosstab Query Wizard, 172
Ctrl+key combinations. *See* keyboard
    shortcuts
currency fields
  described, 56
  formatting, 103–104
  validating input, 112, 348, 353
current date (Ctrl+;) or time (Ctrl+:), 95
Customers (sample table in Table
    Wizard), 72
cut, copy, and paste operations, consoli-
    dating tables into single database,
    345–346

data. *See also* formatting; importing data
  described, 52–53
  field types for, 55–58
  redundancy, 59
  validation of input, 112–113, 348, 353
Data Access Page Wizard, 303–306
data access pages, 303
database files, 54
Database view, switching to Design view
    (Ctrl+Enter), 344
database window
  described, 27, 28–29
  navigating in, 14–15
Database Wizard, 60, 65, 68

databases. *See also* formatting; importing data; queries
  building, 63–68
  closing, 14
  consolidating tables into, 345–346
  described, 54
  documenting for your future sanity, 351–352
  documenting structures with Analyzer, 336–337
  finding "lost," 94
  flat file, 58, 59, 60, 80
  naming, 66, 353
  opening existing, 12–13, 90–92
  publishing on Web, 296
  relational, 59–60, 80, 167–168
  saving, 21
  sorting, 145–146
  style of display, 66–67
  tables, adding to, 68–73
  terminology, importance of, 51–52
Datasheet view
  caution on making changes in, 130
  described, 73
datasheet window, 29–31
datasheets
  exporting as static HTML pages, 307
  navigating, 115–117
date/time fields
  described, 56
  entering current date (Ctrl+;) or time (Ctrl+:), 95
  formatting, 104–105
  formatting with Input Mask Wizard, 107
  formatting with input validation, 112–113, 348, 353
.DB, .DBF file imports, 324
dBASE file imports or exports, 54, 324, 325, 328, 349
decimal place formatting, fixed and standard, 104

default printer, 231
Delete queries, 212–214
deleting
  columns, 124
  with extreme care!, 353–354
  fields (with caution!), 133–134
  records, 95, 96–97
Design view. *See also* formatting
  advantages, 130, 251, 273
  aligning items to grids, 267
  aligning text, 264
  bold, italics, and underlining, 255, 263
  borders, 260–263
  color, 257–258
  dates, 291–292
  described, 73, 100
  detail data, 254
  formatting toolbar, 255–257
  forms, 318–321
  headers and footers, 254, 271, 274, 275–280, 282–283, 285–289
  labels for report data, 253
  Layout Preview, 265
  lines, drawing, 269–270
  opening selected objects in (Ctrl+Enter), 344
  page breaks, 270–271, 285
  page numbers and dates, 291–292
  Print Preview, 265
  rearranging items, 258–260
  Report properties dialog box, 282–284
  section formatting, 284–285
  section summary functions, 289–290
  sections and markers, 253–254, 274–276, 281
  special effects for text, 255, 261–263
  switching between Print Preview, 225
  switching to, 252
  text boxes, 253
Design View button, 252
detail records, 248

Details sections of reports, 275
documenting database structures
  with Analyzer, 336–337
  importance of, 351–352
donut charts, 240
double-clicking the mouse, 4
duplicate records, allowing or not, 87
dynamic Web pages, 303

• E •

Edit menu
  Copy, 34
  Delete Record, 95
  Delete Rows, 133–134
  Delete Tab, 151
  Find, 16, 142–145
  Replace, 210–211
  Undo Property Setting, 256
  Undo Saved Record, 95
  Undo Typing, 19
editing
  with automated editing queries,
    210–217
  automatic saves of, 18, 21
  caution recommended, 18, 21, 95
  importance of backups prior to, 22, 97,
    209–210
  records, 18–19, 95–96
  recovering with backups, 97
e-mail
  address data for, 57
  AutoReports sent as, 228
Employees (sample table in Table
    Wizard), 72
employment data, 57
End key for last field in current
    record, 116
Enter key to save edits, 95
Equals (comparison operator), 158
Escape key to cancel edits, 95
etched text on reports, 262

Events (sample table in Table Wizard), 72
*Excel 2000 For Windows For
    Dummies,* 272
Excel (Microsoft)
  exporting Access reports to, 225, 272
  importing files from, 324
exclamation point (!)
  for adding fields in Expression
    Builder, 206
  for mask-filling from left, 111
exiting Access 2000 for Windows, 23
exponentiation (^), 206
Export Table dialog box, 329–330
exporting data, 327–330. *See also*
    importing data
exporting reports
  to mail merge, 272
  to MS Word or Excel, 225, 272
  to other programs, 228
  as static HTML pages, 307
Expr1, Expr2, Expr3, etc., 199, 200
Expression Builder, 204–207, 288–289
Expression function, 194

• F •

FastTips faxed help, 45–47
Favorites list, 91
fax number data, 57
faxes from FastTips help, 45–47
Field Properties, 100–101, 112
field types for data
  date/time, 104–105
  described, 55–58
  importance to formatting, 101
  numbers and currency, 103–104
  text and memos, 102–103
  yes/no, 105
fields in tables
  adding to tables, 130–133
  caution on excessive number, 195
  caution on excessive size, 352

fields in tables *(continued)*
  as columns, 131
  deleting (with caution!), 133–134
  described, 30, 52–53
  displaying contents in red, 103, 105
  entering @;"Unknown"[Red] indicator
    for fields to be filled later, 103
  key, or linking, 59, 80–81
  naming, 58, 353
  performing calculations on, 195–207
  in records, 54
  renaming, 134–137, 353
  selecting for tables, 70–71
  sizing so data will fit, 249
  truncation of data in, 249
  type examples, 57
  types, 55–56
  validation of input, 112–113, 348, 353
fields on forms, 318–321
file:// (hyperlink type), 297
file formats
  for exported data, 328
  for imported data, 324–327
File menu
  Close, 14, 23
  Exit, 23
  Export, 307, 329–330
  Get External Data, Import, 326–327
  New, 63–67
  Open, 69, 74–75
  Open Database, 13, 91–92
  Page Setup, 229
  Save, 75, 87
File Name searches, 94
files
  caution on excessive folder layers, 354
  finding "lost," 94
  troubleshooting corrupted, 349–350
Fill/Back Color button, 255, 257
Filter by Form button, 148
Filter by Selection button, 147
Filter menu, Apply Filter/Sort, 159

Filter window, 156
filtering records. *See also* queries
  with Advanced Filter/Sort, 155–159
  described, 147–151
Find and Replace dialog box, 16, 143,
    210–211
Find button, 16
Find Duplicates Query Wizard, 172
Find Next button, 211
Find Unmatched Query Wizard, 172
finding. *See also* queries
  with Ctrl+F for Find command, 142
  with "Go to field" button, 255
  "lost" databases or files, 94
  "lost" records, 347–348
  missing options on menus, 348
  records with filtering, 147–151
  and replacing data, 16, 143, 210–211
  and saving searches as queries, 151
  specific data in tables, 16, 142–145
  table records, 15–18
First function, 194
Fit view, 226
Fixed decimal format, 104
flat file databases
  converting to relational, with Analyzer,
    331–335
  described, 58, 59, 60, 80
folders, caution on creating too
    many, 354
font weight, 237
Font/Fore Color button, 255, 257
fonts
  described, 125–127
  selecting from Formatting toolbar, 255
  TrueType, 126
footers. *See* headers and footers for
    reports
Force New Page option of Group Header
    properties dialog box, 284–285
form window, 31
Form Wizard, 311–314

Format menu
  Align Left/Right/Top/Bottom, 268
  Datasheet, 127
  Font, 125–126
  Freeze Columns, 125
  Hide Columns, 122
  Horizontal Spacing, 269
  Size, 269
  Snap to Grid, 268
  Unhide Columns, 123
  Vertical Spacing, 269
formatting. *See also* Design view
  with AutoFormat, 266–267
  by hiding columns, 122–123
  calculated results, 199–200
  column rearranging, 120–122
  column width, 118–119
  date/time fields, 104–105
  described, 101–102
  fonts, 125–127
  with input masks, 106–111
  with input validation, 112–113, 348, 353
  number and currency fields, 103–104
  report columns, 231–232
  report margins, 229–230
  row height, 119–120
  text and memo fields, 102
  3-D look, 127–128
  Yes/No fields, 105
Formatting toolbar, 255
forms
  adding hyperlinks to, 307
  creating with AutoForms, 314–316
  creating with Form Wizard, 311–314
  customizing, 316–321
  described, 310
  exporting as static HTML pages, 307
  running, 14
formulas. *See also* calculations
  including values in, 202
  using field names in, 203
FoxPro file imports, 54, 324, 325, 349

freezing columns on screen, 124–125
ftp:// (hyperlink type), 297
Function keys. *See* keyboard shortcuts
functions
  built-in, 206
  mathematical, 194

• G •

General Date format, 104
General Number format, 104
gopher:// (hyperlink type), 297
graphics. *See* images
graphs. *See* charts
greater-than symbol (>)
  as comparison operator, 158
  in expressions, 207
  for uppercase, 102
grid settings, 231, 232
gridlines, 127
Group By function, 186–188, 194
Group Header properties dialog box, 284
group headers and footers, 275–276,
      277–280
Group On option of Sorting and Group-
      ing dialog box, 280
group sections of reports, 275–276,
      277–280
grouping for customized reports
  caution on changes, 279
  described, 245–247
Grp Keep Together option of Report
      properties dialog box, 282–284

• H •

headers and footers for reports
  described, 254
  for each page, 274, 276–277, 282–283
  on first page only, 274, 276, 277
  for group sections, 275–276, 277–280
  with images, 271

Height option of Page Header properties
    dialog box, 283
help. *See also* troubleshooting
  accessing (F1), 21, 38
  Answer Wizard, 42
  Contents tab, 41–42
  FastTips, 45–47
  Index tab, 42–44
  knowing when to holler for, 355
  Office Assistant, 21, 27, 38–40, 207
  online services, 45
  phone support, 47–48
  from ScreenTips, 33
Help menu
  Microsoft Help, 40
  What's This, 44
Herma label stock, 234
hiding columns, 122–123
highlighting
  entire field with F2, 95, 341
  with the mouse, 4
Home key for last field in current
    record, 116
.htm, .html file imports, 325
HTML 4 For Dummies, 302
HTML (HyperText Markup Language),
    303, 307
http:// (hyperlink type), 297
http addresses. *See* Web sites
hyperlinks and hyperlink fields
  adding to reports and forms, 307
  adding to tables, 298–300
  described, 56, 297
  ineligibility for indexing, 86
  ineligibility for primary key, 78
  types available in Access, 297
  typing, 300
  using, 301

• *I* •

icons
  for Access 2000 for Windows, 10
  used in this book, 5
Image button, 270
images on reports
  adding, 67, 271
  adding hyperlinks to, 307
Import dialog box, 326–327
importing data. *See also* exporting
    reports
  compared to linking, 328
  file format translations, 324–326
  troubleshooting key violations, 349
Index tab, 42–44
Indexes button, 87
indexes to tables
  creating, 86–88
  deleting, 88
Input Mask Wizard, 106–108
input masks
  manual, 108–111
  with wizard, 106–108
input validation, 112–113, 348, 353
Insert menu
  Date and Time, 292
  New Record, 93–94
  Page Number, 291
  Rows, 131–133
Insert Picture dialog box, 271
installing, Chart Wizard, 239
IntelliMouse, 5, 95, 116, 118
Internet. *See also* hyperlinks and
    hyperlink fields
  accessing with Access, 296–297
Internet Explorer, 296–297
The Internet For Dummies, 45, 295
Internet Information Server, 306
intranets, 302
Italic button, 255, 263

• J •

Java, 296
job data in database fields, 57
Justify button, 255

• K •

Keep Together option
  of Report properties dialog box,
    282–284
  of Sorting and Grouping dialog box, 279
key fields
  described, 59, 168
  troubleshooting violations during
    imports, 349
keyboard shortcuts
  Alt+underlined letter for menu
    access, 34
  Ctrl++ (plus sign) for new record, 343
  Ctrl+: (colon) for current time, 95, 342
  Ctrl+; (semicolon) for current date,
    95, 341
  Ctrl+' (apostrophe) for same field value
    as last record, 342
  Ctrl+- (minus sign) to delete current
    record, 343
  Ctrl+C for Copy command, 34
  Ctrl+End to end of datasheet, 116
  Ctrl+Enter for line breaks, 342
  Ctrl+Enter for opening selected object
    in Design view, 344
  Ctrl+F for Find command, 142
  Ctrl+Home to top of datasheet, 116
  Ctrl+PgDn to scroll right one
    screen, 116
  Ctrl+PgUp to scroll left one screen, 116
  Ctrl+W for Close command, 14
  Ctrl+Z for Undo command, 18, 95,
    343, 347
  F1 for help, 21
  F2 for highlighting entire field, 95, 341
  Shift+Enter to save record, 343

keys
  multifield, 78
  primary, 78–80
  troubleshooting key violations in
    imported data, 349

• L •

labels (for mailing, nametags, etc.),
    creating with Label Wizard, 233–239
labels on reports
  adding hyperlinks to, 307
  creating, 253
Landscape orientation of printing,
    230–231
Last function, 194
Layout Preview, 265
Left Justify button, 255
less-than symbol (<)
  as comparison operator, 158
  in expressions, 207
  for lowercase, 102
line breaks (Ctrl+Enter), 342
line charts, 240
Line tool, 270
Line/Border Color button, 255
Line/Border Width button, 255
lines, borders, or boxes
  on forms, 319–320
  on reports, 260–263, 269–270
linking fields, 59, 80–81
linking of tables
  caution on index files for FoxPro and
    dBASE, 349
  compared to importing data, 328
  described, 82–86
  to external data files, 326–327
  and referential integrity, 214
  undoing/canceling, 84
Long Date format, 104
long integers, 346
Lookup Wizard, 56
Lotus 1-2-3 file imports, 324
lowercase, 102

• M •

Mail Merge Wizard, 272
mail merging reports, 272
mailing list for Access 2000 for
      Windows, 46
Mailing List (sample table in Table
      Wizard), 72
mailto:// (hyperlink type), 297
main menu, 27
Main Switchboard screen, 14–15
main window, 26–27
Make-Table queries, 212
many-to-many relationships, 81
many-to-one relationships, 81
markers, 253
Match Whole Field button, 211
mathematical operations. *See*
      calculations
Max function, 194, 289
.MDB file imports, 324
Medium Date format, 104
memo fields
  described, 55
  formatting, 102
  ineligibility for indexing, 86
  ineligibility for primary key, 78
menus. *See also menus by name*
  accessing options, 4
  context-sensitive, 34
  finding missing options, 348, 350
  Start menu of Windows, 10–12
Microsoft Excel, exporting Access
      reports to, 225, 272
Microsoft Help, 40
Microsoft IntelliMouse, 5, 95, 116, 118
Microsoft sales department, 47–48
Microsoft Word, exporting Access
      reports to, 225, 272
Min function, 194, 289
MOD (modulus) function, 206

mouse
  Microsoft IntelliMouse, 5, 95, 116, 118
  operations in Windows programs, 4
  right-clicking, 4, 34–35
MS Excel, exporting Access reports to,
      225, 272
MS Word, exporting Access reports to,
      225, 272
multifield keys, 78
multiple-table queries, 167–176

• N •

names
  combining first and last, 203–204
  in data fields, 57
naming
  databases, 66, 353
  fields, 58, 353
  fields used in formulas, 201–202, 353
  importance of understandable
      names, 353
  indexes, 87
  primary keys of tables, 79
  renaming columns, 124
  renaming fields, 134–137, 353
  tables, 70, 75, 353
navigation buttons, 30
New Database window, 64
New Form dialog box, 311–312, 315–316
New Record button, 93
New Report dialog box
  for AutoReport type, 223
  for labels, 234
news:// (hyperlink type), 297
newsgroups: online help, 45
Not Equal To (comparison operator), 158
number fields
  described, 56
  formatting, 103–104
  long integer, 346
  single precision, 346

turning off automatic rounding, 345
validating input, 112, 348, 353
versus text fields with numbers, 58, 353

• *O* •

Objects bar, 28–29
ODBC file imports, 325
Office Assistant
   described, 21, 27, 38–30, 207
   finding advanced Web publishing
      topics, 307
OLE object fields
   caution on exports, 328
   described, 56
   ineligibility for indexing, 86
   ineligibility for primary key, 78
OLE (Object Linking and
      Embedding), 296
OLE object tool, 271
one-to-many relationships, 81, 214
one-to-one relationships, 81
online services for help, 45
Open Database button, 69
Open dialog box, 13, 91–92
opening
   existing databases, 12–13, 90–92
   existing tables, 14
   from Favorites list, 91
operators
   arithmetic, 206
   Boolean, 177–184
   comparison, 158
   various, 206
OR Boolean operator, 180–184
Oracle (ODBC) file imports, 325
Order Details (sample table in Table
      Wizard), 72
Orders (sample table in Table
      Wizard), 72
orientation of reports (portrait or
      landscape), 230–231

• *P* •

Page Break button, 270
page breaks on reports, 270–271
Page Header properties dialog box, 283
Page Headers and Footers for reports,
      254, 274, 276–277, 282–283
page numbers and dates, 291–292
Page Setup dialog box, 229–232
paper feed specification, 231
Paradox file imports, 324, 325
Part of Tens. *See also* keyboard short-
      cuts; troubleshooting
   common crises and solutions, 345–350
   described, 3
   favorite keyboard shortcuts, 341–344
   tips from database nerds, 351–355
Per Column option of Report properties
      dialog box, 284
Per Page option of Report properties
      dialog box, 284
Percent format, 104
performance enhancement suggestions
      with Analyzer, 338
Personal Web Server, 306
PgUp/PgDn keys for next/previous
      screen, 116–117
phone number data, 57
phone support, 47–48
pictures. *See* images
pie charts, 240
plus signs (+) as related table
      indicator, 30
Portrait orientation of printing, 230–231
postal code data, 57, 353
pound sign (#) around dates, 178
primary keys of tables
   described, 78–80
   indexed automatically, 87
   troubleshooting violations during
      imports, 349
Print button, 225

Print Preview, in Design view, 224–228, 265
Print Preview toolbar, 225
printers, default, 231
printing
  and paper feed specification, 231
  and Print Preview, 224
Products (sample table in Table Wizard), 72
Properties dialog box, 290
province data, 57

• *Q* •

queries. *See also* filtering records; finding
  caution on use!, 209–210, 212, 213–214
  as Advanced Filter/Sorts, 155–159
  Append, 212
  for automated edits/updates/deletes, 210–217
  backups, importance of, 210, 213
  with Boolean operators AND and OR, 177–184
  calculations in, 185–194
  comparison operators, 158
  crosstab ("cross tabulations"), 189–190
  with Crosstab Query Wizard, 172
  Delete, 212–214
  described, 153, 154
  documenting, importance of, 352
  with Find Duplicates Query Wizard, 172
  with Find Unmatched Query Wizard, 172
  Make-Table, 212
  multiple-table, 167–176
  previewing before running, 212
  as reports, 223
  reports based on, 223
  reusable, saving filters as, 159
  reusable, saving searches as, 151
  running, 14, 176

Select queries, 160–164
  with Simple Query Wizard, 164–165
  sorting results, 163
  troubleshooting weird results from, 346–347
  Update, 212, 214–217
  using special functions, 193–194
Query menu
  Delete, 213–214
  Run, 176
  Update Query, 215
Query Type button, 211
Query View button, 212
query window, 32
Query Wizard, 169–172

• *R* •

raised text on reports, 262
Raised/Sunken Cell Effects, 127
record numbers, indexes to, 86–88
records
  adding (Ctrl++), 343
  adding to tables, 92–95
  deleting, 95, 96–97
  deleting current (Ctrl+-), 343
  described, 53
  detail, 248
  duplicate, allowing or not, 87
  editing, 18–19, 95–96
  finding with filtering, 147–151
  grouping for reports, 277–280
  saving (Shift+Enter), 343
  sorting, 145–146
  in tables, 54
  troubleshooting "lost," 347–348
Records menu
  Filter, 147–151
  Filter-Advanced Filter/Sort, 157–159
  Sort, 145–146
red, displaying field contents in, 103, 105
redundancy of data, 59
referential integrity, 214

relational databases
  described, 59–60, 80, 167–168
  from flat file, with Analyzer, 331–335
relationships
  advantages, 168
  many-to-many, 81
  many-to-one, 81
  one-to-many, 81, 214
  one-to-one, 81
  and referential integrity, 214
Relationships button, 62, 82
Relationships menu, Show Table, 82
renaming
  columns in tables, 124
  fields in tables, 134–137, 353
Repeat Section option of Group Header
    properties dialog box, 285
replacing data throughout table, 210–211
Report Headers, 274, 276, 277
report headers and footers, 254
Report properties dialog box, 282–284
Report Wizard, 249–250
reports. *See also* Design View
  from AutoReport, 221–232
  based on queries, 223
  with charts, 239–242
  controls on, 257
  customizing in Design View, 251–271
  customizing with Report Wizard,
    242–250
  documenting, importance of, 352
  exporting as static HTML pages, 307
  exporting to mail merge, 272
  exporting to MS Word or Excel, 225, 272
  exporting to other programs, 228
  formatting columns, 231–232
  formatting margins, 229–230
  formatting with AutoFormat, 266–267
  with graphics, 67
  labels, creating, 233–239
  paper size/orientation, 230–231

  printing, 19
  queries as, 223
  running, 14
  selecting, 19
  sending as e-mail, 228
  style of display, 66–67
  zooming, 226–228
Reservations (sample table in Table
    Wizard), 72
Rich Text File imports, 325
Right Justify button, 255
right-clicking the mouse, 4, 34–35
rounding of numbers, turning off auto-
    matic, 345
row height/width adjustments
  in datasheets, 119–120
  in reports, 232
.rtf file imports, 325
Running Sum option of Properties dialog
    box, 290

• S •

Save As Query button, 151, 159
Save button, 87
saving
  automatic, for edits, 18
  formats as AutoFormats, 267
  tables, 75
ScreenTips, 33
scroll bars, 30, 116, 117
searching. *See* finding
sections (bands) on reports
  customizing footers, 287–289
  customizing headers, 285–287
  described, 253, 254, 274–276, 281
  formatting, 284–285
  page numbers and dates, 291–292
  running sums for, 290
  summary functions, 289–290
Select queries, 160–164

Service Records (sample table in Table
	Wizard), 72
shadowed text on reports, 263
Shift+key combinations. *See* keyboard
	shortcuts
Show Table button, 82
sideways orientation of printing, 230–231
sigma ( ) as mathematical symbol for
	"Sum," 186
Simple Query Wizard, 164–165
single precision numbers, 346
sixteen-bit Winsock, 297
Size menu, 269
Social Security Numbers (SSNs), 57
"Some data may not be displayed"
	message, 232
sorting
	in customized reports, 247–248
	databases, 145–146
	query results, 163
Sorting and Grouping dialog box, 278, 280
spaces
	inserting between first and last
		names, 204
	padding fields with, 102
Special Effect button, 255, 261–263
Special Effect option of Page Header
	properties dialog box, 283
square brackets ([]) around field names
	for calculations, 196–197
SSNs (Social Security Numbers), 57
Standard decimal format, 104
Start menu of Windows, 10–12
state information, 57
static Web pages, 303
status bar, 27
subfolders, caution on creating too
	many, 354
Sum function, 190–192, 194, 289
summary functions, 289
sunken text on reports, 262
switchboard, 14–15, 29, 92
Sybase (ODBC) file imports, 325

• T •

Tab key, 93
Table Analyzer Wizard, 332
table names, 30
Table View button, 110
Table Wizard
	described, 58, 68–73
	sample tables in, 72
tables. *See also* Analyzer; queries
	adding fields, 130–133
	consolidating into single database,
		345–346
	creating "by hand," 73–76
	creating/adding to databases, 68–73
	described, 29–30, 54
	designing, 61–62
	documenting structure, importance
		of, 351
	formatting, 101–102
	hyperlinks in, 298–300
	indexes, 86–88
	joined (linked), 32
	linking, 82–86
	naming, 70, 75
	opening existing, 14
	picking primary key, 78–80
	primary keys, 78–80
	records, adding, 92–95
	records in, 53
	samples from Table Wizard, 72
	saving, 75
	viewing relationships, 62
tabular AutoReports, 222, 274
Taskbars, 27
Tasks (sample table in Table Wizard), 72
technical support, 47–48
telephone number data, 57
Telex data, 57
text boxes on reports, 253

text fields
  described, 55
  examples, 57–58
  formatting, 102
  formatting with Input Mask Wizard, 107
  versus number fields, 58, 353
text file imports, 325, 326
"There is no primary key defined"
      message, 75
thirty-two-bit Winsock, 297
3-D look, 127–128
time. *See* date/time fields
title bar, 27
titles in data fields, 57
toolbars
  Apply Filter button, 159
  AutoReport tools, 225
  described, 27, 32–34
  Design View button, 252
  Filter by Form button, 148
  Filter by Selection button, 147
  Find button, 142
  Formatting, 255
  Indexes button, 87
  Open Database button, 69
  Print Preview, 225
  Query Type button, 211
  Relationships button, 62, 82
  Save As Query button, 151, 159
  Save button, 87
  Show Table button, 82
  Sort Ascending/Descending buttons,
      145–146
  Table View button, 110
Tools menu
  Analyze, Documentor, 336–337
  Analyze, Table, 331–335
  Find File, 94
  Office Links, 272
  Relationships, 82–85

totals, 186–193
Totals button, 186
troubleshooting. *See also* help
  automatic rounding of numbers, 345
  key violations during imports, 349
  "lost" records, 347–348
  startup problems with Access, 349–350
  startup problems with Wizards, 350
  tables misplaced in different data-
      bases, 345–346
  weird results from queries, 346–347
TrueType fonts, 126
.TXT file imports, 325

• U •

Unbound Object Frame tool, 271
Underline button, 255, 263
Undo last changes (Ctrl+Z), 18, 95,
      343, 347
Undo Saved Record command, 95
Update queries, 212, 214–217
updating. *See* editing
uppercase, 102
utility buttons, 27

• V •

validation of input, 112–113, 348, 353
values. *See* calculations
View menu
  Design View, 176
  Form Design, 318
  Pages, 227
  Sorting and Grouping, 278
  Tab Order, 321
  Totals, 186
Visible option of Page Header properties
      dialog box, 283

• *W* •

Web addresses. *See* Web sites
Web browsers, Internet Explorer, 297
Web publishing, 302–306
Web servers, 306
Web site data in database fields, 57
Web sites
  Access databases as, 296
  creating with Data Access Page Wizard,
    303–306
  Microsoft ServicePacks, 1
Web (World Wide Web). *See also*
    hyperlinks and hyperlink fields;
    Internet
  advantages, 302
  online help, 45
Where function, 194
Windows 95, 1
Windows 95 For Dummies, 4, 65
Windows 98, 1
Windows 98 For Dummies, 4, 26, 65
windows
  Answer, 42
  Start menu, 10–12
Windows NT, Service Pack 3 or 4, 1
Windows NT For Dummies, 4, 65
Windows NT Server, 306
Wizards
  troubleshooting startup problems, 350
  turning "on," 257
  Answer, 42
  Chart, 239–242
  Crosstab Query, 172
  Data Access Page, 303–306
  Database, 60, 65, 68
  Find Duplicates Query, 172
  Find Unmatched Query, 172
  Form, 311–314
  Input Mask, 106–108

  Label, 233–239
  Lookup, 56
  Mail Merge, 272
  Query, 169–172
  Report, 249–250
  Simple Query, 164–165
  Table, 58, 68–73
  Table Analyzer, 332
.WKS, .WK1, .WK3 file imports, 324
Word 2000 For Windows For
    Dummies, 272
Word (Microsoft), exporting Access
    reports to, 225, 272

• *X* •

.XLS file imports, 324
XY charts, 240

• *Y* •

Yes/No fields
  caution on exports, 328
  described, 56
  formatting, 105
  not useful as primary key, 79

• *Z* •

Zip code data, 57
Zoom button, 225
zooming on reports, 226–228
Zweckform label stock, 234

Notes

Notes

Notes

Notes

Notes

Notes

From PCs to Personal Finance, We Make it Fun and Easy!

For more information, or to order, please call 800.762.2974.

www.hungryminds.com
www.dummies.com

Dummies Books™
Bestsellers on Every Topic!

TECHNOLOGY TITLES

INTERNET

Title	Author	ISBN	Price
America Online® For Dummies®, 5th Edition	John Kaufeld	0-7645-0502-5	$19.99 US/$26.99 CAN
E-Mail For Dummies®, 2nd Edition	John R. Levine, Carol Baroudi, Margaret Levine Young, & Arnold Reinhold	0-7645-0131-3	$24.99 US/$34.99 CAN
Genealogy Online For Dummies®	Matthew L. Helm & April Leah Helm	0-7645-0377-4	$24.99 US/$35.99 CAN
Internet Directory For Dummies®, 2nd Edition	Brad Hill	0-7645-0436-3	$24.99 US/$35.99 CAN
The Internet For Dummies®, 6th Edition	John R. Levine, Carol Baroudi, & Margaret Levine Young	0-7645-0506-8	$19.99 US/$28.99 CAN
Investing Online For Dummies®, 2nd Edition	Kathleen Sindell, Ph.D.	0-7645-0509-2	$24.99 US/$35.99 CAN
World Wide Web Searching For Dummies®, 2nd Edition	Brad Hill	0-7645-0264-6	$24.99 US/$34.99 CAN

OPERATING SYSTEMS

Title	Author	ISBN	Price
DOS For Dummies®, 3rd Edition	Dan Gookin	0-7645-0361-8	$19.99 US/$28.99 CAN
LINUX® For Dummies®, 2nd Edition	John Hall, Craig Witherspoon, & Coletta Witherspoon	0-7645-0421-5	$24.99 US/$35.99 CAN
Mac® OS 8 For Dummies®	Bob LeVitus	0-7645-0271-9	$19.99 US/$26.99 CAN
Small Business Windows® 98 For Dummies®	Stephen Nelson	0-7645-0425-8	$24.99 US/$35.99 CAN
UNIX® For Dummies®, 4th Edition	John R. Levine & Margaret Levine Young	0-7645-0419-3	$19.99 US/$28.99 CAN
Windows® 95 For Dummies®, 2nd Edition	Andy Rathbone	0-7645-0180-1	$19.99 US/$26.99 CAN
Windows® 98 For Dummies®	Andy Rathbone	0-7645-0261-1	$19.99 US/$28.99 CAN

PC/GENERAL COMPUTING

Title	Author	ISBN	Price
Buying a Computer For Dummies®	Dan Gookin	0-7645-0313-8	$19.99 US/$28.99 CAN
Illustrated Computer Dictionary For Dummies®, 3rd Edition	Dan Gookin & Sandra Hardin Gookin	0-7645-0143-7	$19.99 US/$26.99 CAN
Modems For Dummies®, 3rd Edition	Tina Rathbone	0-7645-0069-4	$19.99 US/$26.99 CAN
Small Business Computing For Dummies®	Brian Underdahl	0-7645-0287-5	$24.99 US/$35.99 CAN
Upgrading & Fixing PCs For Dummies®, 4th Edition	Andy Rathbone	0-7645-0418-5	$19.99 US/$28.99CAN

GENERAL INTEREST TITLES

FOOD & BEVERAGE/ENTERTAINING

Title	Author	ISBN	Price
Entertaining For Dummies®	Suzanne Williamson with Linda Smith	0-7645-5027-6	$19.99 US/$26.99 CAN
Gourmet Cooking For Dummies®	Charlie Trotter	0-7645-5029-2	$19.99 US/$26.99 CAN
Grilling For Dummies®	Marie Rama & John Mariani	0-7645-5076-4	$19.99 US/$26.99 CAN
Italian Cooking For Dummies®	Cesare Casella & Jack Bishop	0-7645-5098-5	$19.99 US/$26.99 CAN
Wine For Dummies®, 2nd Edition	Ed McCarthy & Mary Ewing-Mulligan	0-7645-5114-0	$19.99 US/$26.99 CAN

SPORTS

Title	Author	ISBN	Price
Baseball For Dummies®	Joe Morgan with Richard Lally	0-7645-5085-3	$19.99 US/$26.99 CAN
Fly Fishing For Dummies®	Peter Kaminsky	0-7645-5073-X	$19.99 US/$26.99 CAN
Football For Dummies®	Howie Long with John Czarnecki	0-7645-5054-3	$19.99 US/$26.99 CAN
Hockey For Dummies®	John Davidson with John Steinbreder	0-7645-5045-4	$19.99 US/$26.99 CAN
Tennis For Dummies®	Patrick McEnroe with Peter Bodo	0-7645-5087-X	$19.99 US/$26.99 CAN

HOME & GARDEN

Title	Author	ISBN	Price
Decks & Patios For Dummies®	Robert J. Beckstrom & National Gardening Association	0-7645-5075-6	$16.99 US/$24.99 CAN
Flowering Bulbs For Dummies®	Judy Glattstein & National Gardening Association	0-7645-5103-5	$16.99 US/$24.99 CAN
Home Improvement For Dummies®	Gene & Katie Hamilton & the Editors of HouseNet, Inc.	0-7645-5005-5	$19.99 US/$26.99 CAN
Lawn Care For Dummies®	Lance Walheim & National Gardening Association	0-7645-5077-2	$16.99 US/$24.99 CAN

For more information, or to order, call (800)762-2974

Hungry Minds™